R2004r28423

W9-BWA-493

ALSO BY JOHN BRANT

Duel in the Sun

THE BOY WHO RUNS

THE BOY WHO RUNS

The Odyssey of Julius Achon

JOHN BRANT

 Ballantine Books • *New York*

Published in the United States by Ballantine Books, an imprint of
Random House, a division of Penguin Random House LLC, New
York.

BALLANTINE and the HOUSE colophon are registered trademarks of
Penguin Random House LLC.

LIBRARY OF CONGRESS CATALOGING-IN-PUBLICATION DATA
Names: Brant, John, author.
Title: The boy who runs : the odyssey of Julius Achon / John Brant.
Description: New York : Ballantine Books, 2016.
Identifiers: LCCN 2016009316 (print) | LCCN 2016026304 (ebook) |
ISBN 9780553392159 (hardback) | ISBN 9780553392166 (ebook)
Subjects: LCSH: Runners (Sports)—Uganda—Biography. | Child
soldiers—Uganda—Biography. | BISAC: SPORTS & RECREATION /
Running & Jogging. | HISTORY / Africa / General.
Classification: LCC GV1061.15.A34 B73 2016 (print) |
LCC GV1061.15.A34 (ebook) | DDC 796.42092 [B]—dc23
LC record available at https://lccn.loc.gov/2016009316

Printed in the United States of America on acid-free paper

randomhousebooks.com

987654321

FIRST EDITION

Book design by Simon M. Sullivan

For Jim Fee, always running point

Pause you who read this, and think for a moment of the long chain of iron or gold, of thorns or flowers, that would never have bound you, but for the formation of the first link on one memorable day.

—CHARLES DICKENS, *Great Expectations*

THE BOY WHO RUNS

J ulius Achon almost sat out the biggest race of his life.

It was early May 1996, and Julius was preparing for the NCAA track and field championships. They were going to be held at the end of June, and he was favored to win both the 800 and 1,500 meters.

In anticipation, he engaged in a tear-down phase of training, when a middle-distance runner trashes his muscle fibers and drains his glycogen stores before building them back up for the big event. John Cook, the George Mason University coach, drove Julius through taxing days of drills, sprints, and strength training sessions. By design, the heavy work temporarily dulled his edge for racing. Following convention, Cook decided to hold his prized athlete out of a low-stakes conference meet that GMU was hosting the next weekend.

On Thursday, two days before the meet, Cook put Julius through an especially searing workout: twenty repetitions of 200 meters, each rep run at a full-tilt 26-plus seconds, with an almost sadistically scant 45 seconds of rest between each rep. Afterward, Julius staggered back to the apartment he shared with a few other foreign runners. Mattresses and box springs lay flush on the floor, ranks of training shoes waited by the door, and a pot of rice and beans simmered on the stove.

He grabbed some ice for his legs, flopped down on the couch, and was just drifting off to sleep when the phone rang. It was Coach Cook. "Chief"—for some reason, he always called Julius "Chief"—"I've been reconsidering. How do you feel about running the 800 on Saturday?"

How did Julius feel? As a boy in his native Uganda, during his forced servitude in the Lord's Resistance Army, his rebel commander often whipped him with a switch fashioned from a tree limb. His present pain recalled those beatings.

"I don't know," he replied carefully. "I'm pretty fried, coach."

"That's fine. I don't expect any fireworks. Look, we need the points," Cook continued. "You could finish fourth in the 800—that's three points—if you did fucking back flips the whole way."

Julius understood that Cook wasn't *asking* him to run; he was *telling* him to. "Coach, you don't have to cuss."

"Thanks for this, Chief. I owe you one."

"Come to church with us on Sunday, coach."

"No way, Chief. I'll never owe you that much."

◆ ◆ ◆

So Julius toed the line of the 800 meters. Deep-chested and rope-muscled, he resembled a middleweight prizefighter more than a middle-distance runner. Three faint parallel lines scarring his cheeks, the product of a witch-doctor ritual in his childhood, contributed to the warrior effect. He ran with a stride at once flawless and electric, his hardened feet, only recently sheathed by training and racing shoes, clawing the track surface like a leopard's paws. Julius possessed the strength to lead a race from wire to wire and the speed to win with a devastating final kick. In bearing and aspect he seemed mature as a king, yet Julius was only nineteen years old. His future appeared limitless.

Today, though, no magic was likely. Due to the recent grinding labor, Julius felt like he was wearing a forty-pound vest. After the first lap of the two-lap race, he was running dead last. Midway through the second lap, with just 200 meters to go, he remained buried at the back of the pack. It appeared that Julius would fail to deliver any points for his team.

Then something happened. By habit, Julius stepped to an outside lane, gaining position to launch his kick. And somehow he started passing people. Normally a fiercely focused competitor, Julius felt oddly detached, as if he were standing by the side of the track, watching himself accelerate. Rounding the final turn, with 150 meters to go, he still trailed five runners. But an eyeblink later, with 100 meters remaining, the path ahead had magically cleared. To his own amazement, Julius had seized the lead. In fact, the gap was ten yards and growing.

He wasn't running; he was floating. He couldn't feel his legs. He moved in slow motion, swaddled in a cone of effortless silence. Later he would marvel that it felt so easy.

Julius glided across the finish. He slowed to a stop, laced his fingers together behind his head, and cast a reluctant eye at the digital race clock.

But the numbers on the clock made no sense. He wasn't even supposed to run in the race, so how could ... ? His thoughts were interrupted because his teammates were rushing toward him, and across the infield Coach Cook couldn't stop grinning.

◆ ◆ ◆

Today, during the presentations he gives around the world as head of the Achon Uganda Children's Fund, Julius talks sparingly about his world-class athletic career. More often, he engages his audiences with accounts of Uganda and its anguish: his escape from the LRA under a rain of machine-gun fire, the morning he discovered eleven orphaned children lying underneath a bus.

But in many ways that race exemplifies the life that Julius has led off the track: Attending to duty before taking care of himself. Rising to a challenge that is both physical and spiritual. Finding a way to keep moving forward even as the road bends in unexpected directions. Accepting the grace of a power beyond his agency, even when that power proves more immolating than merciful.

While he doesn't speak often of running, Julius Achon speaks always of a journey. And the story always starts in the same place: a village called Awake. . . .

PART ONE

AWAKE, UGANDA, 1988

It was Saturday, which meant that Julius would be spared the shame of school. He would not be hectored by a teacher demanding tuition and thus wouldn't have to jump out a window to escape a caning. He wouldn't feel humiliated by his lack of a school blouse, he wouldn't grow light-headed because he had nothing to eat between dawn and evening, and his guts wouldn't seize because he'd drunk out of a ditch where the cattle wallowed.

On the other hand, there would be no games during recess, no joking with friends on the three-mile walk to school, no pretty girls to watch shyly from a distance, and no moment under the mango tree when, scratching out numbers in the dirt, he suddenly recognized their order and pattern—a thrill of insight that would inevitably be wiped away by the teacher dragging his shoe over Julius's work so that the next child could take his turn with arithmetic.

Saturday, so none of that, but still Julius rose early. The Achon family—Julius was the oldest of nine children—occupied a complex of circular huts, dried mud at the base and dried grass woven into a roof, spread over an acre-sized clearing about a mile off the

main road between the city Lira and the border with Sudan. Clansmen occupied similar clusters of huts within a ten-minute walk.
Together, the huts formed the village of Awake. There was no com-
mercial center to mark the place; its boundaries were engraved in
the memories of the village elders.

The family slept inside last night because the Karamojong were
not active in the area. During the time of the Karamojong—herders
infamous for thieving cattle—you had to leave at night to sleep in
the elephant grass; there was no resisting their savagery when they
came. You could smell the Karamojong before you saw them, that
sickening grease smell from the cattle fat they slathered over their
naked flesh. They used to attack with bows and spears, but now
they came with AK-47s. Julius once saw a friend, a classmate, a
Langi boy his own age, fall like a bird from the branch of a shea nut
tree when a Karamojong scout shot him. The boy landed with a
sickening thud, bounced once, and then lay still and dead.

At that point Julius Achon had already seen a number of dead
people, especially dead children, but they had all died from cholera
or typhus or AIDS or dysentery or pneumonia or malaria or any
number of other preventable diseases that afflicted Uganda, where
60 percent of the population was under the age of twenty and the
life expectancy was forty-six. But that was the first violent death
the boy had witnessed. It would not be the last.

◆ ◆ ◆

On this Saturday morning in January 1988, there was no school, no
Karamojong, and no lion track in the packed dirt by the fire pit
outside the hut. The lion had come only once, but Julius never forgot the immensity of its pawprint—nearly twelve inches across.
The air seemed to shimmer above the track, just a few steps from
where Julius and his family had been sleeping.

His father explained that the lion had likely been an aged male
cast out from its pride and posed relatively little threat. Still, the
pawprint seemed to pulse with a malevolent force of its own, fright-
ening Julius more than the notion of seeing the beast itself. Every
morning, the boy looked down apprehensively as he stepped from

the hut. When the lion's mark wasn't there, he would say a quick prayer of thanks. And yet at the same time he felt a faint, inexplicable throb of disappointment.

Julius moved into his day and its long chain of chores: tethering the goats, turning over the garden soil for planting, cutting sugar cane, snaring birds, and twice a day, without fail, humping the clay jar down to the spring. He would fill the jar with water, balance it on top of his head, and pick his way barefoot over the mud and rocks and razor-sharp grass for the half mile back to the hut, careful not to spill a precious drop or, worse, drop and break the even more precious jar, made out of mud and shaped and baked with painstaking care by his mother.

The job put steel in his hips, back, neck, and abdominal muscles and taught him to run with a sinuous, efficient, straight-backed stride that would serve him so well in the future. But now Julius resented the jar. Children in neighboring villages bore their family's water in five-gallon plastic jugs that rode easy on their heads or could be balanced, yoke-like, on their shoulders.

Why couldn't Julius use a plastic jerrycan like other children? The same reason he couldn't afford tuition and a school blouse, or a few pennies to buy a mango or cassava root at lunchtime: because Charles, his father, drank up all the money, pounding home-brewed banana beer with his buddies in the nearby town of Otuke. Charles drank all day, every day. That Saturday was no exception.

Julius returned from the spring, carefully balancing his forty-pound cargo of water. His father was up and tending to the cattle. When sober, Charles was a respected herdsman, a broad-chested man known for his strength and endurance, who displayed shrewd judgment and a sharp intelligence. With these traits and his ample landholdings—his farm was among the largest in the area—and the sizable herds he'd inherited from his father, Charles should have prospered in a place where wealth was measured by the number of cattle a man possessed and the number of wives his cattle allowed him to buy. Some Langi men accrued as many as nine wives and sixty children. With all his advantages, Charles easily should have been good for five wives and thirty kids. Instead, due to his drinking and gambling, Charles, at age forty, had amassed only twenty cows, fifteen goats, nine children, and one wife—Kristina.

In the Langi tradition the men took care of the cattle, while the women and children attended to the garden, goats, huts, and everything else. Now, before heading to Otuke, Charles fed and watered his herd. As he worked, he ignored his son; only mothers dealt with the children. Despite the silence, Julius prized these moments with his father. For Charles, however, the silence weighed more heavily. He was painfully aware that, due to his drinking, Julius and the rest of his family suffered. All the more reason to lose himself in the *kongo arege*, the bush brew with an obliterating 20 percent alcohol content.

Beyond fetching water and tending the garden and goats, Julius raised sugar cane to sell at the local market. Along with the clay jars sold by his mother, that was the family's sole source of income. Also, by Langi custom, Julius, as oldest son, looked after his younger siblings. Most boys performed this task grudgingly, but Julius took his protector's role to heart. "Even as a baby, Julius had an old soul," his father would remember later.

◆ ◆ ◆

Julius Achon was born in 1976, five years into Idi Amin's reign of terror. Amin came from northwestern Uganda, a fatherless boy who as a young man served the British soldiers in the elite King's African Rifles regiment, in which he later enlisted and distinguished himself with exceptional courage and brutality. After independence arrived in 1962, the semiliterate Amin, who was also a champion light-heavyweight boxer, bullied his way to a general's rank in the army of Milton Obote, the Lira native with leftist leanings who became Uganda's first president. In 1971, when Obote was traveling abroad, Amin, with the tacit backing of the United States, staged a coup and seized control of the country.

Amin was a paranoid sociopath who saw threats to his rule everywhere, especially among his predecessor's closest allies and advisers, the army officers who were predominantly Langi and Acholi. The fish of Lake Victoria, feeding on the corpses of Amin's victims, swelled to grotesque size. He summarily ordered all Ugandans of

Asian descent—the backbone of the merchant class—out of the nation. Amin and his cronies ransacked the treasury, living in gross luxury while the people starved. Due to Amin's paranoia, however, the usual pattern of patronage and sycophancy was stood on its head: Eventually, inevitably, getting close to the president equated to a death sentence.

According to various estimates, Amin murdered between 150,000 and 300,000 of his countrymen. His rule lasted for eight years, until 1979, when his army lost a war with Tanzania and he fled in exile to Libya.

So Julius Achon lived his early years under a killing moon. Two days before his birth, his mother, Kristina, walked almost five miles to the hospital at the Aliwang Catholic mission, which had the area's only maternity ward. Two days after Julius was born, Kristina, again on foot, carried her infant son back to Awake. His first memory, formed when he was around four or five, was of the boom of artillery, a distant rumble like a storm approaching at the start of the rainy season.

After Amin, Obote returned to power and, in revenge for Amin's persecution of Acholi and Langi soldiers, wrought havoc on people from the south. To counter him, Yoweri Museveni, who would later become president, was leading a fresh insurgency, his forces including fierce warriors who had been exiled from bordering Rwanda. Beginning in 1981, the Luwero War, which pitted a rebel army led by Museveni against a government army headed by Obote, raged across Uganda, eventually killing hundreds of thousands of civilians. Perhaps the young Julius heard the boom of ordnance related to one of that war's many battles.

At that point, however, the distant thunder of artillery was the only direct sign of war in Otuke district, where Awake was situated. The region seemed a world apart, with no mail service, newspapers, or television; no mineral wealth to exploit, no forests to clear or major rivers to drain; and a single, often impassable road supplying access to the rest of the nation. Northerners died wholesale in Uganda's wars, but almost always in the south, where things were deemed worthy of dying for.

The Langi raised cattle, chickens, and goats. They grew cassava (a fibrous white root vegetable), mangoes, and sweet potatoes and trapped birds and other small game, subsisting on the yield and selling any surplus in local markets. Awake exemplified this way of life. Julius, the firstborn, was doted on by the women of the clan. His grandmother had a dream in which Julius was flying in an airplane, an impossible notion for a villager. A great destiny was augured for the boy.

At age seven, Julius contracted measles, a disease which, in the bush of central Africa, was most often fatal. In fact, the village witch doctor proclaimed the boy deceased, and the women wrapped him in sheets for burial. But then a woman heard the child sneeze. And then he sneezed again. The women unwrapped the boy and embraced him. They sang with joy because he had risen like Jesus from the dead, a sign that God had a plan for Julius Achon. A glorious future was again prophesied.

Perhaps Julius would learn a trade and work in Lira as a plasterer or a shoemaker. Maybe he would make it as far as Kampala, where he could serve as a porter at the airport or at a hotel. Otherwise, a boy from a northern village had only three career options: Join the army, join the police, or become a farmer, like his father.

◆ ◆ ◆

Charles hustled off to Otuke, leaving Julius, age eleven, as the man of the house, responsible for helping his mother look after the children. He would make sure they got their handful of beans, carry the little ones on his back down to the cane fields, and keep an eye out for danger, which usually arose from three sources: the pythons, the big cats, or the Karamojong. The trouble most often visited at night, the time that all Langi feared, when evil—they call it *lujoji*—prevailed and families drew close around the fire for comfort and protection.

The Karamojong were avatars from the stone age, or perhaps the outriders of a terrible new age to come. They ranged far from their homeland in the savannah of northeastern Uganda, on a mission to claim all the cattle in Africa, which they believed that their god had vouchsafed to them. They slaughtered the cows and drank the hot blood as it coursed from the beasts' slit necks. They roasted the meat and slathered their flesh with the rendered fat. They wore no clothes, which they believed to be the cloak of the devil.

The Karamojong sent their scouts out by day—one of those scouts had shot the Langi boy that Julius had watched fall from the tree—but attacked at night, advancing in columns of hundreds of warriors, killing anything that stood between them and their prize. There was no resisting the Karamojong, no police to turn to for protection. The only recourse was to leave your hut as darkness fell and range out to the bush to sleep or try to sleep, waiting for the raiders to claim their quota of cattle blood. In the morning, you could emerge from the elephant grass and return to your hut and patchwork fields.

Julius assumed that, along with low-grade hunger and perpetual toil, the Karamojong would always be part of his life, a life that in all probability would entail getting married in the next few years. He hoped that his parents would pick him a pretty bride. Then it would be time for him to build his own hut and start his own family. He was good at farming, strong and handy like his father, and his other two career options—the army and the police, professions of the rifle—held little appeal for him. Perhaps, in following the traditional Langi way, Julius could eventually rebuild the family holdings that Charles had neglected. Due to his intelligence, integrity, and industry, Julius might even ascend to a position of clan leadership, arbitrating disputes and settling grievances.

The boy could cope with a future caught between the government threatening from the south and the Karamojong raiding from the north. It would mean continual vigilance, listening for every breaking twig and altered tone of birdsong, a life of work, danger, disease, and want, but it would also secure certain rewards and comforts. Clan and family formed a refuge; you were never alone or orphaned, as some hut would always take you in. The labor, while unending, was performed according to deliberate daily, weekly, monthly, and seasonal rhythms. Due to the suffocating heat, the searing sun, and the deficiency of calories and protein, you could work only so hard and for so long. There was no pressure from a boss or overseer, because you farmed your own land for subsistence and perhaps a modest surplus to sell on market day. Finally, what was the point of hurry or worry, if only more work waited tomorrow? Instead, you struck a pace and rhythm that sustained you through the days and seasons.

A reasonably healthy Ugandan, one not suffering a malaria attack or the onslaught of a waterborne disease, rarely stopped moving. You saw them walking out on the road or along the paths among hut clusters, moving neither proudly nor desperately, neither quickly nor slowly. In towns such as Lira, you saw them walking toward the market and hospital, the prison and the police barracks. In Kampala, amid the clout and clamor of the African city, people walked for the sheer sake of walking, because their homes were too cramped and stifling to sit in or because they did not have a home.

Always walking, always watching, always listening, always socketed by custom and clan: Julius was reconciled to this traditional path because he could imagine no other way to live, and because he was good at it. The sugar cane grew like weeds under his hand, and he could carry water all day and run like the wind pursuing a guinea hen or on the wing of a piebald soccer pitch. As long as the cattle grew and the rains came, this life remained open to him. The Karamojong would leave enough cows, and the outside world would leave the Langi alone because they possessed nothing worth stealing.

But now there was a third column rising. A force in some ways similar to the Karamojong, but more dangerous. Julius had heard the whispering among the boys at school and among the elders at dusk around the fires.

They would come at night, like other invaders, but their quarry wasn't cattle, or at least not solely. They came for people. They came for the boys. They liked the ones between the ages of ten and fourteen: old enough to walk long distances and bear heavy loads, young enough to mold. The rumor was that in battles they sent the boys out first. They gave the boys ganja to smoke so that they wouldn't be afraid.

Unlike other military threats, this one didn't originate south of the Nile, and it wasn't conceived by a customary Langi enemy. These raiders came from the neighboring Acholi tribe, traditional Langi allies, based near Gulu town, only about sixty miles to the north. They were farmers, or disaffected government soldiers who had grown up on farms. Unlike the case of Idi Amin, a secular despot, this force was led by a supposed holy man in communion with powerful animist spirits. The raiders were nocturnal by habit, but when they encountered little resistance they also operated during the daylight hours.

Julius heard the stories but didn't pay them much heed. The danger seemed vague, as far away as the rains. Compared to the Karamojong or Amin, how bad could these guys be? Other threats lay closer at hand—as did one unalloyed pleasure.

Saturday was soccer day in Awake. Late that afternoon, around four o'clock, as the sun faded from its overhead intensity and slanted diffuse through the mango and shea nut tree canopy and the insects intensified their chant, the boys of the village would leave their respective chores and jog down the paths to a clearing about a half mile from Julius's family compound. There, the boys would play soccer. While the girls had to stay at the huts to help prepare the evening meal, all the boys would play, even one whose leg was withered by polio.

His blood pumping with anticipation, Julius finished turning the soil in the bean patch and asked his mother to be excused. Kristina nodded stone-faced assent. She was not a great deal more demonstrative than Charles in expressing love for her children.

◆ ◆ ◆

In fact, toward Julius, Kristina showed little restraint with the cane. Her frequent ill temper was understandable. Kristina was a handsome woman with some education. She had gone to boarding school in Lira for several terms and had thus cost Charles's family seven cows, the maximum dowry around Otuke district. It had seemed like a promising match. Soon after the wedding, however, instead of building up the herd and taking care of his family, Charles began spending his days with the *kongo arege*.

In some ways, Kristina's life resembled that of an overwhelmed single mother in the United States. Along with caring for the children and running the household, she served as the breadwinner—her clay pots, each of which took days to make, were the chief source of family income. One day a few years earlier, Julius had committed the unpardonable sin: He had dropped and broken one of the pots. Kristina's eyes had blazed. She grabbed the flexible tree limb that she used for caning. She reached for Julius but he bolted away and tore off into the bush, with his mother in lithe, wrathful pursuit.

"My mother was a very fast runner," Julius remembers. "If she had the chance, she could have won many races. I inherited my strength from my father. But my speed, I think, comes from my mother."

Indeed, Julius's canings often started with a footrace, with the boy rarely making it more than thirty yards before Kristina collared him. But on the day he broke the jar, goosed by fear, Julius maintained a five-stride lead over his mother as they blasted past the garden and into a field of elephant grass. They ran for what Julius remembers was a long distance—perhaps half a mile. They ran for so long that the grievance seemed to fade. The transgression was forgotten and Kristina seemed to be running to vent rancor of a deeper stripe—or maybe she was simply enjoying herself: the swing of her hips, the glide of her breathing, and the whisper of her bare feet through the tall grass.

Julius never broke another jar, but Kristina continued to be strict with her son. She had little time or inclination for affection. Also, if she were too lenient, Julius might stray from his virtuous ways and follow his father's path. Despite Kristina's severity, Julius deeply loved his mother and knew that his love was returned. The depth of their bond showed most clearly in times of crisis. When Julius appeared to have died from the measles, for instance, Kristina had wailed as the women wrapped him in the burial sheets. That bond was about to manifest again.

◆ ◆ ◆

Soccer-bound, Julius jogged down the trail past the mud flats where men labored bare-chested, smeared with mud, fashioning bricks that were used to anchor the hut foundations. He continued past a giant old mango tree, under which villagers convened for Sunday religious observances and to discuss jurisdictional matters, and past a mango sapling that Julius had recently planted, which would likely bear its first fruit about the time his future bride bore the couple's first child.

The field was an uneven expanse of dirt perhaps half the size of a regulation soccer pitch. The ball was a worn rubber bladder patched so many times that it barely rolled. But to Julius and his friends, the field might as well be a World Cup stadium and the ball made of the most expensive calfskin, as hard and smooth as a goat's udder at milking time.

They chose teams and rolled out the ball; they forgot themselves in the ebb and flow of the contest. Julius ran the right wing in his light-footed stride, exploding away from the defender marking him, drilling centering passes that his striker teammate couldn't handle, but it didn't matter. What mattered was the moving, the release of running, at once unfettered and meted by the geometry and boundaries of the game.

After forty minutes they took a break, sweating and laughing in the shade of the big mango tree. One of the boys had brought a clay jar, and they took turns drinking chaste mouthfuls of water because water was scarce, and the boys had trained themselves to require only a little.

◆ ◆ ◆

Julius can't remember who first saw the men. Maybe they didn't really see them; maybe they felt them. They seemed to seep out of the bush like water from the clay pot that Julius had broken so many years ago. He heard no warning sounds—no dog barking or twig snapping. It was still broad daylight, but the men seemed to move in the manner of the night, with a dreamlike speed and sure intent.

They surrounded the soccer pitch. Julius was startled but not frightened, because by facial marking and stature and manner of dress, he could tell that they were Langi and Acholi, fellow northerners. For a moment, Julius thought that they might even be kinsmen arrived on a sociable visit or piece of tribal business. They appeared the same as the Awake villagers except for one thing: The men carried rifles, AK-47s. They handled the rifles with a fluid ease, as if the weapons were no more exceptional or dangerous than a shovel.

The rebel soldiers surrounded the patch of dirt, and the boys froze. The scuffed, patched ball came rolling toward Julius, but he let it roll into the bush. The rebels stepped forward and claimed the boys. They must have been lurking in the bush for a long time, choosing their victims. Each of the boys appeared to be assigned to one of the soldiers. It was like a cattle market—or a slave market from centuries past. They grabbed the boys by the shoulder and herded them together. They were very fast and sure, and the boys had no choice but to comply.

The man who claimed Julius appeared to be a few years older than the other soldiers, perhaps in his mid-twenties. The man towered above six feet and was enormously strong, his grip like the squeeze of a python on Julius's thin shoulder. Julius instinctively thought of his mother and father: They would protect him. But Kristina was at the hut a quarter mile away, too far to hear any cries for help. And what would the rebels do to her if he did cry out and she ran to him? Charles was finishing his day of drinking in Otuke town. Other parents were on the scene: two men who'd been making bricks and mothers who'd been tending the cook fires and cleaning beans. They left off their labors and stood watching, mouths open, as frozen and shocked as the newly captive boys. One of the fathers stepped forward, holding his hand up to the rebel who had claimed his son.

"No!" the father cried.

The rebel looked amused. He slouched, his weight on one hip, his AK-47 slung jauntily across his shoulder. "No?" he said. "Okay, then I will shoot him right here where he stands. Then after you have watched your son die, I will shoot you."

The rebel grinned. The father backed away. Die on the spot, or die inside by watching your son be taken away forever.

The rebels hustled the boys beyond the line of thorn trees bordering Awake village—a perimeter that Julius had once traveled with his father, who knew it so intimately that he could walk it with his eyes closed—and out of sight of the huts. Until this point events had moved too swiftly for Julius to be afraid, but now panic seized him. His mother, his father, his young sisters and brothers—would he ever see them again? Who would bring them water? Who would protect them from the pythons, the big cats, and the Karamojong?

But as quickly as the fear arose, Julius forced it out of his mind. In another instant, he realized that his old life was finished. An animal instinct for survival took hold. To cling to his old life, even for a moment, would lead to death. Suddenly, the stories he had ignored around the fires and at school burned clearly in his mind. He must be vigilant. He must pay attention every moment and not overlook the smallest detail.

◆ ◆ ◆

They strode through the elephant grass. The sun was sinking to their left, their shadows falling behind them, so he knew that they must be moving in a generally northeastern direction. There were fifteen boys, ranging in age from eleven to around fifteen. Julius was one of the youngest boys and among the smallest. But his physical size was in inverse proportion to his stamina and agility. How could he turn this discrepancy to his advantage?

Each boy was commanded to follow the soldier who had claimed him. Julius followed the big soldier. His previous life had ended, and his new life—however long it would last, maybe only moments remained—depended on this big man striding in front of him. The markings on his face, where a witch doctor had cut his cheeks and applied a poultice of herbs, indicated that he was a Langi. The man wore military fatigues that suggested he had once served in the government army. The other rebels were dressed in a more motley fashion.

The procession was barely out of sight of the village when the rebels abruptly halted. The giant man in the army fatigues turned to Julius. "I am Captain John," he said.

He thrust his rifle into Julius's hands. Not in the manner of punishment, but as if he were presenting a gift. And in fact, throughout most of Africa, the rifle was the ultimate tool and totem, even more indicative of a man's worth than cattle. With a rifle, you could steal the cattle of an unarmed farmer; you could steal his wife and daughter, too. With a rifle, you could serve a warlord patron who, once in power, would reward you with a sinecure granting license to plunder. What other path to wealth, or even comfort, was open to a boy from the bush?

True, living by the rifle most often ended in dying by the rifle, but wasn't that preferable to dying from AIDS, typhus, cholera, or an infected cut? At the Ugandan military garrisons, the boys would flock around the barracks, hustling any odd job, hoping to win favor and a coveted spot in the army, which would grant them the prize of a rifle. This was the prize that Captain John offered Julius Achon.

The AK-47 gleamed in the fading afternoon light. Julius shrank from it. Not that he was delicate or shirked the necessary killing that was part of life in the bush; he was an adept spear hunter. "Something inside told me it was wrong," Julius says. "Once you accepted the life of the rifle, there was no going back."

Seeing the boy hesitate, Captain John's eyes flared. But before the man went deeper into his anger, Julius took the rifle.

Taking wild aim at a thorn tree, he closed his eyes and let fly. The writhing force of the recoil knocked him flat on his back. Captain John gave a disgusted shake of his head but appeared mollified. The boy had felt the godlike killing power, and now Captain John could feed him more chances with the weapon until he'd been converted into a soldier.

Julius tried to hand back the rifle, but Captain John again shook his head. It was now Julius's job to caddy the weapon. He lifted the rifle onto his shoulder and followed his captain into the bush, into the gathering night.

◆ ◆ ◆

They quick-marched, each boy behind his captain. The boys weren't told anything—no explanation, no hint of their destination or what lay in store—and were granted no gesture of comfort or reassurance. They kept moving in the same direction, avoiding the road in favor of the paths worn by animals and the villagers who pursued them. They forged through sharp grass as high as Julius's chest. The AK-47 felt as heavy as a log and stood even taller than the grass; its strap had already raised a welt on his shoulder. The time for the evening meal came and went with no whisper of food.

They kept on at a furious clip. Even in his fog of fear, Julius marveled at how much ground they were covering, the miles they had ranged from home. The huts in the distance looked strange to Julius, and they splashed across streams from which he'd never filled his mother's clay pot. He found the pace oddly exhilarating.

When night fell, the darkness closing down all at once, Julius assumed they'd stop to camp, because every Langi knew that darkness bore the *lujoji*. But the rebels did not stop. Julius suddenly realized that they *were* the evil. The night multiplied his woe. Now Julius's great fear was separation from his abductor, Captain John. Who else was going to protect the small boy from the lion, the python, the crocodile?

Finally, at the first touch of dawn, the soldiers called a halt. They gathered the boys in a bunch and encircled them. They gestured for them to lie down. Julius froze. *Now I am going to die,* he thought. But the rebels also lay down, and in moments all were crashed out for an hour's nap. Then they rose and moved on at the same relentless pace.

The day seemed as terrible as the night. Julius heard the snakes slither through the elephant grass. He saw crocodile eyes in the river shallows. The rocks sliced his ankles and bare feet, and the pitiless sun drilled down through the tree canopy. The day passed in hours of deliriously paced marching and staccato bouts of sleep. The boys were fueled by a single handful of dried beans and a scoop of tepid water from a malarial pond.

◆ ◆ ◆

As they marched, the soldiers appraised their captives, observing which boys held up under the ordeal and which ones faltered. Through the first day and night, none of the boys lagged or stumbled. When the captains roused them from their brief sleep, all fifteen boys jumped to their feet to resume the trek. Like Julius, they were hard-footed and inured to the privations of the bush. But on the morning—or was it evening? afternoon?—of the third day, one of the boys, Samuel, could not rise when commanded.

Samuel was around fourteen, a kinsman of Julius. The two boys would walk to school together. Sometimes Samuel would give Julius half of a banana or sweet potato that he'd brought from home. Now Samuel was sick. A bout of malaria had caught him. Malaria was universal in the villages, and a mosquito could reinfect you at any time, bringing on days of racking fever and arctic chills. Samuel shivered now, his teeth chattering, twitching uncontrollably. There was no goatskin to cover and warm him. Samuel was clearly incapable of walking or even standing.

"Finish him," one of the captains said. The boys looked up. The captain pointed to a pile of rocks by the trail. "Finish him," he said again. "There is no point wasting a bullet on that fellow."

The boys froze as the meaning came clear.

"Don't worry," the captain said. "You'll be doing him a favor. Besides, he won't be dead forever. Samuel will just be resting."

The captain handed a rock to the youngest boy. "Go ahead," he said.

The little boy, addled with exhaustion and fear, not knowing what to think or believe—maybe here in this unknown country the dead really weren't dead forever—took the rock. If he did not take the rock, moreover, there was every reason to assume that the captain would use it to finish *him*. Reaching similar conclusions, several other boys picked up rocks.

Julius, however, did not pick up a rock. Captain John watched him but didn't say anything. The boys armed with rocks surrounded the shivering, chattering Samuel and finished him.

◆ ◆ ◆

For three more days they marched, covering a hundred miles. They crossed into Soroti district, dominated by Lake Kyoga, a great swamp full of hippos and water buffalo and pine trees jutting out of the scrub trees. They entered a forest so deep that the trees shut out the equatorial sun. Even at midday, shade dappled the reeds and the marshy earth. Here, out of sight from government aircraft and infantry patrols, the rebel army had established a base camp. The three-day shakedown cruise from Awake was finished. Seemingly chaotic, a fevered overland stampede, the journey was in fact carefully plotted, conforming to the best practices, as it were, of African guerrilla warfare. It was primarily staged to test and mold the incoming class of boy soldiers.

The marathon march on minimal food and sleep was meant to disarm and disorient the boys. Forcing them to bond with their captains cut emotional ties with their homes and families. The forced killing of one of their friends bound them together in guilt. Rifles and marijuana were introduced as rewards. The ordeal of the trek weeded out the weak ones, who, subsequently speared or smashed to death by their friends, formed fodder for the rebels' psychological manipulation. Terrorized, guilt-ridden, the surviving boys would lose their physical and psychic bearings, transferring trust and allegiance to their captors. By the end of the march, when they reeled into the camp, the first and hardest stage of basic training would be concluded. They were primed to begin their apprenticeship in Joseph Kony's army.

◆ ◆ ◆

Kony: His name meant "help" in his native Luo language. The Acholi and Langi were cultural siblings. Both tribes spoke Luo, their dialects differing only in inflection and idiom, similar to the difference between the American English spoken in Georgia and in California.

Kony was born around 1962 in the village of Odek, not far from Gulu, a city about twenty-five miles north of Awake. Like Julius, he grew up in a circular thatched hut, humping jugs of water and cutting cane, and also like Julius he was baptized Catholic. Religiously inclined, Kony served for a time as an altar boy for the local parish priest. He then became a witch doctor, a profession of high stature in rural Uganda. The young man apparently thrived in the calling. He seemed to possess the third eye, a special insight into diseases and suffering, and could place himself in a dream state that empowered him to heal. Away from his occult duties, Joseph Kony seemed like just another villager, a slender, loose-limbed man who loved to dance.

And the population was primed to follow such a guru. Alice Auma, Kony's distant cousin, had developed into a sorceress of national renown. In 1986, Museveni drove his rebel army into Kampala to take command of the country, deposing Obote, the hapless champion of the north, for a second time. Museveni started a ruthless campaign of reprisal against the Obote faction that had ravaged the southerners. In opposition, Alice Auma rallied a ragged blend of northern villagers and disaffected soldiers into a force called the Holy Spirit Movement.

Combining disparate elements of Acholi and Langi religion, Christian doctrine, colonial history, and Western pop culture, Alice mixed a bizarre but potent cocktail that, for a time, achieved a striking military success. She convinced HSM soldiers to smear themselves with shea nut butter, promising that it would shield them from enemy bullets. She invoked James Bond, the fictional 007, as a protective talisman. She equated the cause of the Langi and Acholi to that of the Old Testament Israelites. She sought counsel from the ghost of an Italian colonel who had explored Uganda at the turn of the twentieth century.

Alice preached that she had been sent by the divine to rescue the Acholi and Langi from the consequence of their sins. Alice Auma became Alice Lakwena, or Alice the Messenger. Adhering to the principle of *gwooko dog paco* (defending the homestead), Holy Spirit Movement warriors marched into combat chanting the name of an imaginary British secret agent. Museveni intended to slaughter the northerners, and they had nothing to lose.

Somehow, to the considerable embarrassment of the government troops, the Holy Spirit Movement was able to win a few battles, gain some momentum, and mount an offensive toward the south. In October 1987, however, the train ran out of steam. Chanting James Bond and slathered with shea nut butter, the HSM warriors got splattered in a decisive battle, just fifty miles north of Kampala. Alice was driven into exile in Kenya, where she died a few years later, having returned to poverty and obscurity. While the Holy Spirit Movement seemed a freakish anomaly, its rise and fall proved pivotal. It served to drain order and discipline from the Uganda wars. It opened the door to unhinged religion and uncontrolled mayhem.

◆ ◆ ◆

Following the HSM's defeat, most Langi and Acholi reluctantly accepted the Museveni government. But there were some holdouts, northerners who out of fear or calculation chose to continue the struggle. One of these diehards was Kony.

It's not known whether Kony fought in the front lines of the Holy Spirit Movement—if he was one of those ravers smeared with shea nut butter—or if he observed the action from back in Gulu. Clearly, however, he made a close study of Alice's charismatic appeal and unorthodox but effective leadership style. Editing out the looniest elements of his cousin's doctrine, Kony composed his own Catholic/animist creed. Collecting the scattered remnants of the HSM, he started a fresh guerrilla insurgency.

Many Acholi were willing to join him. The British, Obote, and Alice had all failed them, and now Museveni, the latest nemesis from the south, was threatening them again. There was nothing left in the seen or unseen realms to protect the people, and Kony spoke to their animist faith in the dead. Rather than overthrowing the government, his goal was to reclaim territory. He started to fight and plunder on a small scale, working the seams among the villages of far northern Uganda, picking up adult conscripts by persuasion and boys by kidnapping.

◆ ◆ ◆

Kony hardly invented the tactic. Children had long been exploited in central and eastern African conflicts, including long-running wars in Sudan and Congo. Warlords favored boy soldiers because they hadn't learned to value life and thus were heedless in battle. Modern automatic weapons proved manageable for smaller arms and hands. You could readily brainwash unschooled boys from the bush. Sturdy and uncomplaining, they made excellent footmen and porters. Finally, with the average female in northern Uganda giving birth to seven children, boys were in bountiful supply.

Combining charisma, bush savvy, and sociopathic ambition, Kony quickly built his child-centered army. He had luck and timing on his side. Early in 1988, disaffected soldiers of Obote's defeated army began to join Kony's militia, boosting a ragged band into a more legitimate fighting force. Meanwhile, the fledgling Museveni government chose to aid insurgents battling the Islamic government of neighboring Sudan (which, at the time, hosted a budding jihadist named Osama bin Laden). To retaliate, the Sudanese began funneling aid to Kony, not out of enthusiasm for his cause but due to the precept that any enemy of my enemy is my friend.

For the moment, the Kony militia remained a relatively conventional central African guerrilla force. As a matter of policy, Kony was not yet torturing and murdering the people for whom he was ostensibly fighting. He kidnapped boys, but he killed them only in a case like Samuel's, when the boy proved too weak to be of service, or when he disobeyed orders and angered his captain, or if he tried to escape and return to his native village. But if a boy went with the program, he might survive for a while. Boys were of immediate value as porters and valets, and some developed into reliable warriors. After going to the trouble of stealing a boy, it made little sense to kill him.

Similarly cold-blooded thinking drove Kony's treatment of girls. Because the insurgency seemed a short-term enterprise, his militia did not require females for sex, procreation, or servitude. Kidnapping girls, at that point, seemed like more trouble than it was worth—a policy that would change radically in the years to come. When Julius Achon and his thirteen hungry, exhausted, terrified friends arrived at the Soroti camp in January 1988, it was an all-male enclave.

It was a big camp by guerrilla standards, composed of a few hundred men and boys, hidden deep in the forest by a lake and a swamp. Kony had chosen the location because government troops were reluctant to penetrate the swamp, and because pilots of the *sombiye*, the jet fighters greatly feared by the rebels, couldn't spot their targets under the dense tree canopy. Museveni could deploy helicopter gunships, supplied through the friendly U.S. arms industry, but they were vulnerable to rocket-propelled grenades that the Sudanese government provided the rebels.

The camp also held a strategic position, less than six miles from Soroti town, on the main road leading south to Kampala. If an attack on Soroti succeeded, Kony could then contemplate an offensive probe across the Nile. Such a frontal assault entailed considerable risk, but if Alice's crackpot army could advance so deep into the south, anything was possible.

Julius and the other boys from Awake settled into the camp routine. The captains called them "bodyguards," but they were really personal servants. The boys rose at dawn, built fires, and prepared tea and breakfast for their captains. After breakfast, most mornings, the boys followed the soldiers out of the camp to raid nearby villages for food and other supplies—the guerrilla equivalent of grocery shopping.

The boys were required to enter the huts and gardens to steal whatever lay at hand: chickens, goats, eggs, beans, bananas, cassava roots. Julius hated this job. He hated looking into a villager's eyes as he robbed him. In an instant, Julius was reaping what a family had invested months of toil in sowing. He knew full well how much work it took to raise a chicken: sheltering it from foxes, snakes, and birds of prey, husbanding it to the day it was fit to slaughter for a family feast. But the boy had no choice. If the farmer balked at surrendering the chicken, Julius had to cane him.

Captain John showed him how to use a tree limb, tapered at the end to raise welts. The farmer had to lie on his stomach in the dirt. It was humiliating, ludicrous, a small boy whipping a grown man. Even when he reared back and swung with his full weight, Julius couldn't bring enough force to really hurt the villager. But Julius had to go through the motion of whipping, and the farmer had to fake wails of pain. They enacted this grotesque charade because Captain John was watching, AK-47 in hand.

Kony's soldiers were always watching. In camp, the soldiers watched the boys clean and cook the chickens they had stolen. The soldiers watched the boys as they tended the fires, making sure they didn't talk among themselves. Even in the dead of night the soldiers were watching: To prevent escape, they made the boys pee in jars rather than go out in the bush. The boys were forbidden to talk about home. If they were caught doing so, they received a caning. But unlike the sham beatings that Julius inflicted, these punishments left scars. While the soldiers were watching their captives, however, the boys were studying them.

◆ ◆ ◆

Julius, of course, made a special study of Captain John, one of the professional soldiers who had defected to the rebels when Museveni took power. Knowing that Museveni would seek revenge on Langi troops who'd been loyal to Obote, Captain John—to avoid being summarily shot or skewered by a *panga* (machete)—had left the government army to join Kony's rebel force.

By the standards of an organized military, he had deserted, but most Ugandans understood that the average uniformed soldier or police officer was more of a self-employed entrepreneur than a disinterested public servant. Governments rose and fell as often as the tide in Lake Victoria, and amid the chaos a trooper or a cop might go months without getting paid. To make do, he relied on bribes from citizens or hired out as a private security guard or to a warlord allied to his tribe. Captain John had no interest in Kony's mysticism, his Alice-derived shea nut butter moonshine. Captain John wanted to save his own skin and play the best hand available.

"He was a big lover man," Julius recalls. "He had a girl in every village."

Captain John also liked his ganja. He was a powerful fighter but possessed an indolent nature. He was willing to overlook small transgressions and, most important, did not enjoy killing for its own sake. Captain John realized that soldiering offered an infinitely softer life than farming. Instead of going to the trouble of raising a chicken, he could just tell Julius to steal one. He could have his way with the village girls. If Kony's rebellion succeeded—if northerners could wrest control of the government from the southerners, or perhaps share power—then Captain John might one day sit behind a desk and skim development money. He would own a villa and a car, just like the Museveni sycophants who presently held sway in Kampala.

Stoked on weed, Captain John would sometimes lecture Julius. *I did you a big favor by stealing you away from your sorry village! You are a smart, tough, capable boy—you might go far as a soldier if you stick with it!*

The other boys from Awake weren't so lucky. Their captains might get a spliff inside them, yawn and scratch, and decide that they felt like killing. Then the next villager they saw would end up *panga*-hacked or with his skull crushed by a rifle butt. To avoid being killed themselves, the boys had to assist in the murders. Captain John, by contrast, resorted to violence only when it was necessary or suited his interest. During that winter, there were relatively few engagements with the enemy. Like so many armies, Kony's mostly waited.

◆ ◆ ◆

The days wheeled by in terror and routine. By dint of constant vigilance and assiduous effort, Julius managed to fly under the radar and to keep on Captain John's good side—until the day the villager rebelled.

The raid began like any other. The rebels approached a village and the boys filtered past the huts, looking for food to steal. In front of one hut, Julius came upon a man holding a chicken. When Julius reached to take the bird, the farmer tightened his grip on it.

"No," the man said. "I need this chicken to feed my family."

As Julius and the farmer faced off, Captain John came upon the scene. In the script, the villager, intimidated by the soldier's appearance, quickly surrendered the chicken, and Julius caned the man for his brief insurrection. But this villager changed the story. He stubbornly held on to his chicken.

Instead of reacting with anger, Captain John smiled, as if he'd been hoping for such a moment. He handed his rifle to Julius. "Shoot him," he told the boy.

Julius felt a bolt of terror. The game was over. Captain John had been on to him all along. He had noticed and remembered everything: how Julius only pretended to suck at a spliff when one was handed to him; how he avoided picking up a rock when it had been time to finish Samuel. Here was another test, one Julius saw no way of ducking.

He accepted the AK-47 from his captain and fingered its trigger. Over the weeks of Julius's captivity, the welt on his shoulder where he caddied the weapon had toughened into a callus.

"Shoot him!" Captain John ordered again. His eyes had grown hot and angry. The farmer held his chicken, too terrified to move or speak, waiting to die. Julius was also frozen, knowing that he could not squeeze the trigger and that therefore he would also die. The moment stretched on. A black sheet of fear enveloped Julius. Finally Captain John grabbed the AK-47; the boy closed his eyes. But instead of shooting Julius, the rebel turned the rifle on the farmer. With an almost careless gesture, as if he were tossing a plate of dirty water to the ground after washing, Captain John shot the man in the leg.

The man screamed, a high keening scream that rose and fell with the pulse of blood from his shattered leg. "Take the chicken!" Captain John roared. Julius did as he was told, grabbing the chicken, wringing its neck, and following his captain into the bush toward the next village as the man continued to scream behind them.

They had walked only a short distance when Captain John stopped, lifted Julius as if he weighed no more than a frog, and flung him to the ground. Tearing off a tree branch, the soldier whipped Julius, all his ease and indolence vanished, his thick muscles pumping, sweat sprouting on his forehead, cords rising out of his massive neck, hitting the boy so hard that he grunted with each blow.

In camp that evening, as Captain John ate the chicken that Julius had prepared, he told the boy that he'd been lucky to escape with the caning. The captain would have shot Julius instead of the farmer—or really, after he shot the farmer—but since Julius was a fellow Langi, he had chosen to be merciful.

"But don't disobey again, boy," Captain John said. "Next time, I promise I will shoot you."

◆ ◆ ◆

Chastened, Julius returned to his duties. The days became weeks, the weeks slipped into months, and the dry winter season gave way to the rains. He would see Joseph Kony around the camp. At that point, Kony was still gauging his power, developing his craft. He would speak often to his militia, declaiming in a rhythmic church-style call-and-response. He told his soldiers that it was their turn to be rich, that God wanted *them* to rule Uganda, not the infidels of the south. At times the leader would fall into a trance and speak in the tongues of the four spirits guiding him: *Divo, Silindy Makay, Who are you?*, and *Juma Oris.*

Kony waved his finger as he preached, harangued, and free-associated. Because he was Acholi, a farmer from the north, he intimately understood his listeners' fears, grievances, hungers, and dreams. Although he sought comfort and plenty for his soldiers, material wealth appeared to mean little to him personally. He did not pursue the usual warlord's path of patronage and corruption. He had never served in the regular government army and didn't seem interested in coming out of the bush and into the city and living large like Idi Amin.

◆ ◆ ◆

"Kony mixed the gospel with the devil," Julius says. "But love does not allow you to kill."

◆ ◆ ◆

At its peak, Julius estimates, about 250 men and boys occupied the camp. Although gratuitous killing was increasingly common among the soldiers, it had not yet become epidemic. There was plenty of death, but it traveled via the usual avenues: typhus, cholera, AIDS, infected wounds. In general, morale among the men seemed high. They hoped to prevail in the looming attack on Soroti town.

Something big was brewing. Julius and the other boys were never informed of any plan, of course, but they could sense something in the air, in the tone of the captains' voices as they talked in the ganja circles, in the tension of their shoulders, in the way they cleaned their weapons, in their impatience with the boys if they dawdled while performing a chore. Joseph Kony was more visible and talked more often to his troops.

Julius remembers that Kony was frequently ripped on weed. In photographs from that period, he has the same red-eyed, slack-jawed, stone-killer look as thugs in the Mexican and Caribbean drug cartels. Like most prospering organizations, the militia took on the habits and personality of its chief executive: The soldiers also loved their weed—and only that, as Kony forbade alcohol in the camp. Captain John and his buddies would blow ganja and start honking and waving their rifles around. Julius knew that his captain's heart wasn't in it, that he was just putting on a show, but ultimately what was the difference?

The rhythm of the days continued: Go out on patrol, steal a chicken, bring it back to camp, clean and boil it, and serve it up to Captain John, who would sit on one of the wooden bush stools that villagers often carried on their heads and that reminded Julius of home.

It seemed like Captain John was always stoned and always talk-ing, mostly bragging about his prowess as a cocksman, but now there was an edge to his voice. Since the scene with the villager and the chicken, Julius worried that Captain John, for all his seeming indolence, was just waiting for the slightest excuse to kill him.

If death didn't come by disease or his captain's hand, it might be delivered by the *sombiye*, the dreaded government fighter jets that kept flying closer to the camp. Now, instead of starting each morn-ing by looking for a lion's pawprint, Julius woke up thinking that this might be the day he would die.

◆ ◆ ◆

Life in the camp had grown desperate, but escape—even the idea of escape—was more terrifying. Assuming you got away from the camp—a huge assumption, because the soldiers were always watch-ing, well aware of the thoughts running through a boy's head, be-cause many of them had been in the same position themselves, and not that long ago—assuming you escaped, your troubles were just beginning. Once you were on your own, away from the rebels, with no rifle, you were fair game for the villagers seeking retribution. The farmer you stole a goat from at gunpoint yesterday wouldn't hesitate to slice you with a *panga* today.

And once you were exposed and on the run, the *sombiye* pilots could spot you and strafe you into ribbons. If you avoided the venge-ful villagers and circling government deathships, the Soroti swamp, with its malarial mosquitoes and aggressive water buffalo and lurking razor-toothed crocodiles and twelve-foot pythons, might do you in.

Beyond all that, if you did make it to your village, you could hardly rest easy, because you knew that, back in the rebel camp, your friends were being tortured and killed in retaliation for your escape. Finally, once back home, your clansmen would likely shun you. You had become *orum*, forever infected by the curse of the bush.

So Julius stuck with the camp, waiting and watching. The boys from Awake saw each other only glancingly; each boy remained tethered to his captain. After months away from home, months of rebel brainwashing, a few of the boys were turning. They were smoking the ganja and brandishing the AK-47s and showing off for the captains. But not Julius. Although careful not to appear prudish, he continued to avoid the marijuana.

At the same time, he couldn't appear delicate or unmanly. He pulled his weight during the raids on villages. Although it pained him to do so, he would cane and shove terrified farmers when they showed resistance. Julius was in survival mode, doing enough to get by but not enough to get singled out for either exceptional bravery or timidity.

◆ ◆ ◆

The day before the battle, Joseph Kony addressed his army. "We are going to fight and overthrow the government." He spoke in that hypnotic singsong. "We are going to get rich ourselves."

As Kony spoke, standing on one of the towering, ancient anthills, Julius looked out over the camp. Soldiers and boy soldiers, as far as he could see. All eyes were locked on Kony. Even Julius was mesmerized. On the one hand he fantasized escape every moment, but on the other hand he wanted the rebels to win the battle—for the militia to succeed so that they could romp into Kampala and rule. Julius wanted to ride around in a car. He wanted to fly like a god in a big airplane.

Soldiers on the winning side got rich after a war. You pledged your loyalty to your captain or general and in return, if you survived the war, you were appointed to a government post. You were given an office, a title, and permission to steal. Ugandans had learned this behavior years earlier from observing their colonial masters. A boy from the bush had no middle-class job ladder to climb.

The boys in camp now outnumbered the men. Contrary to the rumors, Kony had not yet begun to send boys out front during a firefight, especially for a key battle like the one the next day. In that conflagration, the seasoned troops would fight while the boys stayed back in camp, awaiting the outcome.

◆ ◆ ◆

The rebels attacked Soroti on an April day a month into the rainy season. It was one of the few head-to-head engagements with government troops in the history of the Lord's Resistance Army. Kony much preferred to work by ambush.

The soldiers set out early in the morning, before dawn, while the boys waited back in camp, guarded by a skeleton crew of older combatants. They waited in great suspense for their fate to be decided. Part of Julius hoped that the rebels would be routed so that he might escape his bondage and return home; another part hoped that the rebels would prevail and that somehow Kony's promises would come to pass—the hard times in the north would finally end. It was difficult for Julius to envision what being rich would look like. He imagined eating meat every day and carrying water in a plastic jerrycan instead of his mother's clay pot.

Hours passed; the boys sat and waited, hearing the booms, blasts, and howls of ordnance. Far in the distance jets looped and screamed. It was like that first suite of artillery explosions Julius had heard as a small child. He sensed disaster. He had learned to expect calamity, terrible dark forces pursuing him.

Rebel soldiers soon started reeling in, sweating, bleeding, panic-stricken, and wild-eyed, blowing past the boys who awaited the verdict. For months the rebels had watched the boys every moment. Now they were invisible to the captains; they might as well have been rocks or bush stools. And here came Captain John, sprinting wildly, no longer indolent or spouting braggadocio.

"*Toka, toka!* Move, move!" he roared. Not to warn Julius to flee, but just to get him the hell out of the way.

Defeat, Julius realized. He was just beginning to process this fact, to calculate what defeat meant, what the militia's next move might be and how he should move in response, when he heard a rending noise. A terrible sound seemed to swallow him.

The red earth shook, the pine trees trembled, and it seemed that the swampy ground would split open. On the heels of this cataclysmic howl came the patter of a hard rain. The world must be ending,

Julius thought, because the morning sky was cloudless. A gust of rain swept over a stampeding soldier, and the man fell as if shot. Then Julius understood: The man *had* been shot; the rain was made of steel, not water. Julius looked up and saw a *sombiye* pulse overhead as if flung by an angry god. The jet had trailed the routed rebel soldiers back to the camp, and now it would slaughter them all.

Along with the other boys, Julius dove for cover. They huddled under trees on the edge of the great swamp, adjacent to a quarter-mile-wide swath of elephant grass, which had grown dry and prickly, waist-high on a grown man and up to the necks of the boys. The jet fighter circled out after its first pass. Julius prayed that it would fly away, but his prayers sank into the dirt. The jet returned, dropping another gust of bullets. The boys cowered. The captains would not protect them; they had fled in desperation.

This could be the chance to escape. For the first time since their abduction ten weeks earlier, the children weren't being watched by their captors. After months of raiding the local villages, the boys knew the area and the general direction of home.

The government jet still raked and screamed. Death from the sky, or death on the ground, if not today then someday soon, when, red-eyed and ripped on ganja, the boys would be sent by their captains to run point on an attack and the government soldiers would cut them down. Or if the boys hesitated to attack—or maybe even if they didn't hesitate but simply because their captains were bored, possessed of a devilish whim—then the rebels would shoot them instead.

Julius felt especially vulnerable. Sooner or later—probably sooner—Captain John would grow weary of toying with Julius, batting him around like a cat playing with a crippled mouse, and finish him.

The boys made their break, fleeing from the cover of trees and into the field of elephant grass. The jet swooped down. Wouldn't the pilot recognize that they were not the enemy but fleeing children desperate for home? But there was no way to know. The boys tore through the elephant grass, hearing the jet close behind them, praying that God for once would be merciful and that the steel rain wouldn't fall. But again death rained down.

Julius dove into the grass, covering his head with his arms as if that could protect him, burrowing into the earth like a bug. The jet strafed and strafed again, the pilot likely grateful for the easy targets. Amid the relative quiet, when the jet banked and turned between strafing runs, Julius heard his friends screaming. He glanced up once as the jet circled out and saw that the grass had turned red with blood. Blood jumped from the grass in crimson spurts.

Crawling, Julius finally reached the forest on the far side of the field. Fourteen boys had started across the field, and nine had made it to the trees. Three of the surviving boys were badly wounded. The boys burrowed in and waited. The jet made several more passes over the camp, circling with an observant, buzzard-like aspect. The pilot seemed reluctant to leave such an abundant hunting ground. Finally, he flew away.

Across the field, the rebel camp was silent. The boys tensed, waiting for the captains to come striding across the field to reclaim them, but no men appeared. The boys waited the rest of the day, gnawing on wild roots that they grubbed from the soil. At nightfall they rose from their hiding places. The three wounded boys were too weak to walk. There was no choice but to leave them behind.

Closing the day's horror into an emotional box to open later, Julius and the other five boys turned away from the strafed and bloody field, away from the bodies of their friends, away from the rebel captains, away from the AK-47s, and started trekking back toward Awake.

There was only one road, so they couldn't get lost.

◆ ◆ ◆

In reverse, the boys repeated the forced march they'd performed a few months earlier. Now they were free, but now they were even more afraid.

And yet neither the soldiers nor the airplanes chased them, so the boys settled into their journey, blending among the villagers traveling the road at a pace and rhythm set long before the advent of Joseph Kony. They kept their eyes down, avoiding notice, ever vigilant for a passerby sounding an alarm by ululating—*Uganda 911,* went the joke. They ate no food during the three-day trek. At night they slept in the bush at the side of the road, shivering in the rain.

In the morning, reckoning by the sun, they would strike a general northwesterly heading. When unsure of their course, they resorted to traditional bush craft, tossing dry leaves into the wind, spitting, and following the direction that fate pointed.

As they neared Otuke district and home, another danger arose. The government army had reclaimed the territory from the rebels and had established checkpoints. To determine if the passing boys and men were serving with the rebels, the soldiers inspected the flesh of their right shoulders. A welt indicated the strap-mark of an AK-47. If they found such a bruise, the government soldiers would "detain" the traveler, who would never be seen again.

Now Julius approached the checkpoint, manned by three red-eyed government soldiers as frightened, addled, and violent as the rebels Julius had just escaped. The soldiers' eyes fastened briefly on Julius and then moved on—even Kony, they decided, couldn't make a killer out of such a slip of a boy. The soldiers waved Julius through the checkpoint without inspecting his calloused shoulder.

When the boys finally reached Awake, they paused at the edge of the open place where, on that afternoon three months earlier, they had innocently played soccer. The village women looked up from their cook fires and stiffened, thinking at first that these boys were rebels raiding to claim more children. The women were right to fear him, Julius thought. He knew that he'd changed, that he projected a different kind of force than before. A long moment passed before the women recognized their sons and ran, weeping, to embrace them.

◆ ◆ ◆

Julius was back in Awake, returned again from the dead. Death, so insatiable and indiscriminate in Uganda, oddly seemed to have no taste for Julius Achon.

Kristina rejoiced. When Julius was gone, she told him, the family had prayed for his deliverance. The entire family, even his father. Yes, God had been merciful, returning both Julius and Charles to Kristina. One day during the rains, she explained, Charles had drunk so much *kongo arege* that he became sick and nearly died. Since that day he hadn't touched a drop. He had resumed working hard and was now providing for the family. He prayed every day for forgiveness, Kristina said, and for Julius's welfare and return. Now all of their prayers, praise God, had been answered.

But what of the prayers of their neighbors? Out of the fifteen boys kidnapped, only six had returned. It fell to Julius to deliver the dreadful news to the parents of his slain friends. "The spirit of killing was not so general then in northern Uganda," Julius says. "A person's death still meant something." The mothers wailed, out of both grief and the fact that they could not bury their sons in Awake, their native place. How then could the boys' spirits find rest? After bearing these tidings to the mothers, a profound weariness fell over Julius Achon.

"My mind needed a vacation," he says. "I was tired of being chased."

He felt as if he'd been pursued his whole life. The teachers chased him at school because he couldn't pay his tuition fee. The Karamojong chased him because they wanted cattle. Kristina chased him because he'd broken one of her pots. Captain John chased him because he wouldn't shoot the villager. The *sombiye* chased him because he was an easy target.

A quiet, chrysalis-like spate of time ensued. After their setback at Soroti, Kony and his militia suspended attacks, retreating north to Gulu and the ungoverned borderlands of Sudan. Museveni's forces took sporadic stabs at the rebels, but mostly the war faded, gestating before blooming again with renewed violence in the 1990s. Life in Otuke district resumed its familiar rhythm. Julius, however, couldn't bring himself to return to school. Too much had happened. He didn't feel like a child anymore. Also, he'd begun to question the certainty of his future in Awake.

Sensing her son's state of mind, Kristina hurried to find Julius a bride, a girl to bear him babies and pin him down to life in the village. Just as he'd shrunk from the rifle when Captain John first offered it, however, Julius recoiled from the idea of marriage. He just wanted to sit still until things became real to him again.

◆ ◆ ◆

He couldn't talk about his experiences. The Langi believed that a warrior returning from the bush possessed malevolent, superhuman powers. What manner of darkness had Julius brought back with him? Even if the boy were an unwitting carrier, the sickness might lay waste to Awake. His clansmen didn't regard Julius with the outright hostility that would greet returning LRA boy soldiers and bush brides in the years to come; Julius wasn't shunned, but they remained wary of him. And Julius kept silent about his time in the war. He understood that when you talked about the devil, you risked inviting him into your hut.

Still, his months with the rebels haunted him. Scenes replayed in his mind. Ripping through the bush in a fever dream. The slither of the python. The hatred on the villager's face as Julius awkwardly caned him. The farmer's scream when Captain John shot him in the leg. The wail of the *sombiye*. The jump of blood in the elephant grass as Julius crawled to freedom. But now, safely back home in Awake, he wondered: Was this truly freedom?

It was more than taboo that kept Julius from talking about his time with Kony. It was guilt. Because at odd, fleeting moments during his servitude, as he trailed Captain John from village to village, never knowing where the day or night would deliver him, Julius had felt an exhilarating sense of adventure and release. Fate had sprung him from Awake, delivered him a glimpse of a wider world. Now, back home, Julius hungered to escape again, on his own terms, and to never return.

Besides the war, however, what other way out beckoned? School? Scratching figures in the dirt under the mango tree with fifty other barefoot boys? And if Julius did make it through the equivalent of sixth grade, what advantage would that give him? What sort of career or future would open? Julius bleakly envisioned tending bar at a Lira hotel or joining the white-shirted traffic police, who made their living by shaking down one-hundred-shilling bribes from truck drivers.

◆ ◆ ◆

The weight of all these questions, all these memories, pulled down Julius, almost to the point that a witch doctor had to be summoned to exorcise the dark spirit that blighted the boy. Eventually he rallied, at least outwardly. He had no choice; he was the eldest son, counted on by his family to haul water, tend goats, and cut sugar cane. He resumed his chores and again walked the three miles to school each morning.

Julius saw no release or escape. He was the firstborn hope of his clan, the boy who rose from the dead when he had measles, who carried his younger sisters and brothers on his back, who would inherit his father's holdings and restore their luster. But at the same time, he felt the tug of a greater calling. Why had God chosen him to be abducted by the rebels? And why, amid so much death, had his life been spared?

One evening, after the day's work was finished, Julius sat with his father outside their hut. The smoke from the village fires hung above the shea nut trees. In the forest, the daytime sounds were giving way to the racket of the night creatures.

It was the time of evening when, in the lucky parts of the world, children worked their mobile devices while their parents glanced at the TV news—pixel images of conflict in the unlucky nations. There were no televisions in Awake; there were none within twenty miles. Julius had never watched TV or worn a pair of shoes. He was only dimly aware of the shape and lineaments of the outside world.

At that moment a jet airliner soared above the village, its wing lights glowing, its contrail tracing a graceful arc, and a faint, fierce whisper of its engines audible amid the bush cacophony. Julius watched the airplane with a longing that felt like a knife in his ribs.

"What must you do to ride in one of those jets?" he asked his father.

"That is not possible," Charles said.

"There must be a way. Somebody rides in that airplane."

His father looked into the fire. "Airplanes are for people from the south," he said.

Father and son were silent for a time. Charles felt guilty about his erstwhile drunkenness. He felt ashamed for not protecting Julius from the rebels. Charles recalled the longing he felt as a boy, when, during brutal days picking cotton for the British, he had dreamed of foreign lands.

"There is only one way for a boy from the north to have money and ride in an airplane," Charles said finally. "He must learn to run. He must become like John Akii-Bua."

◆ ◆ ◆

In Uganda in the 1980s, John Akii-Bua was almost as well known as Idi Amin. Other Ugandans were famous among their tribes or regions, but no writer, artist, actor, or musician—and certainly no statesperson—had emerged to arouse collective national pride. But in 1972, as Amin rose to power, John Akii-Bua, a Langi from Lira district, a farm boy just like Julius, won the gold medal in the 400-meter hurdles at the Munich Olympic Games.

Akii-Bua had trained for his triumph on the pitted dirt track around the dusty soccer pitch in Lira town. He had worked with legendary intensity. In order to learn proper hurdling form, he hung a pole above each barrier, banging his head if he held it too high. Working out in ninety-degree heat, he wore a twenty-pound weighted vest. He set his practice hurdles a foot above the height of the one used in competition.

At the Munich Games, the style of Akii-Bua's gold-medal run was as impressive as its substance. After blasting across the finish line five meters ahead of the silver-medalist, Akii-Bua kept on running, clearing two more hurdles, as if the stadium couldn't hold him; as if, by extension, the old world order could no longer suppress the boundless creative energy bursting out of the new, liberated Africa.

Uganda went wild. After the Games, throngs welcomed Akii-Bua home at the Entebbe airport. Policemen stopped him on the street to shake his hand and thank him. He was showered with money and gifts and traveled to European capitals. He drove a big car and amassed eight wives and more than forty children. He was favored—and eventually doomed—by the patronage of the most important and powerful Ugandan of all: Idi Amin.

By the 1980s, Akii-Bua was enshrined as a national hero. Ugandan children learned about his magnificent Olympic victory and the fame and wealth he gained as a reward. Less reported was the misery he suffered at the hands of Amin. Inevitably, the president grew to mistrust those close to him. So it was with John Akii-Bua, whose popularity provoked intense jealousy in Amin.

On the eve of the 400-meter finals at the 1976 Olympics in Montreal, where Akii-Bua was poised to win a second consecutive gold medal, Amin pulled Uganda's runners out of the race, ostensibly to protest South Africa's invasion of Angola. From then on, Akii-Bua's fortunes declined precipitously. He lost his money, his villa, his cars, his women. To avoid execution, he fled in exile to Kenya.

Charles didn't tell Julius about the Olympian's fall; he probably didn't know about it himself. The point was that if Julius dreamed of transcending the village, if he wanted to ride in cars and airplanes, he had to become like John Akii-Bua.

Julius wasn't quite sure what the 400-meter hurdles was, but he knew there was a stadium in Lira named after John Akii-Bua. If one boy from the bush could learn to run so fast, then why not another?

Julius Achon started to run.

◆ ◆ ◆

He had been running his whole life, but he never realized it, was never conscious of it, and never thought about it. Now he ran purposefully and with single-minded intent: It was all or nothing; either he had to become the next Akii-Bua or there was no point running at all.

He began by running back and forth on the dirt track between the family hut and the main road, roughly a two-mile round-trip. He ran early in the morning, before going to school. It felt strange, paying attention to something that had been as automatic as breathing. Julius knew nothing about track, beyond that the goal was to get from Point A to Point B faster than the next boy. So on his first morning of training, he tore away from the hut at a dead sprint, his bare feet hitting up puffs of dirt; he ran as he had that morning in the rebel camp with the hellhound *sombiye* overhead. After a quarter mile he was spent. He stopped, hands on knees, panting—grabbing his shorts, he would later learn to call the gesture. This wasn't good; his goal was to make the Olympics, and he couldn't even run a mile. He'd have to try a different tactic.

He began to experiment. One day he'd run the entire distance at a steady pace, perhaps three-quarters of his maximum speed. The next day he would blast through the first leg of his run and slow down during the second half. The day after he'd reverse the order, and the day after that he tried mixing speeds: fast-slow-fast, slow-fast-slow-fast, and so on. Julius intuitively sensed that the key to winning a race was to finish strong. He taught himself to always hold a portion of energy in reserve.

He started to build his days around these sessions. He would awaken earlier each morning, impatiently waiting for dawn. He already realized he was good at running, but more important, running belonged to him. A boy from the bush typically possessed nothing of his own, no tool or toy, no technique, praxis, or skill beyond the range that daily village life offered. Running seemed one thing he could claim for himself. He needed will and desire, nothing more.

Soon he gained an audience. Nothing in the bush stayed private for long. You always had eyes on you, especially during the times when you most wanted to be alone. First his younger sisters and brothers came out to watch, squatting in the dirt, eyes big and intent. It was as if they expected Julius to conjure some wonder, deliver rain out of the cloudless sky, or produce a baked sweet potato out of thin air. Julius would put on a little show, planting his feet and tensing his muscles as if starting a race, assigning one of the little ones the task of shouting "Go!" As Julius took off running, they would chase after him, laughing and shouting and throwing clumps of dirt at one another. This continued for a few days, until the children grew bored with the game, treating their older brother's odd behavior as a natural part of bush life, like bringing the cattle in from the fields.

Next, his brother Jimmy, number three of the siblings, came to see about the fuss. Stocky, calm, stolid, Jimmy stood watching one morning, his hands on his hips. He carefully studied Julius as he ran back and forth, reached the conclusion that running had nothing to do with him, and returned to the hut and his practical pursuits.

Jasper, a year older than Jimmy and a year younger than Julius, watched with more interest. Jasper was tall and rangy, a good natural athlete, among the first to be chosen at the village soccer games. He watched Julius with a wistful expression. Julius invited Jasper to join him.

"I'll race you," Jasper responded.

"You have to get strong before you can race," Julius said. "It's longer than you think, from the hut to the road and back." Julius never relinquished his big-brother role; he always looked out for the younger ones. But he was also a little put out by Jasper's cockiness.

"No, I don't mean that kind of race. I'll race you to the shea nut tree." It was a much shorter distance, perhaps a hundred yards. Julius accepted the challenge. He wanted to beat Jasper, and he also wanted to test himself, learn where his strength lay as a runner.

Julius drew a starting line in the dirt. The two boys crouched and leaned forward. One of their little brothers shouted go and they tore off sprinting. Moving with his galloping long-legged stride, Jasper pulled away halfway toward the shea nut tree, flashing across the finish ten feet in front of Julius.

The little children jumped up and down. Jasper and Julius shook hands. "Come train with me," Julius said. "You could be a champion, Jasper."

Flushed by his success and flattered by his older brother's attention, Jasper came out the next morning. He ran with Julius on just one out-and-back repetition and then, daunted by the effort, sat down in the shade. He never showed up for another morning work-out. Julius returned to solitary training, and each morning he was able to make it to the road and back a little faster than the day before. He didn't own a stopwatch or any timer, of course, other than the clock in his head.

Each morning he would chafe and turn on his sleeping mat, itching for the time to rise and run. He loved the swing and rhythm and the chuff of his breath, the feeling he imagined his mother experienced as she chased Julius through the elephant grass after he'd broken her pot. When running, Julius could re-create the strange exhilaration he felt in the first hours after his kidnapping; those moments when, despite his terror, he was thrilled at how fast he was moving, how much ground he was covering.

Running gave Julius the same physical pleasure that he felt while playing soccer, but he didn't need a dozen other boys to play with, nor did he have to wait until 4 P.M. on Saturday to experience it. Best of all, when Julius ran, the flood of images from his time in the bush finally ceased. He was in control. Rather than being pursued, Julius was on the hunt.

◆ ◆ ◆

After a month of training, Julius was eager to test himself. Each day at school he hoped that Mr. Tomba would announce a field day, when lessons would be suspended for the afternoon and races held on the dirt path around the soccer pitch. Julius knew it was around the time of year for the big event, but Mr. Tomba kept his students in suspense, enjoying the power he held over them. Finally he announced that today was the day. The event would be canceled, however, if the children didn't mind their lessons and generally behave in the morning. Therefore, all morning, Julius sat perfectly rigid and still, raising his hand at every question and problem, even when he didn't know the answer. When the other boys started to goof and roughhouse during arithmetic, he shot them a glare that instantly silenced them. Noon came and Mr. Tomba, after a final moment of suspense, led the class out to the field for the races.

Of the hundreds of races that Julius would eventually run all around the world, none thrilled him more than that first one. His stomach flipped, and every fiber of his being thrummed with anticipation as he set his bare toes to the line.

The teacher clapped his hands and Julius leapt forward. He had cautioned himself not to start too fast—the race was comparatively long, 600 meters, two laps around the soccer pitch. But Julius couldn't hold back. He jumped out in a dead sprint and immediately ran all alone, as if he were floating over the ground and soon might simply levitate, like one of the jet airplanes he watched soar over the huts in the evening. He told himself to slow down, but he couldn't do it. He ran at a flat-out sprint the entire distance, winning the race by 100 meters.

Mr. Tomba and the other children were astonished. A stunned silence ruled the field.

After that day Mr. Tomba held more field days and arranged rudimentary track meets against nearby schools. There was no track, of course, but with Julius's help he measured off distances covering 600, 800, and 1,500 meters. The results were always the same. Julius won each race by a gaping margin. He never needed to employ the changes of pace and rhythm, the surges and retreats, that he practiced on his private training ground, the strip of dirt track stretching a mile between Awake and the main road. Julius would just blast away from the start, achieve a big lead, and then cruise to the finish. His reputation started to build. People looked at him differently. Delphina, the popular girl in school, smiled at Julius, and Mr. Tomba no longer chastised him about school fees.

◆ ◆ ◆

When anyone in Langiland started to stand out and apart, exhibit a special talent, that person became a target of abuse. His clansmen were determined to cut him down to size; in track parlance, to reel him back into the pack. So it happened in Julius's case. Rumors started to swirl that his speed was a product of *orum,* the infectious malevolent power he'd brought back with him from the bush. Others whispered that a witch doctor was dosing Julius with an herbal potion that lent him this unreckoned power, but that in Faustian fashion would poison and kill him within a year.

Julius wasn't the only target. His family got abused as well. The women at the spring teased Kristina. What is wrong with Julius? That boy is always running. Has he gone crazy from his soldiering?

His mother fumed in silence. She hated the derision but in large part agreed with the women. The truth—that her eldest son aimed to become like John Akii-Bua and fly like a god in a jet airplane—would make him sound crazier than he already appeared. Moreover, she had her own concerns. Julius had refused the bride that Kristina had selected for him. True, age thirteen was a little early for marriage, but with the rebels and the Karamojong taking so many of the family's cattle, there would be little to offer in dowry when the proper time for marriage came.

Most boys were quite willing to accept the perks of marriage; in the villages boys were no longer boys by age thirteen. But when Kristina and Charles made their pitch, Julius immediately and adamantly refused. It wouldn't have mattered if they had chosen the fair Delphina. A wife would only lock him in to the life he was so desperate to escape.

And every day presented a fresh reason to leave. One afternoon after school Mr. Tomba brought out a boom box and held a disco dance for the teens. Since Julius had emerged as a star athlete, arousing commingled admiration and jealousy, he'd been exchanging looks with a quiet, pretty girl in his class, but he remained too shy to speak to her. But now, as the music rose, he summoned his courage and asked the girl to dance. To his delight she accepted, and after the dance he walked on air. But then another boy approached her. Julius could hear their conversation.

"Why are you dancing with that bum?" the boy said, gesturing to Julius. "He carries a clay water pot because his family is too poor to buy a plastic jerrycan."

Julius burned with humiliation. He wanted to thrash and throttle that boy, but he refrained. He would not be distracted from his goal. The slight only made him run harder.

◆ ◆ ◆

Within a few months of beginning to train, he had beaten all the other runners around Otuke. Many adolescent boys would have grown arrogant or complacent at that point, but Julius's fascination with running, his confidence in his destiny, grew stronger by the day. He wasn't a natural long-legged sprinter like John Akii-Bua or his brother Jasper, nor had he been endowed with the light, lilting stride of the superb long-distance runners that Kenya and Ethiopia produced in such profusion. Instead, Julius possessed a combination of speed, strength, endurance, and will. In short, he was a natural for the middle distances.

Now he needed to test himself in a wider arena. Mr. Tomba found out about a regional junior championship track meet to be held in Lira town. The winners from that meet would advance to the national junior championships a week later in the capital city of Kampala. The teacher told Julius and a few other boys that he would drive them to the meet, where they would represent Otuke district. Julius had qualified to compete in three events, the 800, 1,500, and 3,000 meters. The meet was all Julius thought about for weeks. On the Thursday before they were to travel to Lira, however, Mr. Tomba came to Julius with a sheepish expression. The truck had broken down. The trip to Lira was canceled.

By Langi tribal custom a grown man never deferred to a boy. No other explanation was required and certainly nothing approaching an apology or acknowledgment of failure. But this situation was different; Julius was different. He just looked at the man. He wasn't angry. He wasn't even disappointed, in the usual sense of the term. There was simply no way Julius could accept this information.

"I am sorry, Julius," Mr. Tomba said. "I know how much this meet means to you. There will be another one next year. And next year, you will be even faster and stronger."

Julius said nothing, just kept looking at his teacher. He couldn't wait another year. During the next year, how many times would the Karamojong raid? What was to stop the rebels from attacking again? Perhaps Julius's worst nightmare would be realized, and Captain

John would appear one day to recapture him and this time finish him for good. Or perhaps in the next year he would finally give in to his mother and take a bride and build a hut of his own. By next year he might even have a child. The nature of time had changed. His months in the bush with Joseph Kony had altered traditional rhythms. Life moved faster now, and he had to run to keep pace. Julius wasn't going to miss this track meet.

He went to see his uncle, a district administrator, who had access to a Land Rover. Julius stood in his office in Otuke and asked if he could please provide transport to Lira town. The man glanced up at Julius, a spindly-legged fourteen-year-old slip of a barefoot boy in baggy shorts, not even wearing a proper school blouse. Turning back to his papers, he told Julius to go away.

He stepped out into the afternoon sunshine, the hammering sunshine of central Africa, and trotted three miles home to Awake. Running now felt as natural as walking. Outside the family hut, Kristina had just finished glazing a clay pot and had set it in the sun to dry. Beads of moisture glittered like diamonds in the dappled gray surface of the setting clay. Julius hesitated. He knew how his mother felt about his running. But if anyone could help him now, it was Kristina.

Julius told her that he'd won three races at the Otuke qualifying meet, the 800, 1,500, and 3,000 meters, and there was a good chance he might win those same events at the big meet in Lira. He told her about the truck breaking down, and how his uncle had rebuffed him.

"There is no transport but it doesn't matter," Julius said. "I'm going to find a way to get there."

Kristina was quiet for a long moment. Julius took her silence as another refusal. He was turning away to leave when she finally spoke. "There is another official in Otuke," she said. "He has a truck." She glanced at the sun; it was nearly 4 P.M. She looked at her son with an appraising glint. "But you just came from Otuke."

Julius brightened. He said he was more than ready to run back to town. "All right," Kristina said. She pointed to a hen pecking in the dirt by the fire pit. "Take the man that chicken and ask him to drive you to Lira."

In the bush of central Africa, chickens trailed only cattle and goats in value. Julius started to protest, but his mother gave him a look that precluded further discussion.

Gripping the hen by its legs, rendering it immobile, Julius trotted back to Otuke town—a few squat concrete buildings baking in the sun—and presented himself to the official. Despite all the effort, the running back and forth, he felt deeply engaged in this project. He was on a mission. Destiny had called, and Julius was responding.

"Good afternoon, sir."

"Good afternoon, my boy. What can I do for you?"

Julius told his story, made his pitch, holding the chicken at an angle at which the official could readily appreciate its plumpness.

The man considered for a moment, but then shook his head. "I'm sorry," he said. "I am hauling a load of peanuts on Saturday."

Julius trotted home. The continued presence of the chicken revealed the outcome of the mission. Kristina was washing clothes in a pot on the fire in front of the family hut. Julius set down the hen and watched it scramble away.

"Tomorrow," he said, "I am going to run to Lira."

His mother laughed and continued with her washing.

◆ ◆ ◆

The next morning, Friday, Julius rose at dawn as usual. Outside the hut there was no sign of the lion. The morning racket rose from the bush, and on the lip of the tree canopy, the equatorial sun was poised to detonate. Julius briefly recalled the day of his abduction, the quiet routine preceding the moment that had changed his life. Would today mark another turning point?

Charles was up, tending to the cattle. His back was turned to Julius and, following custom, he didn't call to his father. He just grabbed the water pot, trotted without thinking down to the spring, and returned with the load balanced on his head. A boy from the bush possessed nothing of his own, and village life permitted him no secrets. This morning, Julius owned both.

He quietly scooped a handful of cold cooked beans into the pocket of his baggy shorts. Then, heart pounding, he set out at a trot on the path to the main road, just as he did each morning in training. When he reached the road, however, instead of turning around and running back to the hut, Julius broke left, starting his forty-mile run to Lira.

In all respects, it was a journey into the unknown. Julius had never been down the road farther than Aliwang Mission, three miles distant, where he'd been born and baptized. He had never traveled south of Aliwang, but there was only one road, and if he had trekked for three days from the Soroti swamp, dodging jets, rebels, and water buffalo, he should be able to find his way to Lira town.

He knew that the distance was around forty miles. If he jogged at a steady pace, eight to ten minutes per mile, he should make it to Lira in about five or six hours, arriving around midday. Julius had worked out the rough calculations, he had a rudimentary plan, but as he settled to his pace he let all that go. Dwelling on the details would lead to considering the vastness of his undertaking. Better to keep his head in the mile he was running now. The outcome was in God's hands.

Hitting his rhythm, running with that easy swing that felt as natural as walking. His bare feet chuffing over the rutted dirt, his soles hard as Kevlar. The road was busy; it was always busy. Men carried sugar cane and drove herds of goats. Market-bound women carried baskets of bananas and cassava and sweet potatoes on their heads, moving in groups of two and three, talking among themselves, swaying, wearing the wildly colored *busutti*, traditional flowing dresses requiring twenty feet of cloth. And outnumbering the men and women fivefold, flashing around the adult travelers like pilot fish around a whale, children walked toward school or chores, the students wearing vivid bright blouses, the children who couldn't afford school wearing ragged T-shirts bearing the faded logos of U.S. corporations, universities, and sports teams.

In the miles north of Aliwang, many of these travelers knew Julius, or at least knew him by reputation: Look, there is the boy who runs, and today he is running to Lira. The bush telegraph would kick in, and within an hour the entire subregion would know about his mission; word might even filter back to the family hut in Awake. The notice strengthened his resolve. He had never felt more socketed into his place, at one with his people, but at the same time he had never felt as separate, moving in a private cone of grace and intent. He trotted steadily through the early morning. He thought about his mother's offer of the chicken; he was running for Kristina, too. Every few miles he bent to scoop a handful of water from a ditch. His vitals were as inured to bacteria as his feet were impervious to rocks.

He ran down the familiar miles to the mission and into the unknown regions beyond. Had he fully realized the scope of his journey, he never would have set foot on the road that morning. But now, working south, strangers' eyes marking his passing, Julius felt emancipated. Rattling motorbikes and roaring trucks. Mangoes, chickens, bolts of cloth. Villagers traveling on workaday errands, Julius moving clandestinely among them, like a spy on a secret mission.

Had anyone ever tried to run this distance before? He didn't know and didn't really care. Julius wasn't trying to prove anything. Had a truck been available he would have much preferred to ride. He wasn't trying to be a hero, yet he gave no thought to failure.

He was still in Langi country, but he'd outrun the boundaries of his clan. He drew down deeper into himself and ran. As the morning lengthened the sun lifted, striking the road with unholy force. The traffic started to thin, the travelers peeling off to find shade. Julius trotted on, trying to forget that he was alone, to deny the risk and audacity of his journey, but fear and doubt encroached. A gorge of panic rose, tasting the same as the fear that struck when Captain John first clutched his shoulder. Julius had tamped down the fear on that day by opening his eyes, paying attention to details, meeting the demands of the moment. Now he employed the same tactic. Instead of following his mind's instinctive course—How much farther? When will I get there?—he winnowed his thinking to the road in front of him. He would run only as far as he could see. He fastened his eyes on a hut or thorn tree or anthill in the near distance and set that as his lone goal.

Just make it to that tree, and after the tree to the slough, and after the slough to the rock . . . and when the tree or rock started to shimmer and blur in the furnace glare he narrowed his vision further, confining it to the stride he was taking, one step at a time. All he was doing was moving. All he had to do was keep moving.

Finally, as noon approached, Julius was alone on the road. All other travelers had retired to the shade. His mind was his body, his body was a spear. In the distance, he saw a limestone hill jutting above the scrub and beside it a silver river. Instead of the brackish brown seep of the Otuke sloughs and ditches, this river surged with clear shining water. Why hadn't anyone told Julius of this wonder? It had to be a mirage. But no, it was real; the first paved road he'd ever seen. The heat shimmer that looked like water dried and vanished as the boy waded into it, running the final mile into Lira town.

◆ ◆ ◆

Julius had woken up in one world and run forty miles into another.

Lira seemed like a great metropolis, vibrant and thronged beyond imagining. The welter of the marketplace, the clamor of so many voices—the town at first seemed overwhelming. But after drinking his fill of water from a pipe outside the hospital and resting in the shade of a tree beside a tin-roofed shebeen, he felt refreshed and ready to explore the town.

He had no contacts, but at that time, before the worst of the war blighted the north and changed the heart of Langiland, no child was ever alone or orphaned. Someone would shelter Julius. But for now there was only one place for him to go—the track where tomorrow's meet would take place. He inquired at the marketplace and a woman pointed the way to John Akii-Bua Stadium, which turned out to be a weedy soccer field enclosed by a packed-dirt running path. A rickety stand of bleachers might accommodate fifty spectators if they sat cheek by jowl. To Julius's eyes, however, the venue appeared worthy of the Olympics; indeed, the great Akii-Bua himself once trained here, batting his head on a pole to learn proper hurdling form. Luck was on Julius's side. He saw a boy he knew from the village whose family had recently moved to the city.

"Achon! How did you get here?"

Julius told him. The boy laughed in the same manner that Kristina had laughed when Julius announced his plan the day before.

"Where are you staying?" the boy asked.

Embarrassed, Julius made no reply. "Come with me," the boy said. He took Julius to his home, where he received hospitality of unimaginable luxury: rice and beans for dinner and a cowhide on which to sleep. The next morning, refreshed and confident, Julius reported to the stadium and registered for the track meet. Maybe it was adrenaline, but he felt neither sore nor weary from the previous day's trek. Julius was the lone athlete from Otuke subregion, and with three races on his docket, he stood to be the busiest runner of the day.

First up was the 1,500 meters. He eyed his competition at the starting line. Only a few of the boys wore shoes of any kind, and their shorts and shirts were about as ragged as the ones that Julius wore. They seemed different than he'd imagined—more ordinary. But looks could be deceiving. These other boys had to be formidable, and Julius would have to perform beyond his best to keep up with them. But at the same time he felt confident and oddly curious. Today, finally, he could employ the various tactics that were unnecessary to succeed up in Otuke.

A man clapped his hands and the field set out, four loops around the soccer pitch. For the first time, instead of bolting straight to the lead, Julius held back, moving in the middle of the pack. The initial pace seemed impossibly slow. That meant either that the final lap would be furiously fast, or else that these runners weren't any better than the boys in Otuke. There was no way the latter could be true, Julius thought, so he stayed with the pack, conserving his energy.

One lap passed, then the second and third at the same sedate pace—not much faster than the rate at which he'd covered forty miles the day before. Now they were into the final lap. One boy made a move to the lead but remained within striking distance. He had to have more inside of him, Julius thought, and if not, then one of these other boys would make a definitive move. Through the first half of the final lap, however, the race remained unchanged. With only 200 meters remaining, Julius could wait no longer.

He pulled around the front-running boys and launched his kick, pouring everything into it. Recalling how Jasper had out-sprinted him on that day in Awake, Julius expected a boy with Jasper-like sprinting talent to appear at his shoulder, blow past him, but no such rival appeared. To his own astonishment, Julius blasted across the line in first place, winning by a margin of ten meters.

The spectators and coaches exchanged looks. Who was this boy? Julius, for his part, felt numb. There must have been some mistake, he thought. Perhaps he had simply won some sort of junior varsity race. How else to explain the ease of his victory? For the next forty minutes he laid low, his mind blank, waiting for the 800 meters. The same boys as in the 1,500 lined up against him, and he ran the same type of race, holding back through the first 600 meters although the pace seemed absurdly slow, then kicking over the final half lap to win by a wide margin.

After the race the buzz got louder. *Where do you come from?* demanded the officials of Julius. *Who is your coach?*

The meet paused for a lunch break. The other athletes retreated to shady spots to eat and drink with their teammates. Julius had no teammates, no one to talk to. He chewed a few stalks of sugar cane that his friend's mother had given him. He poured a cup of water over his head.

That afternoon, after the break, Julius lined up for the 3,000 meters. The rigors of the past few days had finally caught up with him. He felt light-headed; his legs seemed to be encased in concrete. He was too tired to be nervous and had nothing to prove at this event, which was longer than his optimal distance. He had already punched his ticket to the national junior championships in Kampala, had already made his mark. No longer anonymous or invisible, Julius could feel the eyes of the crowd on him as he stepped to the line.

His fatigue showed through the early stages of the two-mile race. He hung near the back of the pack, running on a sort of automatic pilot. That left an opening for another runner to throw down a surge and take control of the race, but no one stepped forward. Three hundred meters from the finish, Julius came alive, delivering one more kick, sealing his day's third victory.

◆ ◆ ◆

At the invitation of sports officials, instead of going home to Awake, Julius remained in Lira to prepare for the national junior championships to be held in Kampala one week later. He continued to lodge with the family from his village. Astounded at his good fortune, his sudden breathtaking success, he kept waiting for some authority to knock on the door and tell him that the fantasy was over, that it was time to return to Awake.

No such authority arrived, and the dream continued. Each day he trotted down to the "stadium" to train, and in the morning or evening—sometimes morning and evening—he ran the streets and lanes and paths of Lira town, marveling at all he saw: schools, the regional hospital standing beside the prisons, both institutions forbidding in aspect, and in contrast the bright, teeming market stalls overflowing with goods and viands of all description. Shopkeepers waved to him as he ran. He'd already made a mark, due both to his unprecedented run from Awake and to his startling success at the meet on Saturday. Here in town, at least thus far, no one tried to pull him down or discredit his achievement.

Julius reveled in the attention, yet at the same time sensed the danger of yielding to it. He tried hard to stay in the moment, as he had during his run from Awake and the months he'd spent in the bush. But that proved difficult, given the elation he felt at his success and the novelty and richness of all he encountered in the city. And if Lira was so attractive and welcoming, he reasoned, then imagine the marvels of Kampala!

Julius couldn't resist daydreaming. He envisioned conquering the capital in the manner that he'd won over this provincial city. Why couldn't another star lift from dusty Lira town? After all, John Akii-Bua had trained on these same hard roads. Someday Julius would match the achievements of the Olympic champion. He would drive a fine car and live in a villa atop a hill in the capital city. The newspapers would publish stories about his exploits and he would marry a dazzlingly beautiful woman, one combining the seductive beauty of Delphina and the fresh-faced goodness of the girl he danced with at the school disco back home. What else? The classmate who had berated Julius for his poverty, who now scratched along as a farmer like his father, would jealously watch Julius returning in triumph.

Julius told himself to knock it off. Attend to business. Focus on his training in the way he once homed in on the habits, appetites, and movements of Captain John. Similar to his time in the bush with Kony's army, Julius had entered a new world fraught with traps and hazards. He must remain vigilant. But at the same time, it was all too easy to embrace the comforts of town. Fried beans for dinner, a cowhide to sleep on, and the wonder of drawing water from a tap instead of humping a half mile down to the spring with a clay jar balanced on your head. Mastering the workings of the water tap, Julius gloried in a daily shower.

At odd moments he thought about the village. In fact, he thought about it more than he had during all the time he'd spent with the rebels, when he couldn't afford that luxury. Back in Awake, his brothers would now be fetching the water, turning over the soil in the garden patch, gathering the sugar cane, and looking after the younger children. His father would be herding the cattle, his mother washing the sweet potatoes. There was no way of contacting his parents, no way of telling them of his triumphs. North of Lira there were no phones, fax machines, newspapers, and certainly no television.

However, nearly everybody had access to a radio. Perhaps his parents had learned of his achievement due to a brief broadcast announcement. And then there was the bush telegraph. Almost as fast as on the radio, a choice piece of news or gossip could fly from market stall to gasoline kiosk to shoe repair stand along the clay road connecting the village to the world.

◆ ◆ ◆

On Friday morning, just one week after leaving Awake, Julius set forth for Kampala and the national junior track championships. Along with six other young athletes, he rode in the open bed of a lumbering cargo truck. He wasn't the youngest of the group, but as usual he was the smallest as measured by physical size. The other boys eyed him coldly as they staked their places for the journey.

"You might have won three races," one boy whispered, "but you've only got one raggedy-ass shirt."

Julius stood his ground, fighting off the boys trying to muscle him out of his place at the front of the truck bed. He had survived Captain John's caning and the lash of the *sombiye*. What could these boys bring that he couldn't handle?

As soon as the truck cleared the town limits, a cold rain began to fall. The rain continued for the next twelve hours, all the way to Kampala. This was Julius's first trip into Uganda's south. His time with Kony had taken him into the nation's northern and eastern reaches. Every mile delivered a new vista. Facing the wind and rain, as if standing at the prow of a frigate, Julius watched the towns and fields sail by. After four hours they came to a crossroads. A sign pointed a right-hand turn to Murchison Falls National Park.

Every child in Uganda, even those in the north, learned all about Murchison Falls. Named for a British geologist, the falls didn't form the fount of the Nile but lay close enough to the true source to have acquired that cachet. In 1907, thirty-three-year-old Winston Churchill, then Britain's colonial administrator, while following the Nile from present-day Kenya to its mouth in Egypt on the coast of the Mediterranean, made pilgrimage to Murchison Falls.

"The kingdom of Uganda is a fairy tale," Churchill wrote in the book recounting his journey. "You climb up a railway instead of a beanstalk and at the end there is a wonderful new world."

Britain called Uganda a "protectorate" rather than a colony. One day in Berlin in 1885, the foreign ministers of England and France had peered at a map of the continent and drew up the Africa we recognize today. Among their creations was Uganda: landlocked, about the size of Oregon, tucked between Kenya and Ethiopia to the east, Sudan to the north, and Congo to the west. Lake Victoria sat on its southern border, feeding the headwaters of the mighty Victoria Nile, which bisected Uganda in every conceivable way.

Uganda lay at the fulcrum of Africa, at the intersection of the Islamic north and the Bantu south, on the crossroads of the Arab, white, and African slave trade routes. With its mango groves and bamboo and pawpaw trees, its savannah and deep forests providing a home to lions, giraffes, and tree gorillas, Uganda represented the Africa of the West's collective unconscious and popular imagination. Forty-seven tribes were native to the territory, roughly divided into two main groups, the pastoral tribes north of the Nile and the nomadic tribes to the south. For centuries before the arrival of the Europeans, these two groups—farmers and cattlemen, the traditional cultural poles of Africa—alternately coexisted and battled. Their weapons had been spears, machetes, and knives, and a kind of center held.

Although Britain "protected" Uganda on both sides of the Nile, it followed the time-honored imperialist tradition of concentrating its favors and resources on the one tribe or ethnic group that best suited its national interests; in this case, that was the Buganda of the south. The Buganda got the education, the healthcare, the civil service jobs, and the bonds to the bwanas. The northern tribes, chief among them the Langi and Acholi, were judged capable of just two things, farming and soldiering, and their land was deemed valuable for a single purpose, growing cotton to feed England's textile mills.

As long as the British ruled, the tensions between north and south were largely stifled. Then came the 1960s, then came independence, and the lid blew off. The northerners' long-repressed anger and resentment blossomed, and within its first few decades of sovereignty, Uganda, like so many other emerging African nations, descended into a rending cycle of sectarian war. Now, along with spears and machetes, the warriors wielded grenade launchers and semi-automatic rifles.

In the fifty-plus years of its existence, the small "fairy tale" of a country had produced no Mandela or Tutu but had conceived its own Stalin and Mao, a pair of world-class war criminals who could stand among those of any age or nation: Idi Amin and Joseph Kony. For various reasons, both of these men took special aim—directed their most loathsome violence—at the Langi and Acholi, who thus easily qualified as two of the unluckiest groups of people in history.

But in 1907, when Winston Churchill traveled through Uganda, such a bleak future seemed unimaginable. At first riding the newly constructed Uganda Railway (which he described as "one slender thread of scientific civilization, of order, authority, and arrangement, drawn across the primeval chaos of the world") and then traveling by boat and on foot, with native porters humping his gear in a hundred-man safari, young Winston had the time of his life, blasting away at elephants, lions, giraffes, crocodiles, and rhinos, gathering trophies for his London home.

One night in his tent, Churchill opened his map and saw that his planned route would bypass Murchison Falls. He ordered the safari to make a three-day, dagger-thrust detour so that he could take in the fabled sight. It meant three extra days of sweating and suffering for the porters, but few white men had ever visited the falls, and Churchill was determined to bag the experience.

The falls were of such force and magnitude that Churchill could hear their roar from miles up the rocky, spray-slick trail. The drop-off into the river was so precipitous that Churchill negotiated the final quarter mile on his hands and knees and the very last feet on his belly (much as, eighty years later, Julius slithered through the elephant grass while the bullets rained down from the *sombiye*).

Finally reaching trail's end, Churchill beheld the cataract, the full force of the river channeled into a twenty-foot-wide chute of bedrock. The water roared into the chasm, crashed down the falls, and spilled onto the plain below: the Nile honed into a spear. Churchill lay transfixed, drenched by the spray, so close to the roar that he must have felt inside of it.

He then had his vision. Churchill saw Murchison Falls powering a paradise within a paradise, a world of gleaming dams and turbines run by native work crews, flooding the Ugandan economy with purposeful jobs, allowing families to educate their children and clothe their nakedness, irrigating vast fields that would grow cotton of Egyptian-grade quality, which would be shipped on the shining new railway, eventually reaching the textile mills of England, further enriching the benevolent white "protectors" who were delivering the benighted Africans into a twentieth century that, in its early years, still promised to be utopian.

"Uganda is the pearl [of Africa]!" Winston Churchill famously wrote in his travel book. "Concentrate upon Uganda!"

Eighty years later: no dam, no turbines, no cotton, no railway. Instead: Amin, Kony, AIDS, boy soldiers. Grinding past the cutoff to Murchison Falls, standing drenched and near-naked with his shivering fellow athletes, Julius resolved that one day he'd return to see the famous sight.

◆ ◆ ◆

Twelve miles farther south, the truck crossed the Nile. The setting wasn't as dramatic as Murchison Falls, certainly, but it was still impressive. Westerners think of the Nile as a mammoth, turbid, braided waterway, flowing north through the Sahara past the Sphinx. In Uganda, however, near its headwaters, the Nile shoots out of undammed Murchison Falls in a foam of white water, recalling the Rogue or Deschutes, wild Oregon rivers that Julius would see in his life to come.

Now, he laughed at the monkeys and chimps gathered on the north bank, trolling for handouts from travelers. His laughter died as he regarded the stony looks of the soldiers manning the checkpoint on the far bank, the portal between the blasted north and more fortunate south.

The soldiers inspected the driver's papers and, after a withering look at the boys riding in the back, waved the truck through. Julius fingered the welt on his right shoulder, the faint scar left by the strap of Captain John's AK-47, the mark of Julius's forced service in Joseph Kony's army.

• • •

An hour later they were inching through the outskirts of Kampala, the capital city of 1.2 million people on the north shore of Lake Victoria. At first it was too big, too much of a blaring, weltering mass, for Julius to take in. They rode past enormous hotels and office buildings. Pungent wafts of unfamiliar cooking drifted up from vendors' stalls, the marketplaces they were part of larger than a half dozen Langi villages combined. Julius suddenly lost confidence. He was just a soaked, barefoot boy from the bush standing on the bed of a broken-down truck. His dreams back in Lira now seemed laughable. What made him think that his grubby little provincial victories could translate to success in the big city? Did he really think that he could wear the mantle of John Akii-Bua?

As the truck climbed the hill toward the grand colonial-era campus of Makerere College, where the track meet would take place, his anxiety spiraled into despair. What if he got lost in the city? Could he somehow get word back to his parents in Awake and beg them to arrange for bus fare home? But how could they find the money, and what would happen when they couldn't deliver the funds?

Julius imagined becoming a *bayae*, one of the countless street urchins clogging the cities of sub-Saharan Africa, equipped with no skill, schooling, or contacts, just a feral hunger for a better life than the one they had left behind in the villages. Adrift in the city, they would settle for an overripe banana stolen from a vendor's stall.

But once the truck ground to a halt after the twelve-hour journey and the boys boiled out of the open back and jogged on the turf track, Julius began to feel better. The rain had stopped, and the grass felt cool and springy under his bare feet. Until this moment, the only kind of grass he'd ever experienced was elephant grass. The man in charge of the Lira runners approached Julius. He explained that, unlike the competition last week, where he won three races, he could enter only one event in the national championships. Julius had qualified in the 800, the 1,500, and the 3,000 meters. Which distance did he want to run?

Julius pondered the question. Each event had its advantages and disadvantages. The 800 meters was really a sprinter's race. There were no tactics to speak of. In some ways Julius felt most confident in his 800 speed, but in that short a race one mistake, one misstep, could doom your chances. If he got boxed in on the turn, for example, he wouldn't be able to unleash his kick. Maybe he should choose the 3,000, the longest race in his portfolio. The event was long enough—roughly two miles—to allow ample time to recover from mistakes. But he couldn't employ his speed to full effect at the longer distance. He had raced the 3,000 only once, and he remained unsure about the event's pacing and tactics.

"I'll run the 1,500," Julius told the man. Four laps, requiring a blend of 800 speed and 3,000 endurance. The 1,500, the metric mile, was the most glamorous of all track events and hence the most competitive. Julius would be running against boys two and three years his senior, rich boys who ran in shoes. But the 1,500 was his strength. If he had to go down, he'd go down playing his best hand.

◆ ◆ ◆

In the moments before the race, Julius grew so nervous that he wondered if he'd be able to run at all. As he stepped to the line, however, his anxiety melted away. All his energy and attention crystallized on running four laps around the turf path. He didn't look at the spectators massed on the wooden bleachers or lining the hills around the field. He didn't look at the stately buildings and tall pine trees shading the campus buildings, or the downtown skyscrapers faintly visible through the prevailing haze, or the other runners with their bright spiked shoes. Julius looked straight ahead, his world narrowed to a meter-wide lane.

During a race, he wasn't being chased; he was doing the chasing. Starting with the evening around the fire when his father told him about John Akii-Bua, continuing through his morning runs from the hut and the first races at school and on to the heady events of the last few weeks—running forty miles from Awake, winning the races in Lira, riding twelve hours through the rain to Kampala, and now experiencing his first national junior championship race—through all of this he was moving toward something, not running away.

The starter clapped his hands and the runners jumped from the line. Only now did he consider his tactics. Should he bolt to the lead, release all the pent-up energy from the long truck ride, try to steal the race? Resisting the impulse, he prudently tucked into a lead group of ten boys that quickly separated from the rest of the field. Julius hit his rhythm, running under control.

In the far straightaway of the second lap, he made an exploratory probe, moving up in the pack, but the runners closed rank, their spikes nicking him, seeming to form a force field that Julius couldn't penetrate. After three laps he appeared to be out of contention. A shrill whistle marked the start of the final lap. Now, Julius told himself. He still felt calm. In fact, suddenly, everything seemed to slow down.

Gliding to the outside, he delivered a sustained surge that lifted him past the other runners. He sprinted the final lap in a lightning-fast 62 seconds, blowing by the boys with shoes and winning the race by a ten-meter margin. Julius Achon was the Ugandan national junior champion of the 1,500 meters.

After the race, things speeded up again. There were grudging and admiring nods and handshakes from the runners from the other provinces. As the crowd buzzed and the announcer called the next race on the schedule, Julius didn't know what to do with himself. If he had warm-ups or some other type of clothing, even a sweatshirt, he could have looked busy putting them on. But he had nothing to change into, no coach to greet, no teammate or family member with whom to share his joy. All he could do was stand there, barefoot and glowing in his baggy shorts. Finally, a tall stranger approached.

He said that his name was Mugisha Christopher Banage and that he was a teacher and track coach here at Makerere College Preparatory School. *"Kop ang?"* Mr. Banage said, the traditional Uganda greeting. "How are you?"

How was he? Julius was tripping over the clouds. It was tough to focus, Julius noticed, to bring his attention down to this imposing, dignified man who had administered the meet. He had wide shoulders, big hands, and quiet eyes. He clearly wasn't Langi, nor did he come from another northern tribe. But something seemed solid and trustworthy about the man. "I'm fine, thank you," Julius said.

He expected that the man would congratulate him on his victory, ask some questions about his background. Instead, without preamble, contrary to Ugandan custom, he got right to the point. "Do you want to come to Kampala and study and run here at Makerere College?"

It took a moment for Julius to process what the man was saying. Once it registered, his heart leapt but then, as he flashed on his prior school experience, quickly sank. The central fact of his student life: jumping out of the window when Mr. Tomba came around to collect the fees. His friends teased him about it and he laughed, pretending it was a big joke, Julius the clown, but in fact he felt ashamed and humiliated. But all of that was behind him—it was all back in Awake. He would not go through that again, especially here in the city. "Thank you," he told the man. "I would like nothing better. But I have no money."

"You will be a scholarship boy," Mr. Banage said. "You won't have to pay anything." Julius stared at the man, disbelieving, not able to reply.

"Go home to your village, tell your parents, visit with your family," Banage said. "I will send an assistant to arrange for your bus ticket and travel with you here to Kampala."

Before Julius had a chance to say yes or thank the man, Mr. Banage had turned and walked away, leaving Julius to wander the field for the remainder of the meet, until the awards ceremony at the end of the day. There, Mr. Banage pronounced Julius Achon to be the Ugandan national junior champion of the 1,500 meters and presented his prize: a ten-gallon plastic jerrycan, perfect for carry-ing water.

◆ ◆ ◆

Julius returned to Lira in triumph, again standing in the back of the truck, his set face belying his euphoria, clutching the jerrycan as if it were a chalice. In Lira he hurried to board another truck bound for the northern villages. Already, Lira seemed less exotic and thrilling than it had the previous week; he had seen the bright lights of Kampala, and even brighter lights beckoned. At the spur road to Awake, he hopped off the truck and walked the final mile to his family hut. Julius had left just ten days earlier, but it felt like a lifetime had passed. He told Kristina and Charles about the scholar-ship and that he'd soon be leaving again for Kampala. His tone made it clear that he really wasn't asking for permission.

For the next three days, Julius held court in front of the hut, while villagers and clansmen traveled from far and near to learn about his magical journey. Unlike his nightmare months in the bush with the rebels, Julius could talk freely about this adventure. He described his forty-mile run to Lira, the house with running water where he stayed, his hat trick of victories at the Lira track meet, the truck journey to Kampala, the wonders of the big city, his triumph in the 1,500 meters at the national championships, the jer-rycan trophy, and the scholarship offer.

The villagers listened, slack-jawed with amazement. Of all the marvels that the boy told of, the jerrycan—an object the people could see and touch—impressed them the most. No one in Julius's household would ever have to carry water in a clay jar again.

Kristina watched all this with commingled pride and foreboding. She understood that her firstborn child would not be getting mar-ried after all. When the rebels had taken Julius, she always knew in her heart that he'd return. When Julius left the village this time, she sensed, it just might be for good.

◆ ◆ ◆

In July 1990, Julius again took the long journey across the Nile to enroll at Makerere College School in Kampala. The school term wouldn't begin for another month, and until then he'd board at Mr. Banage's house, not far from campus, where the teacher lived with his wife and three children. He showed Julius the mat he'd sleep on in the front room and the procedures regarding meals. As was the case with the Kony rebels, the coach wanted to break all of Julius's bonds to Awake. Mr. Banage understood the seductive, undermining power of the village—the pressure to get married, for instance. So at all costs, Julius must not go back to Awake, even for a visit. It would be better, in fact, if he stopped thinking about the village altogether.

That suited Julius. It was easy to forget the village. There was so much to explore, so much to take in, and no need to go beyond the neighborhood and school grounds to perceive the vastness and richness of the city. Julius kept his eye out for Langi, fellow tribesmen he could speak to and learn from, but saw none. Indeed, it was as if the north didn't exist in Kampala. There was no awareness of a rebel insurrection. No one knew that people like Alice Lakwena and Joseph Kony existed. If Kampalans thought about the Langi and Acholi at all, they regarded them as heathens. The common derogatory term for northerners was "rebel," an epithet analogous to "nigger" in the United States.

Julius pointedly avoided telling Mr. Banage about his time in the bush, although, ironically, he keyed on the coach as totally as he had on Captain John during his rebel stint. The teacher appreciated the fact that the boy was willing, even eager, to listen to him, and over time, sitting after breakfast while the teacher drank tea, Julius learned Mr. Banage's story.

A native of a southern tribe, a science teacher by training, he had been hired to bring harmony to the fractured student body of Makerere College, where the children of the Kampala elite could sometimes make the bitter ethnic rivalries of the countryside seem tame by comparison. The student body was riven by cliques. The headmaster decided that sports would be the best way to quiet the conflicts and boost school spirit. He brought in Mr. Banage, who had successfully taught and coached at other schools around Kampala, to institute an athletics program.

Mr. Banage first thought to build a soccer team, since soccer was by far the most popular sport in Uganda, and also the one he knew best. But it took time to build a winning soccer team. Allegiances were already established among Kampala's club teams, and the competition to acquire good players was fierce. Mr. Banage decided that it might be easier and quicker to build a track and field program.

He could build a winning team around two or three good athletes, and even one outstanding performer could bring distinction to the school. He scoured the city for prospects and embarked on scouting expeditions to the villages. Perhaps he'd find a diamond in the rough and uncover the next John Akii-Bua.

His first crop of recruits included Francis Ogola, Julius's cousin, a talented 400-meter sprinter. Modest success followed, but the headmaster wasn't satisfied, and Mr. Banage kept searching for a blue-chip athlete. He was starting to think he'd never find one, when this national junior championship meet came to his own front door. He watched a scrawny, ragged boy in baggy shorts blow away a strong field in the 1,500 meters and offered him a scholarship.

It wasn't just that he won, it was the way that he competed. The kid was confident. He was joyful. This boy had the bones of a champion.

The coach was also encouraged by Julius's deportment. He didn't seem arrogant or egotistical. In fact, the other runners from Lira district seemed to keep a respectful distance from him, as if there were something about the boy that set him apart. Sensing that the runner he'd been searching for was standing right in front of him, Mr. Banage made his scholarship offer—which was really more of a command.

◆ ◆ ◆

And now, for the next month, besides nominal housekeeping chores, Julius's only job was to train. He hoped that Mr. Banage would teach him the craft of running. All Julius knew so far, he had taught himself. But the coach couldn't offer much guidance. He knew a lot about science and about life but not much about circuit or interval training. Also, Mr. Banage had his own wife and children to take care of, as well as lessons to plan and a farm outside the city to manage; in Uganda, most men pursued a range of occupations. So Julius trained on his own, following the mostly intuitive plan that he'd used to get this far.

There was one new element, however: hills. The landscape around Awake and Lira had been virtually flat. Kampala, by contrast, was built on a range of hills, with neighborhoods climbing the slopes and plunging down into ravines and canyons. Makerere College sat at the crest of one of these hills. Julius found a half-mile stretch of road above campus with relatively little traffic. It climbed past lean-to market stalls and shanty homes with corrugated metal roofing. Human waste and other liquid refuse ran fast down the open roadside ditches, but by running in the cool of morning Julius avoided the stench that rose later.

During the month before classes started he ran that hill constantly—for the first time in his life he had no other duties. He often trained with Francis, his cousin, the 400-meter runner who'd been enrolled for a year at Makerere.

Julius's father and Francis's father were brothers, which made the two boys first cousins (although the distinction was largely irrelevant in Uganda, where men often had multiple wives and "cousin" was a loosely defined term; around age fourteen, moreover, most boys stopped using their father's surname and chose their own). Francis's father was a police officer in Kampala, where he had a wife and children, and had a second wife and family in the northern village where Francis was born and raised.

Francis told Julius how he got started in the sport. Francis would run from the village to a market about two miles away to buy paraffin. His uncle would spit on the floor. "Make it back before it dries," he would tell the boy.

Julius and Francis quickly grew close, although they differed in temperament. Francis was fun-loving and less disciplined, Julius more serious. Like most boys, Francis often resented looking after his younger siblings. He would seize on shortcuts and excuses to avoid the duty. Julius took the opposite tack. For instance, he always made sure that he and Francis finished folding the younger children's laundry before they went to the hill to train.

◆ ◆ ◆

The month ended and Julius moved into a dormitory at the school. He enrolled in classes—the equivalent of ninth grade. But Julius felt like he was starting school all over again. His English was rudimentary, and he had only a smattering of schooling in other subjects. His social skills, his understanding of city customs, movies, and popular music, any cultural references: zero on all fronts. The lack of sophistication would have put him behind in just about any school in Kampala, but it set him light-years behind the students of Makerere, the most exclusive and prestigious secondary school in Uganda.

The school, founded by the British, originally educated the children of the colonial administrators. When independence neared, it started admitting the children of the Buganda civil servants and Indian merchants and traders. During the Amin years of the 1970s, the school declined but rebounded afterward, regaining cachet among the city's nouveau riche. Some kids arrived at school by chauffeured limousine. The snobbery and status-consciousness and infighting—the conflict that Mr. Banage had been chartered to remedy—often reached Darwinian proportions.

Into this snake pit walked Julius Achon, late of Awake village and the Soroti swamp camp of Joseph Kony, the boy who couldn't afford a school blouse or a pair of shoes, who scooped water from the ditch where the cattle wallowed and was saddled with a past that he couldn't divulge.

◆ ◆ ◆

On one of the first days of the term, hoping to set a more genial tone for the school year, Mr. Banage convened an intramural field day. He organized a series of running events, with each class or form competing separately. Julius's sprits lifted; here was a chance to impress his schoolmates, break the ice, prove himself—running was the one way he had to communicate. But other boys had their own hopes for the day. The established leaders of the class, some of them good runners recruited previously by Mr. Banage, would not deign Julius a glance as they lined up for the first race: the 100 meters.

The event was not Julius's strong suit. His younger brother Jasper had trounced him when they sprinted against each other back in Awake. But Jasper wasn't here, and Julius had been blasting up hills for a month. When Mr. Banage clapped his hands to start the race, Julius shot out of his barefoot crouch and flashed across the finish line with daylight showing between him and the next-fastest boy. Julius was careful not to gloat. He made a point of shaking hands. He gave a modest grin, a sign of goodwill that was not returned. On the sideline, the girls looked on with similarly stony expressions.

Then came the 200. Again, not Julius's specialty. But again, drawing on a month of fast-twitch-muscle development, he won easily. Now, when he offered his hand, his opponents turned away. Reading the boys' verdict on this newcomer, the girls put out crocodile vibes.

The 400 now—should Julius just tank the race? The thought occurred to him, but in the heat of the chase he couldn't hold himself back; he knew only one way to run. Open hostility greeted his third consecutive win. The day's final two races, the 800 and 1,500, were Julius's wheelhouse events. He couldn't even think about throwing these because it would look too phony.

He ran and won both with his face burning in embarrassment. Mr. Banage patted him on the back, another teacher's-pet blow against him.

The taunts came from the girls, impossible to trace. Rebel ... bush monkey ... Langi asshole ...

◆ ◆ ◆

Julius rebounded from these slights, however, and before long his running prowess, along with his self-deprecating sense of humor and general affability, won him a certain degree of popularity. Not the all-around esteem paid one of the smooth, rich boys, the ones whose parents drove them to school in BMWs, who draped their school sweaters over their shoulders with careless elegance, who flirted easily with the girls, and whose fathers took them to vacation apartments in London for winter break, but a certain niche appeal granted to boys with a particular skill.

There were no more bush-monkey or rebel epithets, at least not from his Makerere classmates. Now the taunts came from runners at rival schools, whom Julius unfailingly thrashed at every cross-country race and track meet. The boy soon earned a nickname with a more positive connotation. They called him "Acid" because, in races, he burned all his competitors.

During the term he followed a monk-like routine. He would rise at 5 A.M. and go for a run on the hill, then back to the dorm for cleaning, and then classes and the afternoon workout with the team. Then dinner, studying from 7 to 10 P.M., followed by lights-out. Compared to life in the bush, the one Julius couldn't talk about, this was easy. By any other standard, however, it was an ordeal.

Schoolwork presented a constant challenge. Julius had good aptitude and was eager to learn, but he had no confidence. It was as if the teachers were speaking a different language. He was too shy to ask for help. At day's end he would return to his dorm room and labor over his lessons to the degree that he earned passing grades, but that was his limit in terms of academics.

On weekends and vacations, the school would turn into a ghost town, the rest of the kids going off with their families. Boys would invite Julius to come home with them for the weekend, but he was too shy and embarrassed to accept their hospitality; after a while they stopped asking. Julius stayed in his small dorm room and trained.

That same shyness and anxiety kept him from playing anything but the innocuous clown with the girls. He could make a girl laugh, but once she got beyond the laughing he would turn away. All of Julius's passion, all his desire and anger and frustration and hope and guilt, he channeled into his training.

He would rise at dawn to run his hill in back of the campus.

Then track practice with the rest of the team in the afternoon. In the evening, Francis would often join him for another hard session of hill work. They had no plan or system. Francis might have sacrificed a good chunk of his speed by hitting out the high miles; the training regimen for a sprinter was very different from that of a middle-distance runner, but the two boys worked the same way.

"I used to tease him about being a rebel, but it was no joke for Julius," Francis says. "I didn't know the truth about his experience. I didn't know that Kony's soldiers had taken him. At that time I had barely heard of Joseph Kony. I didn't know about Julius's time in the bush. I would joke, but a look would come over Julius's face. I remember him slamming one boy to the ground who had called another boy 'son of a rebel.' Julius beat the boy who said that."

◆ ◆ ◆

Despite the loneliness and hardships, the years at boarding school in Kampala might have been the happiest of Julius Achon's life. From 1990 to 1994, he could focus on his running with a relatively unworried mind. There were occasional stabs and hauntings such as the "rebel" epithets, but for the most part he could suppress memories of the bush and village. No one in Kampala worried about the Karamojong or Joseph Kony.

Given Francis's sunny laughter and playfulness, Mr. Banage's stern but benevolent guidance (and the teacher's avoidance of all village-related matters and his strategy of discouraging Julius to talk or think about Awake), and the busy routine at school, it was possible to believe that the troubled country north of the Nile didn't exist. Julius sent no messages to Awake, and none arrived from the region. No Sunday phone call or weekly letter to Mom. If something terrible happened, he would've heard about it through Francis's father. Up in Awake, the radio and the bush telegraph informed Julius's family of his continued success.

◆ ◆ ◆

Within a year of arriving in Kampala, Julius had developed into Uganda's top 800- and 1,500-meter runner of any age. In 1990, he made his first national team. In 1993, his times qualified him to compete for a spot on the team that Uganda would send to the senior world championship meet. Due to Julius's youth, however, and the fact that he hadn't served sufficient time in thrall to the corrupt national sports federation, he was denied a spot in the trials. By the next year, however, there was no holding Julius back.

In February 1994, at age seventeen, he made the Ugandan team for the senior-level African cross-country championships to be held in Addis Ababa, Ethiopia. The flight to Addis was his first trip in an airplane. It passed in an anticlimactic blur, with Julius terrified, clutching the armrest. He stayed in a room on the seventh floor of the Holiday Inn, which seemed like a palace to the boy. At the meet, he finished fifty-seventh out of one hundred competitors, and was the top Ugandan finisher. In June, he dominated at the Ugandan national championships, winning the 800 in 1:51, and the 1,500 in 3:53, both times recorded on the pitted dirt track at Makerere College. Those performances qualified Julius for the world junior track and field championships to be held in July in Lisbon, Portugal.

◆ ◆ ◆

One day while he was running on the dirt track under the cedar trees of Makerere College, knocking out easy warm-up laps with his teammates, who no longer hated or resented him but who laughed at his jokes and felt enlarged by his presence, Julius looked up and saw his father.

At first he thought he was hallucinating. Julius blinked and looked again. Yes, it was Charles, standing in the same splayfooted country manner in which he stood in the dirt beside the sweet potato patch in Awake. Mr. Banage was talking to him. Julius trotted over to the two men. Mr. Banage shot him a warning look and went off to work with the other runners. Julius greeted his father stiffly, formally. Langi custom precluded physical contact.

"How are you, my son?"

"I am well, Father." He waited for Charles to declare the purpose of his visit, but the man just looked at him.

Julius felt a jolt of anger. Had his father learned of Julius's success—that he was a step away from the big time—and now, before he got away entirely, did Charles want to make sure that the family got their piece of any action coming the boy's way? For a moment he hated his father.

"Why did you waste your shillings on this journey?" Julius knew he sounded harsh, but he didn't care. "How much did you squander on this fool's errand?"

Charles looked small and old and worn-out. This was the powerful man Julius had feared? Still, Julius resented this invasion. He had worked so hard to get away from Awake; now here was his father, riding all day in a truck to bring him back.

Honoring his filial duty, he settled his father at Francis's house and then hustled back to the track to continue preparing for the most important track meet in his life, the world junior championships in Lisbon.

◆ ◆ ◆

Held every other year for premier track and field athletes aged nineteen and under, the world juniors drew a wide spectrum of talent, ranging from gangly adolescents to physically mature women and men entering their second year of university, along with the occasional teenaged prodigy already embarked on a professional athletic career. The meet gave young African runners the opportunity to emerge before athletes from the developed world could catch up with them.

When a runner from the bush of Kenya, Ethiopia, Somalia, or Uganda was still a teenager, the thousands of miles he'd run and walked as a child gave him a gaping advantage over his peers from the wealthy nations. Within a few years, that head start, while still significant, would lose a percentage of its value, as the West's superior coaching, nutrition, equipment, and sports science kicked in to narrow the gap.

The junior world championships also provided African runners with a marketing opportunity. Potential customers included coaches from U.S. universities offering scholarships; at the 1992 junior worlds, for instance, Francis, Julius's cousin, had won a bronze medal in the 400 meters, which in turn earned him a scholarship to George Mason University in Virginia. Besides the American college coaches scouting the world juniors, there were agents who might sign the most auspicious talents to professional contracts and sponsorship deals with shoe companies, and reps from petroleum-rich Middle Eastern countries hoping to lure promising young performers to become citizens of their kingdoms. Runners from Africa had still another constituency to impress: the officials from their own national sports federations.

In Uganda, for example, it wasn't enough to be fast; you also had to cultivate the right patrons. If your coach belonged to a favored tribe or clan, had the right friends in Kampala, then you had a chance to compete in elite events and build a career. If you weren't connected, didn't play the game, oblivion was most often your fate. Because Mr. Banage refused to engage in payoffs or politics, Julius had been held back from competing for a spot in the 1993 senior world championships. But now his talent was so obvious that the officials could no longer suppress him.

At the Ugandan national championships, he punched his ticket to Lisbon with wins in both the 800 and 1,500, his respective times just barely meeting the qualifying standards for the junior world championships. The stage was set for the most important competition of Julius's life. Mr. Banage helped him deal with the anxiety.

The coach wouldn't accompany Julius to Lisbon; he hadn't played the sycophant or forged the right connections. And he still was no expert on the technical aspects of the sport; Julius had far exceeded Mr. Banage's capacity to provide that sort of instruction. However, the coach did understand the way Julius thought. For all of the boy's discipline and self-sufficiency, he still required structure; a specific plan, just as he had on the day Mr. Banage had first met him.

"Trust your speed," the coach told Julius. "Don't take the lead too early."

◆ ◆ ◆

On the flight to Lisbon, Julius again gripped the arms of his seat, just as he had on his first flight to Addis Ababa earlier that year. On that earlier flight he'd been too overwhelmed to notice much—the journey passed in a silver-blue blur of packaged peanuts and pressurized air. But now he saw everything, marveling at the world sliding by, thirty-seven thousand feet below. The blue plain of Lake Victoria gave way to the variegated green of the bush, and then, as the plane drilled north, the grays and browns and delicate dun shadings of the Sahara. He remembered the evenings as a younger boy in Awake, watching the jets soar above the village, and following the thrilling, heartbreaking trace of the contrails. That memory, in turn, rekindled thoughts of his father and his surprise visit to Kampala.

What was its meaning, what did it signify? It seemed that every time Julius was on the verge of irrevocably stepping away from Awake, something drew him back. A ghost from the north would appear. Were the ghosts sent to strengthen or undermine him? Remind him of where he came from, or confirm his decision to leave his past behind? Mr. Banage, along with every other voice in Kampala, warned him not to trust the ghosts. Still, Julius wasn't sure.

There was no doubt, however, concerning his immediate mission. He stepped off the plane in Lisbon determined to follow Mr. Banage's advice. Don't go out too fast; blend into the crowd; strike at the opportune moment. Similar to the moment of his abduction, and his forty-mile run from Awake, Julius allayed his anxiety by channeling his vision to the trail in front of him. As was the case with his time in the bush with Captain John, Julius tried to escape notice.

That wasn't difficult, because of all the athletes in Lisbon, Julius might have been the easiest to overlook. His qualifying times were slower than virtually all his competitors'. Moreover, he still ran barefoot. Because his feet were so small, it was difficult to find running shoes that fit him, especially given the scant selection in Uganda. So he did without. There was a precedent for competing shoeless. Zola Budd, for instance, ran barefoot at the 1984 Olympics, but she was a white South African. People from the wealthy nations equated a black African's bare feet with poverty and ignorance.

However, again as in his time with the rebels, Julius could turn his motley appearance and modest pedigree to his advantage. His qualifying races had been logged on an improvised turf track at Makerere College. How much faster could he run on a regulation Tartan Track?

The 800 meters came first on the schedule. Sticking to his plan, starting conservatively and relying on his kick, Julius performed well enough in the heats to secure a slot in the finals. The unexpected success earned him a long-distance telephone call.

"Hey, Chief, hello from Virginia! I got Francis sitting right here telling me how great thou art. . . ."

The voice belonged to John Cook, the track coach at George Mason University, where Francis went to school. Cook had established his Division I program, one of the best in the United States, on a foundation of foreign athletes, with a special reliance on East African middle-distance runners. Most prominently, Cook had discovered and developed Abdi Bile, who, after competing for George Mason, won a gold medal in the 1,500 meters for his native Somalia at the 1987 world championships. Now Cook was offering the pearl of great price, the dream of every Ugandan, to Julius Achon: Come on over and join us, Chief!

Cook's offhand manner made Julius think that he must be joking. But the coach made it clear that the deal was real—a full scholarship, all expenses paid. A thrill shot through Julius; his chest swelled; he emitted a sound that could be mistaken for a sob. It was like the moment when Mr. Banage offered him the scholarship to Makerere College in Kampala. But now, beneath the surge of euphoria, Julius heard Mr. Banage's quiet voice: *Don't go out too fast.*

Julius forced himself to think: If Coach Cook was so eager to acquire Julius's services, wouldn't other coaches also express interest? He recalled the market stalls in Kampala, in Lira, and even in dusty Otuke town: Neither buyer nor seller ever accepted the first offer; you always negotiated.

Working to keep his voice from shaking, Julius thanked the coach but explained that he was so busy right now preparing for the 800-meter finals and the 1,500-meter heats that he could not make such an important decision. Could Julius please respond after he was finished competing?

There was a beat of silence on the phone. Julius tensed, expecting a blast of wrath, the offer to be rescinded, the dream crushed before it was born. Instead, Cook laughed. "Sure, Chief," he said, and Julius thought he detected a note of approval in the coach's voice. "Let's talk again then."

◆ ◆ ◆

The 1,500: Again, expectations were low for Julius. In fact, they couldn't be lower. Of the sixty-four competitors in the event, he had the slowest qualifying time. Buoyed by his unexpectedly strong showing in the 800, however, and the tentative scholarship offer from George Mason, Julius relaxed and ran exceptionally well in the preliminary heats. In the semifinal he logged a 3:47, lowering his previous personal best by a remarkable 5 seconds (in elite-level track, records were typically shaved by fractions of a second). Now came the finals.

By this time he had lost all his jitters. He no longer felt outclassed or intimidated. Indeed, Julius found that he enjoyed the atmosphere of a world-class track meet. In the hotel he discovered the bubble that runners lived in, a minimalist style—the world reduced to the fundamentals related to training and racing—that could be transposed anywhere. He felt at home among the athletes and the fans, and he could feel the affection returned. The other runners smiled and wished him well and invited him to sit beside them on the bus from the hotel to the stadium. The waitress at the hotel coffee shop smuggled him extra pancakes with his order. The fans cheered when his name was announced before a race.

He felt so relaxed and confident that, before the final, he accepted the offer of a pair of racing spikes, the super-light shoes that gripped the Tartan Track like talons. It was his first time in spikes, and he was skeptical as he laced them up at the warm-up track next to the stadium. The shoes felt like steel springs juicing his stride; could these marvelous things even be legal? But still he wondered if he should wear them for competition. One of the cardinal rules of running was never to make a significant change just before a race. But riding a hunch, the strong, confident feeling that had lifted him during his entire time in Lisbon, Julius decided to take a chance.

◆ ◆ ◆

There were twelve runners in the final. When the starting gun cracked, Julius suffered a flashback moment, recalling the gunfire from his days with Kony's army.

But he quickly recovered and, contrary to his successful formula thus far in the meet, bolted to an early lead. It was partly due to the shoes, partly due to the presence of Kenyans in the race (whom Julius wanted to show that he wasn't intimidated), and partly due to instinct, to the feeling that he should ride this assertive bolt. Let those other guys know he was here, that his performance in the 800 was for real. After two laps—half the race distance—Julius dropped back to a strategic position at the rear of the lead pack.

With each lap, the buzz from the stands grew louder. Julius felt the crowd's energy wash over him. The stands were a blur, and the other runners congealed into a bright-shirted mass. The spikes of his shoes whispered over the track. He did not glance at the big digital clock on the scoreboard, and unlike the other athletes, he had no coach calling out splits (the time for each lap). Julius knew he was running faster than in any previous race, and yet it felt effortless.

He moved up to third place and remained there for the next lap and a half. Waiting, waiting, chasing rather than fleeing, keeping his prey in view. Like Julius, the guys in front of him had run multiple heats of the 1,500. Several had also gone through the grinder in the 800. Now they were weary, their fatigue showing in a raised shoulder or a stride not carried to full extension. Julius, by contrast, still felt full of running. His legs remained fresh. Fate and labor and his time in the bush with Kony had rendered him immune to weariness. Running was easy. He had run forty miles from Awake. He could run forever.

The bell sounded, signaling the final lap. The Kenyan runner in the lead surged, and Julius, shifting to a higher gear, easily matched him. He could have bolted to the lead, but he decided to wait. Two hundred meters out, half a lap to go. Into the final turn he remained in third place, waiting, waiting. . . .

Until the end of the turn, the point where the homestretch started, the straight shot to the finish line. Now, with 150 meters to go, Julius kicked, sprinting to the lead. It was still effortless. A deep percussive roar rolled down from the stands. There was no one in front of him now, just the finish line.

At this stage of the race, when your lungs sear and lactic acid floods each muscle cell with toothache-grade pain, the finish line can seem to move backward, to retreat in a sadistic dance, and for each agonizing step you manage, that pitiless line can appear to take a matching stride-length away from you.

But for Julius, on this day, the finish line was like a magnet, and the more deeply he pierced its force field, the greater its pull. With each step, he felt stronger and more himself.

And now Julius Achon from Otuke district, Awake village, the boy from the bush, the Langi tribesman with three faint parallel scars on his cheek from the witch doctor's knife and a faint bleached crease on his right shoulder from when he caddied the AK-47 for Captain John in the kill-zone camp in Soroti, Julius Achon whipped across the finish line in 3:39.78, an astonishing 14 seconds faster than his qualifying time. He was junior world champion of the 1,500-meter run.

The crowd's thudding surf-like roar coalesced and sharpened. The blur of the stands crystallized into thousands of individual faces transmitting laser beams of love for the boy as he circled the track in his victory lap, waving the black-and-red Ugandan flag that somebody had thrust into his hand. Julius grinned. The smile split open his face, reflecting the affection flooding down from the stands, magnifying it, beaming it back at the faces, and Julius trot-ted a lap that he never wanted to end.

◆ ◆ ◆

Suddenly he was a star, an unexpected champion in the sport's glamour event, the metric mile. The BBC interviewed him. Repre-sentatives from Yemen and Qatar tried to entice him to leave Uganda and run for one of their respective countries. His friends at the hotel held a party in his honor.

Messages started to pile up at the front desk. Congratulations from Ugandan officials Julius had never heard of. At the party there were sandwiches and cold cans of Fanta. Julius was too happy to eat or drink. Messages came in from American colleges other than George Mason: Weber State, Oklahoma, Villanova, Adams State in Colorado, the University of Texas, New Mexico State. There were also cryptic notes from European agents: *Julius, give me a call. I can hook you up with an Italian doctor.*

At the edge of the crowd at the party stood Dalton Eubanks, a native of Jamaica and now an assistant coach at George Mason. Eu-banks had been there all through the meet, encouraging Julius dur-ing the qualifying rounds of the 800, when he was still unknown. Eubanks fed him nuggets of specific, practical advice—how close to hug the rail on the turns, and the optimal pattern for lacing spikes once Julius decided to go with shoes. Now here Eubanks was again, tactfully letting the blasts of adulation and approbation wash over the boy, letting Julius have his moment, before coming close and letting Julius know that Coach Cook was on the phone, hoping to congratulate him personally.

Even amid the postrace excitement, Julius realized what an ef-fort it was for a coach from America to figure out the time-zone differences and put through a personal phone call. He also noticed that George Mason had been the only American university to send a representative to Lisbon; the other schools that had contacted Ju-lius figured it wasn't worth their trouble. Their name and reputa-tion were enough to impress any African kid.

Julius picked up the phone. John Cook's voice again, raspy, strong, warm—from that moment forward, Julius would always think of it as the voice of America.

You're the man, Chief! You nailed that son of a bitch!

When judging people, Julius relied on impressions and instinct. Coach Cook, clearly, was not a godly man, but Julius sensed that he had a good heart. The word around the hotel, around the warm-up track, was that Cook was a master of the middle distances; he possessed the detailed training knowledge that Julius hungered for, that he couldn't get from the well-meaning Mr. Banage or other, perhaps less well-meaning, coaches in Kampala. Moreover, Cook had a wire to African runners, a connection he had proven with his development of Bile and other athletes from the continent.

Julius sensed that he could trust John Cook. Here was a man he could follow into the new wilderness. Julius could pledge Cook his all, just the way he had pledged his all to Kristina, Charles, and Mr. Banage. Coach Cook repeated his scholarship offer, and this time Julius gave a full-throated yes.

◆ ◆ ◆

On the one hand, it didn't seem real that he was on his way to America, that his dream had come true, that he had really made it out of Awake. On the other hand, the development seemed natural and inevitable, an enactment of a master divine plan. On the plane ride back to Uganda, he felt more calm than exultant. As he looked out the window at green Europe sliding into the blue of the Mediterranean, which then became the sere gray-brown of Saharan Arab North Africa and then finally green again, the deep forest green of central Africa, Julius almost relaxed. His fingers unclenched from the seat arms.

By the time he got off the plane at the airport in Entebbe, he was alert again, eyes wide open, at once delighted to greet his supporters and wary of them. Some of his people looked at him differently now; they were proud, but they were also expectant. They hoped to cash in by knowing him. That was the Ugandan way. Julius decided to tell no one at school about the George Mason scholarship. He knew that the Makerere officials would not want him to leave. He didn't even tell Mr. Banage, although he knew that the coach would support him when the time came.

Cook had told him to hang tight, that the school would send him all the necessary information. After a brief rest, Julius resumed his training routine, now preparing for another international competition. After his success at Lisbon, the Ugandan federation decided to send him to Victoria, British Columbia, to run the 1,500 at the prestigious British Commonwealth Games in August. The experience passed in a blur. Even though it was a senior-level competition, open to professional and Olympic-level athletes, Julius, at age eighteen, made it to the final rounds of the 1,500 meters, finishing ninth.

However, the trip was worthwhile because John Cook flew out from Virginia to meet Julius and watch him run. Julius had liked the coach immediately. He was a short, stocky, forthright man, sharply observant beneath a gruff, often profane exterior. The impression that Julius had formed over the phone in Lisbon was confirmed: Cook was a man he could trust.

Returning to Kampala, Julius got ready for his final academic term at Makerere. He also quietly began to prepare for his departure to America, tentatively scheduled for December. Cook had instructed Julius how to complete an I-20 admission form, the visa that the U.S. embassy issued Ugandan students for travel to America. Julius's stomach knotted at the prospect; he recalled the ordeal that Francis went through when he acquired the form two years earlier. It had taken Francis three trips to the embassy and weeks of anxiety and frustration to obtain the visa. Then he had to start all over again, navigating the Ugandan bureaucracy.

So one day in October 1994, Julius slipped away to the U.S. embassy, which wasn't far from the Makerere college campus. Julius now felt at home in Kampala. He knew the back streets and shortcuts, and places to buy a plate of chicken marsala for a shilling. He knew a shack where a barber would shave his head for free, a shop where a traditional healer sold herbs, and a stand where a self-taught dentist pulled teeth. He threaded his way to the embassy door, feeling more anxious than he had at the 1,500-meter starting line in Lisbon.

It was 11 A.M., the appointed time for Ugandan nationals to apply for visas. Julius was prepared to wait for hours, but to his surprise the secretary called his name after only a few minutes. He followed her clacking high heels over floors of polished hardwood into the fragrant recesses of the building, past vases of flowers and a framed photo-portrait of President Bill Clinton. Julius reflexively dipped his head, as if it were the image of the pope. They continued to the innermost reaches of the embassy, where, to Julius's astonishment, the secretary led him into the hushed, cool office of the ambassador himself. The secretary withdrew with an encouraging smile. The ambassador came around his desk to shake Julius's hand in the hearty U.S. manner.

"So you're the young fellow who won the world championship!"

Julius said yes and briefly described the race in Lisbon. He told about the scholarship at George Mason and the I-20 admission form.

The ambassador took the form and placed it on his clean desk. "When do you want to go?" he said.

December, Julius said.

"Okay," the ambassador said, glancing at his watch. "Come back in . . ." Flashing on the day in Otuke, when his uncle had imperiously ignored his request for a ride to Lira, Julius expected the ambassador to tell him to return in two months, or a month if he was lucky. ". . . in an hour," the ambassador said.

Julius went home for lunch. An hour later he returned to the embassy. He assumed there'd be some sort of snag, or perhaps a more serious problem—the Ugandan government had learned of his defection and an agent would be there to detain him. At the embassy, however, the secretary again greeted him with another warm smile. She handed him a signed and stamped student visa.

♦ ♦ ♦

For two more months he kept his secret. Not until December did he tell Mr. Banage; it was too late now, he calculated, for anybody in Kampala to stop him. Mr. Banage was happy for Julius. He understood that the young man had grown far beyond his coaching ability. Julius richly deserved this opportunity. But the Makerere officials, Mr. Banage warned, might think otherwise. Sure enough, once word got out, the dean summoned Julius into his office.

"Achon, don't go to America," he said. "It would be a big mistake. They hate black people there. The Klan lynches Africans. Stay here at Makerere. You can attend the university for free. You can become a celebrity in Uganda."

Julius was prepared for such a gambit. "Sir," he said, "I am grateful for the opportunity you have given me. I have worked very hard to bring good attention to the school. In fact, often, I have suffered. I know other athletes who have gone to America. I know that the Klan is no longer lynching black people. I have my visa, and my mind is made up."

During the autumn, Cook had arranged the details for Julius's move to America. In order to sharpen his English and to make up credits required for admission to George Mason, Julius would spend one year—two semesters—studying and running at Southern University in New Orleans and then transfer. Meanwhile, once they determined that Julius was really leaving, the Ugandan athletics officials did everything possible to send him off with good feelings about the country: After his talent ripened and matured in America, Julius would be in better position to win Olympic glory for Uganda. The federation bought him a first-class plane ticket to New Orleans. A wealthy businessman in Kampala called him into his office and handed him an envelope filled with one thousand dollars in U.S. currency.

"For expenses," the man explained. "Living isn't cheap in America."

Julius knew right away what he'd do with the money.

◆ ◆ ◆

He would travel back to Awake, his first visit in four years, to spend Christmas with his family. He made his way to the central bus station in Kampala to begin the complicated journey. Awake lay less than two hundred miles away, and only one road from the south led there, but in Uganda there was no such thing as a straight line.

At the depot, Julius told a driver where he wanted to go. The driver led Julius to his minivan and collected two thousand shillings, the equivalent of about three U.S. dollars. Then Julius sat in the van for two hours, until the seats had filled up with other travelers. The van left the depot and inched through the dense snarl of Kampala traffic—there were no traffic lights in the city—stopping for the driver to negotiate a bribe with one of the white-shirted traffic police. After an hour the van cleared the city and was on the rumbling, bucking way north to Lira. At the Lira bus depot, Julius got out of the van, collected his bags, bought a goat-meat skewer and a bottle of water, then repeated the process, arranging a ride farther north toward Otuke and Awake.

To think that in July he'd flown in a jet to Portugal. Thousands had cheered him in the stadium, and a fine hotel, with thick towels and color TVs in the rooms, had thrown a party in his honor. Next week he would board another airplane to fly to the dreamland of America. But now he sat in the back of a truck, carrying a massive wad of shillings in his pocket, hoping that no one would try to rob him. In Lira he'd overheard men talking about "troubles" up around Gulu; he was glad he wasn't traveling that far north.

He looked out at the men on bicycles, the women walking, and the spindly-legged children darting among them. Langiland was still at peace. Kony and his army seemed far away. Out of sight, out of mind. It was especially tempting to believe in peace if, like Julius, you had a future to contemplate.

During his time in Kampala he had met people who had risen out of villages to positions of relative wealth and influence. They recalled the bush with derision, swearing that they would never return. Julius assumed that he'd develop a similar attitude, that it would come as a by-product of his worldly success. But, thus far, this way of thinking hadn't developed. He felt no contempt for the life he'd escaped, although he understood that this life was no longer his. To live successfully in the village you could know no other way. Julius could never go back to cassava root and ditch water. And yet he still felt responsible for his family. He remained the eldest son of Kristina and Charles Achon.

He hopped off the truck at the Awake spur and walked the mile to the hut. The land looked the same. When he reached the huts, however, he saw that his brothers and sisters had grown and that his parents seemed older, smaller.

It was a joyful holiday reunion. Julius distributed the small gifts he'd brought for his siblings. He went down to the river and feasted on beef with his clansmen. They sang Christmas hymns around the fire at night, and Charles, who had been saved and now worked as a lay minister, preached on biblical themes. The children led him back to the worn dirt patch where he'd been kidnapped and the boys thrilled to play soccer with the hero of Awake village. The mango tree he'd planted at the time of his abduction was now yielding fruit.

Julius was still a boy himself, only eighteen, but he felt much older. The wind rustled, a twig snapped, and he looked toward the bush, but no rebel soldiers emerged. When the time came for him to return to the city, he presented the thousand dollars to Kristina and Charles. It was enough to pay the school fees for all the children and to buy seeds and goats and chickens and perhaps even a cow or two; enough to support the family for the next several years.

Kristina gasped. Julius tried to explain the money's provenance, that he'd earned it by running around a track faster than other boys, but his mother never quite got it. She kept asking her son if he'd stolen this fortune.

◆ ◆ ◆

Julius returned to Kampala, and on December 29, 1994, at the international airport in nearby Entebbe, boarded a Sabena Airlines flight, bound for the promised land. He carried a single duffel bag and a first-class ticket.

Although he hardly looked first-class. He had on a cheap polyester sport coat bought at the Kampala street market. The jacket's padded shoulders only seemed to accentuate his leanness. His hair was a disaster, spiking out wildly in the manner of Don King, the African American promoter who had brought Muhammad Ali and George Foreman to Zaire for their famous 1974 heavyweight championship bout. Julius nervously eyed the other passengers in the departure lounge. About half black and half white, but all displayed the same sense of gleaming, entitled ease.

Julius fidgeted. He imagined the other passengers giving him a wide berth. He imagined them imagining him as a terrorist like the ones that had hijacked a jetliner in 1973 and landed it at Entebbe to negotiate a ransom.

Now, Julius looked out the window at the airplane. It was a Boeing 747, one of those double-decked aircraft in which you had to climb a corkscrew flight of stairs to get to the first-class deck. When they called for first-class passengers, Julius stood and made his way out of the terminal across the sun-splashed tarmac. Sweat beaded on his forehead, and not just because of the suffocating polyester sport coat. He felt as if every eye in the airport was on him.

Julius climbed up the stairway to the first-class cabin, where his seatmate, a dignified middle-aged black Ugandan woman, possibly the wife of a dignitary heading to London, shot him a dagger look and removed her elbow from their shared armrest. The flight attendant, a tall, dazzling Belgian woman, stalked down the aisle and, with a professional smile and hard eyes, asked to see Julius's ticket.

For some reason, that broke it open. It was like the crack of a starter's pistol at a race—his tension and self-doubt dissolved; all he had to do was run. Now he just started talking. *Madam, thank you. I am Julius Achon from Otuke district, and I belong in this seat because the sports federation bought me a ticket to go to my scholarship in the United States. In fact, madam, please forgive my bragging but I am the world junior champion in the 1,500-meter run and not only that, the federation named me the sportsman of the year, not just among junior competitors, nineteen and under, but among all sportsmen in Uganda of all ages, thank you. The ceremony will be tomorrow. I must travel today so I cannot accept the honor in person, but here is the story from the Kampala* Guardian *newspaper. . . .*

The flight attendant didn't need to look at the clipping. She smiled for real now, smitten by this sincere ragamuffin bound for a new life. She plumped his pillow, smoothed his blankets, and showed Julius how to adjust his seat back and tray table. During the flight she fed him a steady stream of snacks and treats. His seat-mate also thawed, asking about Julius's family and background and tactfully correcting his English.

As the airplane banked over Lake Victoria and attained cruising altitude, he pressed his face against the window. Julius looked down at the blade-like glint of the Nile, and beyond the river at the un-lucky north, where at this moment, around the fire in front of his family hut, a Langi boy might be looking up at the whisper of the jet, dreaming that one day he might fly in one of those magic vessels.

◆ ◆ ◆

During Julius Achon's years of single-minded devotion, as he honed his craft in Kampala, developing from a barefoot adolescent into a world-class athlete, Joseph Kony underwent a similar apprentice-ship in Uganda's far northern provinces, progressing from a provin-cial guerrilla commander into a world-class warlord.

After his force's defeat in Soroti, the rout that gave Julius oppor-tunity to escape, Kony gave up on the tactic of pitched, conventional battles. He withdrew to his native region near Gulu to regroup, and through the early 1990s confined his operations to the far north of the country. No longer hoping to defeat the Museveni-led Ugandan army, Kony shifted his strategy to one of harassment.

There are few biographical details on Kony during this period, but it seems clear that it was a time of exceptional growth for him, albeit of a dark, metastasizing nature. He simultaneously sharp-ened his military skills and his witch-doctor mystique, with one realm complementing the other. He adeptly blended elements of animist beliefs with scraps of Christian doctrine, creating a mix that, while perhaps bizarre to the Western mind, proved intoxicat-ing to many Acholi. Kony dreamed up the sound-bite goal of gov-erning Uganda according to the biblical Ten Commandments. In time-honored false-prophet tradition, he cherry-picked scripture passages to justify his crimes. Preaching that a divine spirit ani-mated and protected his warriors, Kony had branded his militia as the Lord's Resistance Army.

Since it was easier to sell this program to unformed minds, Kony stepped up his abduction of children and his raids on schools and hospitals. When Julius was kidnapped in 1988, children were an adjunct to Kony's platform; now, exploiting kids formed one of the LRA's main planks. The system for stealing and indoctrinating boys as soldiers and girls as sex slaves—known as bush brides—still in somewhat crude form during Julius's forced servitude, was now perfected.

As he developed into a shrewd, efficient guerrilla commander, a master of ambush and evasion, Kony also grew more sociopathic, paranoid, and obsessed with the unseen realms. He increasingly appeared to believe his own quasi-spiritual hype. During his tapped-in moments, as he purportedly communed with one of his four *zoas* or the prophet Abraham, the weed-zonked dancer from Odek really did believe that he would rule Uganda according to his demonic reading of the Ten Commandments. From there, it was a short jump to taking murderous vengeance on any villagers he believed were siding with the government, his unholy enemy. Tearing a page out of Idi Amin's playbook, Kony started to afflict his own neighbors, allies, and clansmen.

◆ ◆ ◆

Meanwhile, a mix of political factors, both domestic and international, boosted Kony's cause. President Museveni, irritated by the LRA's low-grade but persistent harassment, determined that he would squash the insurgency once and for all. He ordered Operation North, a draconian and ultimately disastrous campaign that cut off the three northern regions from the rest of the nation. No travel to or commerce with the area was permitted, and a strict media blackout was imposed. Government soldiers allegedly oppressed the Acholi villagers, with the direct or tacit approval of the administration. There were rumors of killings, rapes, and other atrocities as grievous as those committed by the rebels. Due to the travel and media restrictions, the charges couldn't be verified. What was certain is that the LRA continued its raids and ambushes.

Hoping to capitalize on anti-Kony sentiment, the government started a program that supplied villagers with bows and arrows that they could employ in self-defense against the rebels.

Kony was outraged, by both the government's scheme and the idea that an Acholi might accept such a gift from his adversaries. He swore vengeance on any villager giving the slightest indication of siding with the government. Twisting his witch-doctor doctrines, Kony concocted hideous, symbol-laden forms of revenge and intimidation: hacking off lips so that villagers couldn't talk to government troops; lopping off ears so that the villagers couldn't hear the rebel raiders attacking; and severing arms so that the villagers couldn't point which way the rebels had escaped. These macabre practices reinforced the notions that Kony possessed divine powers and that the Acholi were suffering due to their own sins.

"This is all what he preached, just to disorganize your brain," an escaped LRA boy soldier told an interviewer. "Kony has a kind of invisible magic. Somehow you believe."

LRA child soldiers, many no older than eleven or twelve, now inflicted most of the atrocities. Torture and murder soon became their own justification. The only way to rationalize the violence was to believe unconditionally in the commanders issuing the orders and to double down on the mayhem. Thus the Acholi were tormented from both sides of the conflict, the rebels and the government, with the outside world oblivious to their suffering.

• • •

How did Kony get away with all this? How did he avoid getting killed or captured? Some thought that Museveni and his troops were incompetent, while others believed that the president intentionally allowed the LRA to scourge a population that the government wanted to control. What is certain is that the increased support of the Sudanese government proved crucial to his success.

The LRA maintained its base camp across the border in Sudan, beyond the reach of Museveni's forces. With the largess of Sudan's oil-wealthy government, Kony acquired sophisticated weapons, pickup trucks, and other booty. There were undocumented stories of a brief alliance between Kony and Osama bin Laden, who also found safe haven in Sudan during the early 1990s. In gratitude to his Islamic patrons, Kony added Koranic notes to his Bible-based LRA doctrine. He and his militia gave up eating pork.

The rebels also benefited from the Ugandan government's harsh treatment of the Acholi during Operation North. Some northern villagers freely chose to support Kony rather than Museveni. Later, after the LRA took their daughters to be sex slaves and their sons to be warriors, those same villagers sided with the rebels because they didn't want government soldiers to kill their children in battle.

"1994 marks the turning point in Sudan's relations with the LRA," writes the British journalist Matthew Green. "Sudan gives Kony guns and other support. Kony returns to Uganda heavily armed and supplied, kidnapping villagers like the slave traders of old. The LRA swells from the hundreds to the thousands. The Sudanese government knows Kony could never overthrow Museveni, but he could wreak enough havoc to be useful."

Finally, during the spring of 1994, genocide raged in neighboring Rwanda. Within a period of ninety days, one million Tutsis were slaughtered by rock, *panga,* shovel head, and knife. The Hutu authorities urged civilians to do the killing, so that the entire nation shared the shame and guilt. Across the border in Uganda, Joseph Kony surely paid close attention.

◆ ◆ ◆

As a result of these forces, the stunned, devastated people of Acholiland came to view the LRA like the Langi did the Karamojong: as an inescapable scourge, destroyers that the gods must have set upon them in righteous punishment for their sins.

In the final days of 1994, however, it was still possible for Julius Achon, who had spent the last four years in Kampala, to think that the Kony virus had been confined to a remote, isolated pocket of Uganda. It appeared that the contagion would never spill over to infect the Langi, much less draw the world's attention. The notion that, instead of burning out, the LRA insurgency had burned down to a pure concentrate of evil, seemed unthinkable.

In the day's final light, as his transformative year of 1994 drew to a close, from the godlike height of thirty-seven thousand feet, riding in the first-class cabin of a Sabena jetliner, Julius assumed that he had escaped Awake for good. As he drifted off to sleep, instead of being haunted by the sing-song serpent's call of Joseph Kony, he heard the raspy American voice of John Cook, welcoming him to a new life.

The young man had no way of knowing that, in the land behind him, the war was just getting started, or that, in the country ahead, the coach had traveled his own hard road to America.

PART TWO
AMERICA

PART TWO

AMBER

Hans Schaller watched the ivory-white parachutes bloom against the leaden gray sky over Munich, Germany. He waited in the field below, calculating where the paratroopers would land. He liked this job, at least compared to every other task he had to perform in occupied Munich in 1950, with World War II still an open wound and the Cold War continuing to intensify. Had he not spent most of each day feeling hungry, desperate, and terrified, Hans, who was nine years old, might have even thought the sight was beautiful.

As one parachute neared the ground, the boy saw that he'd judged its descent accurately. He was camped underneath as the paratrooper, a member of the U.S. Army's 11th Airborne Division, met the ground with a whistle, thud, and rustle of collapsing silk. The trooper hit, rolled, and popped to his feet—a landing so textbook he almost took a bow. He looked around to see if anybody noticed and there was the street urchin, Hans Schaller.

The soldier's face, blackened for camouflage, split into a wide grin. Laughing, he shoved a nickel's worth of American-sector scrip into the boy's grubby palm. In return, Hans handed the soldier a bottle of Coca-Cola: America condensed into a seven-ounce globe of fluted glass, bought on the black market for four cents and sold at a penny profit.

◆ ◆ ◆

Hans lived with his war-widow mother in an apartment that had somehow escaped direct bombing or shelling, although the ruined city pressed all around—entire blocks of buildings transformed into towering mountains of rubble and shattered glass, sprawling refugee camps segregated by nationality. In the daily street battles that Hans waged against boys from the various camps, whoever amassed the biggest pile of rocks and broken masonry won.

Decades later, when Hans Schaller was known as John Cook, coach of the George Mason University track team in Virginia, he would tell this story to his runners.

"The American kids would just sort of space out," Cook says. "But the African guys always listened very closely. They understood exactly what I was talking about."

◆ ◆ ◆

Cook was the only child of a BMW engineer and his wife. Through the early years of the war, the family lived comfortably in the graceful Bavarian city. Because his job was crucial to the war effort, Cook's father wasn't drafted until 1943, when he was commissioned as an officer in the Luftwaffe. According to Cook, his father was indifferent to the tropes of fascism. "But in the end, he was a good German," Cook acknowledges. "My father raised his right arm to Hitler, like everyone else." By the same token, because it had fewer military targets than other German cities, Munich was spared Allied bombing until late in the war.

In 1944, however, the family's good luck came to an end. Cook's father was killed in a non-combat-related traffic accident, and Allied forces began their aerial onslaught. During a three-month period in 1944 and 1945, the Allies dropped sixty thousand tons of bombs on Munich. In July 1944 alone, the U.S. Army Air Force attacked the city with a million incendiary bombs. On the night of January 19, 1945, 505 civilian residents of Munich were killed during bombing raids.

By the early spring of 1945, there wasn't much of Munich left to destroy. Every night, Cook and his mother would descend into the bomb shelters, and the little boy would fall asleep to the drone of the B-17s and the thunder of their payloads. In the morning, mother and child would emerge to scavenge their ruined city for food. By April, Allied ground forces were closing in on Munich from the west, while the Soviet army approached from the east. A stunned silence ruled the shattered streets. The only question now was which army would arrive first.

Knowing that Russian occupiers, seeking revenge for the millions of civilians killed by German troops during the siege of Stalingrad, would rape and pillage relentlessly, the surviving citizens of Munich prayed for the Americans. Their prayers were answered. On April 30, 1945, U.S. Army tanks rolled into Munich, beginning an occupation that would last for more than five years, altering the course of contemporary European history—and crafting the destinies of John Cook and Julius Achon.

◆ ◆ ◆

At war's end, the refugee camps sprouted around Munich, one for Germans, another for Czechs, still another for Poles, and so on. On his way to school each day, little Hans Schaller ran the gauntlet between the camps, firing rocks and getting stoned in turn. He worked various hustles for money, including selling Cokes and candy bars to the paratroopers and other soldiers on maneuvers. The Americans came to recognize the boy. "This fucking kid again," they would say to each other in mock complaint.

"That's how I learned my English," Cook explains, "and that's where I picked up my vocabulary."

At first, American commanders forbade fraternization between the troops and civilians. After a few months, however, the ban was lifted. Thousands of destitute German war widows commingled with thousands of triumphant GIs. Cook's mother met a handsome young sergeant from Georgia, but neither a one-night stand nor a dewy-eyed romance ensued. Sergeant Cook, a career soldier, purposefully wooed the woman over a period of years. Eventually they married and, with the growing boy in tow, moved to the United States.

Cook's mother hated living on an army base in Georgia, where the people seemed crude and the sergeant proved not quite as charming as he'd appeared in Munich. Life wasn't much easier for her son. Although he'd changed his name by this point, the boys at school knew that John Cook came from Germany, America's just-vanquished enemy. Cook battled every day on the playground, just as he had among the rock piles of occupied Munich.

While his mother never quite adjusted to America, Cook eventually found a niche in sports, developing into an outstanding schoolboy soccer player. In the 1950s, opportunities in the sport were limited in the United States. At age sixteen, Cook decided to return to Germany to try to make it as a professional player. In Europe, however, Cook quickly learned that he was no better than a minor-league talent. Still, the experiment panned out in an unforeseen manner.

During his time in Germany, Cook received superb coaching at the athletic clubs that sponsored semiprofessional soccer teams. The German system was rigorous and steeped in exercise physiology. The coaches dissected the movements of athletes the way BMW engineers like his late father studied the movements of workers on the assembly lines. Fascinated, Cook returned to America thinking that he might not make it as an athlete, but he could go far as a coach.

◆ ◆ ◆

Cook returned to the United States. He completed high school, enrolled at the University of Maryland, earned a teaching degree, and got a job at a high school in the lumber-mill town of Columbus, Georgia. There were no after-school activities for the students, so Cook started a track and field program. The kids liked it, and Cook soon became hooked. Inspired by the training he'd received at the German sports clubs, he carefully analyzed each event and athlete. He began to study track and field training manuals, translating German articles for American journals. His teams excelled, and Cook grew increasingly fascinated. He had discovered an outlet for his energy and intelligence as well as a vent for the pain and frustration of his childhood.

Moving to a high school in the suburbs of Washington, D.C., Cook developed a special affinity for coaching middle-distance runners. Studying the science of running—the way that an athlete moved and assimilated energy—he developed a theory of stride mechanics and designed a regimen of drills that improved efficiency. "Drills are like playing the violin," Cook says. "You do them over and over again until they're imprinted in the muscle memory and nervous system. There are two main goals, minimizing the foot's contact with the ground and avoiding injury. My runners haven't had a stress fracture in twenty years. The key is to strengthen the connective tissue so you can take the workload. You bake the cake right, it's a lot more effective than going out and running 150 miles a week."

Virginia state championships followed in rapid succession. Still, Cook wasn't satisfied. "You could only take things so far with high school athletes," he says. "I've always been pretty good about moving on when the walls start closing in."

By this time, the late 1960s, the controversy over the Vietnam War raged. Cook, who had seen enough of war as a child, actively joined the protests. Meanwhile, his stepfather was serving two tours of duty in the conflict. Cook and the sergeant engaged in bitter arguments. "Although, after his second tour, my stepfather came around to my way of thinking," Cook says.

◆ ◆ ◆

Had John Cook been a little smoother around the edges; had he not so blatantly challenged the status quo and employed a paratrooper's vocabulary; had he been slightly less opinionated; had he not communicated an ineffable but unmistakable air of foreignness, then perhaps one of the brand-name Division I NCAA programs such as Oregon or Arkansas might have snapped him up.

But despite Cook's growing reputation—his ideas were now discussed at coaching clinics around the nation—and his hunger to appease the restlessness that had dogged him since his Munich boyhood, despite his sense that all was impermanent and he had to keep moving, no college coaching offers arose.

"I could understand why they passed on me," Cook says. "I'm not the easiest guy in the world to get along with."

Finally, in 1978, George Mason University offered him a head coaching job. At the time, GMU was still an obscure commuter school in northern Virginia. "I had lived in the area for years and never heard of it," Cook says. "When they first contacted me, I thought it was another high school."

Indeed, the university had been founded only twenty years before Cook came aboard. Despite the marginal facilities and utilitarian campus, he saw possibilities. Realizing that few talented American runners would pick a workaday campus such as GMU over a glamorous place like UCLA, Cook focused on recruiting foreign athletes. He built an especially productive pipeline from East Africa. His teams began to rack up conference titles and to finish among the leaders at NCAA championship meets. In 1983, he landed the Somalian middle-distance runner Abdi Bile, who developed into a two-time NCAA champion in the 1,500 meters and the 1987 world champion at the distance.

For all his talent, however, Bile was a somewhat fragile athlete. Cook couldn't race him too often, and thus Bile couldn't rack up the points that would deliver the coach his ultimate goal: a team NCAA title. By 1994, after sixteen years at George Mason, Cook, now in his fifties, doubted that he'd ever find the horse that could take him all the way. That summer, however, Julius Achon won the 1,500 meters at the junior world track and field championships. Cook signed the kid to a scholarship. That August, the coach flew out to Victoria, B.C., where Julius was running in the Commonwealth Games, to get a firsthand look at the runner.

Although he was an eighteen-year-old competing against professional athletes five and ten years his senior, Julius advanced to the final round on raw strength and speed. Cook was ecstatic. "Here was a kid who just exploded off the track. He was an unformed talent with limitless room for improvement."

When Cook finally met Julius face-to-face, he was even more encouraged. "You could tell right away there was something special about Julius," Cook says. "A sense of responsibility, a kindness underlined by strength. He was thinking about important things. There was stuff tugging at him. I was impressed, but at the same time I felt worried."

At that point, Cook explains, Julius's visa application was still in flux. "I didn't know anything about what was happening in Uganda," he says. "Hell, how many people in America could even find the place on a map? And of course, Julius didn't breathe a word about what he'd gone through as a kid. I wouldn't learn anything about that for a long time. But I got a sense of how screwed up things were over there and that Julius might get caught up in it.

"He was such a great kid, such a great talent," Cook continues. "I didn't want him to leave North America. I had this crazy thought that I should smuggle him back to the U.S. on the ferry. I worried that if Julius went back to Uganda, I would never see him again."

◆ ◆ ◆

At the airport in New Orleans, Cook had arranged for a British runner named Rob Lotwiss—another foreign recruit who needed to make up credits to gain entrance to George Mason—to meet Julius's flight. Hoping to make the Ugandan feel welcome, Lotwiss shook Julius's hand and said, "So how is Idi Amin?"

Julius laughed, as if the joke were funny. He was eager to seem polite, not to offend, to be the well-mannered African kid everybody liked; this was the same tactic he'd employed with the rich students at Makerere College in Kampala, to be applied even more assiduously here in the United States, a land of prodigal wealth. But perhaps Lotwiss wasn't joking. Maybe he really thought that Amin still ruled Uganda, that he hadn't been deposed more than a decade earlier. Julius had heard that, besides being rich, people in America were notoriously ignorant about the world in general and Africa in particular.

Ironically, of all major American cities, New Orleans felt the most African. In the wards by the Mississippi River, the streets emanated a funky, faintly desiccated allure that reminded Julius of Kampala. And it seemed fitting that he should enter America through a city where, in the days of slavery, so many Africans had been bought and sold. Perhaps some of Julius's own ancestors had passed through here.

"New Orleans isn't like the rest of America," people kept telling him.

That suited Julius, because he wasn't like other foreign students. He was on a different, specific sort of mission. He had been through enough training camps in Africa, and international meets such as the world juniors and Commonwealth Games, to observe the style of elite runners. He saw that they lived in a manner somewhat resembling that of a Ugandan village: a life reduced to essentials, as convenient to tear down and reconstruct as a hut made of straw and mud.

You inhabited a bubble, an uncluttered, self-contained environment in which every element, each detail, was dedicated to training and racing. The same pot of pasta, cornmeal mush, or rice and beans was always bubbling on the stove, and the same clothes (flip-flops, jeans, and warm-ups) filled a corner of your closet. Your duffel bag was always packed so that you could head off to the track, trail, gym, or airport at a moment's notice. The TV was perpetually on and tuned to ESPN, and your mattress and box spring sat flush on the floor.

It was an environment easily transferable to an apartment or room in any hotel or training camp around the world. You didn't really connect with anybody outside the bubble of your sport; on the other hand, your fellow runners provided a ready-made community. You were plugged in automatically to the place where you lived, but at the same time, the bubble kept you from fully experiencing that place. As Julius matriculated at Southern University, he was prepared to strike this bargain and enclose himself in the bubble's comforting, limiting confines.

Southern University was a historically black college founded in the decades after the Civil War. The university's main campus was in Baton Rouge. The New Orleans campus, with about two thousand students, was tucked into an old neighborhood close to the river. Its athletic teams competed in the NAIA, a national network of smaller schools, rather than the larger, better-known NCAA. Artis Davenport, the track coach, was a patriarch in his seventies who had served at Southern for decades.

Cook had worked a deal with Davenport: He would lend Julius to Southern for a year. In exchange for the necessary academic credits and ESL courses, Julius would reward Southern with probable NAIA titles in the 800 and 1,500. Cook would check in weekly to monitor the runner's progress.

◆ ◆ ◆

With the benefit of the bubble, Julius adjusted quickly to his new surroundings. The warm, humid climate of New Orleans helped him acclimate. He shared an off-campus apartment with track athletes from Ghana, Jamaica, and the Bahamas. The professors and students proved kind and welcoming. Davenport let him devise his own training schedule, and Julius locked in to harness.

In January, at his first indoor track meet as an athlete or spectator, he ran a 4:04 mile, finishing second. In February, he traveled to an indoor meet in Missouri. It was the first time he had experienced snow. He went out for a run and afterward soaked his freezing hands in hot water. "Big mistake," Julius recalls. He won the mile anyway. In March, fulfilling Cook's projections, he won NAIA indoor titles in the 800 (1:50) and the mile (4:05). The times were comparable to those logged at the NCAA Division I indoor championships. Up in Virginia, Cook rubbed his hands together in anticipation.

The performances made Julius a star on the small Southern campus, but he didn't try to capitalize on his fame. He mostly stayed in his bubble. The apartment seemed palatial, with a fully equipped kitchen and a hot-water heater that always functioned. He avoided American food, sticking with kidney beans and rice. The guys from Ghana cooked—they laid on the spices—while Julius washed the dishes. His roommates sometimes went out to the clubs and bars, but Julius declined their invitations to join them, although when Mardi Gras came around, he ventured forth to take a look. The masks and beads and general wildness reminded him of the Karamojong.

But this was New Orleans, this was college, and Julius was a recognizable athlete with an exotic background. A Jamaican girl on the track team came on so aggressively, wrestling with Julius, that Coach Davenport had to warn her to back off. There was a fierce undercurrent to her playful attack, as if she sensed the depth of Julius's defenses, the inability of other women to breach them. Julius couldn't read the signals. In Uganda, relations between the sexes were strictly codified; the man made all the advances. In the United States, by contrast, you couldn't tell the hunter from the prey.

Julius thought it best to hang back, remain the seemingly happy-go-lucky guy who washed dishes and won races. He would tell stories about Africa—everybody was curious—but he stuck to a safe tone, as if he were *National Geographic,* describing the lions, giraffes, and pythons. He never said a word about his boy-soldier past, his time in the bush with Joseph Kony. He was certain that no one in New Orleans had ever heard of the man.

◆ ◆ ◆

And from inside the bubble, Julius observed the American racial scene in all its contradictions, tensions, and complexities. Since everyone in Uganda was black, he had never learned to hate or fear white people. Other blacks, from the Karamojong to the LRA rebels to the government soldiers, proved hateful and fearsome enough. Julius trusted and liked everybody, and was liked and trusted in turn. "I became a bridge between black and white," he says.

Meanwhile his running kept getting better and better. There was no dip in performance as he adjusted to his new surroundings. Indeed, Julius had been mentally, physically, and emotionally adjusting to new surroundings since the day he'd been kidnapped. That May, at the outdoor NAIA championships at Azusa Pacific College in California, Julius repeated his indoor double victory, winning the 800 in 1:46 and the 1,500 in 3:43. Coach Davenport was so thrilled that he tried to talk Julius into staying at Southern for his entire college career. Coach Cook, waiting and watching in Virginia, said no way.

Through the summer and fall of 1995, Julius continued at Southern, earning his credits and polishing his English. As long as he was training or going to class, he didn't think about Awake. But at odd moments—washing the dishes, in that twilight moment before drifting off to sleep—haunting images found him. Also, his Ghanaian and Caribbean housemates would talk often on the phone to their families back home. Julius listened wistfully to the happy conversations.

In December of 1995, one year after landing in America, he left Southern and moved on to George Mason University, the province of another war-haunted pilgrim.

◆ ◆ ◆

Julius moved his bubble from an apartment in New Orleans to one in the suburbs of northern Virginia. In Uganda you could travel five miles and be in a different world, one whose tribe spoke an alien language and worshipped unfamiliar gods, where the people eyed you with a hostility and suspicion bordering on hatred. In the United States, by contrast, you could travel a thousand miles and go to the same convenience stores and watch the same TV shows. Not only did everyone speak the same language, they greeted you with the same bland smile and the same injunction to have a nice day.

As soon as Julius was settled in his apartment, Cook called him into his office. It was their first face-to-face meeting since the summer of 1994, at the Commonwealth Games in Victoria, when Cook had been simultaneously impressed by Julius's talent and concerned that some component of his character would keep him from realizing that talent. Of course, every athlete—every human being—faces a similar problem. For the overwhelming majority of runners, a weakness or defect held them back: laziness or overzealousness, a lack of trust, the wrong boyfriend or girlfriend, fear of failure, or, to a surprising degree, fear of success.

But Julius was different. Cook sensed that if Julius fell short of his gift, it would be due to an excess rather than a lack of virtue. "In some weird way," Cook remembers thinking, "this kid might turn out to be too good for his own good."

During the sixteen months since their first meeting in Canada, Julius had affirmed Cook's hunch that he was a special athlete, possessing the combination of speed and durability that might finally deliver George Mason a team NCAA title. Had a year in America bled some of the goodness out of him—the virtue that ultimately might prove his flaw? Cook decided to find out.

"Look, Chief, my wife and I are heading down to Florida to spend a week in the sun over the new year. We need somebody to come to our place to water the plants. Can you help us out?"

Of course Julius agreed. Before departing for Florida, Cook placed a hundred-dollar bill in plain sight on his kitchen table. He knew the bait would prove tempting. His foreign athletes were chronically, desperately short of cash, and draconian NCAA regulations made it certain that they remained poverty-stricken. For instance, the rules allowed Cook to transport his athletes from the gym to a workout site, but giving them a ride to class was an infraction; they had to walk across campus in the rain. When the dining hall closed on weekends and vacations, his runners often went hungry. To help them out, Cook would sometimes slip a small sum of cash into an African kid's pocket and, with a wink, tell him to go shopping.

From the stories he'd heard from New Orleans, Cook knew that Julius was especially strapped. A hundred bucks would mean a great deal to the kid. Cook wouldn't say a word to Julius if the money were to have vanished when he got back home. In fact, in a way, he'd be relieved.

When Cook and his wife returned from Florida, however, he found the house plants flourishing and the hundred-dollar bill on the table, exactly where he'd left it. On a personal level, Cook was gratified. From a competitive perspective, however, the coach wasn't sure this was a good thing.

• • •

The semester started and workouts began. While Julius got acquainted with his new surroundings and teammates, Cook limited the runner's training to base mileage; no drills, weightlifting, or other strength work, just moderately paced tempo runs on the roads around campus. The first important competition of 1996 would be the Mobil Invitational indoor track meet in New York City on February 25. Mobil had hired Cook to organize the meet, and he'd assembled a strong field for the evening's marquee event, the men's mile. Marcus O'Sullivan, a celebrated Irish runner, served as headliner, joined by a half dozen Olympic-level professionals competing for a prize purse.

There was still room for a few more runners, however. Should Cook give Julius a slot? Could the kid compete, given his lack of sharpness, the fact that he hadn't really prepared, and the fact that he was nursing a minor knee injury? This wasn't the NAIA championships at Azusa Pacific; this was Madison Square Garden, Saturday night in midtown Manhattan. Could Julius rise to the occasion? Or, if he got his clock cleaned in his first prime-time race, would he be able to bounce back? Again, Cook decided to find out.

Adding to the challenge, Julius had little experience running indoor races, where the track was only half as long and significantly narrower than a standard outdoor track. There were more turns during an indoor race and more contact with rivals. Not all runners prospered indoors; some avoided the winter track season altogether. Julius gamely accepted the challenge, but in the early laps he appeared out of his depth. He strained to keep contact with the lead pack and seemed reluctant to elbow his way into position to launch his kick.

Over the final two laps, however, as the crowd roared and the lights seemed to grow brighter, Julius came alive. Over the penultimate lap he shot into second place. As the bell clanged to signal the final lap, a British runner named Nigel Bruton led by a stride. But at the first turn, Julius blew by him. O'Sullivan and Jason Pyrah, a standout U.S. middle-distance runner, tried to respond with their own potent kicks, but Julius's lead kept growing. Covering the final 400 meters in 56.5 seconds, Julius Achon hit the tape in 3:57.66, seven meters ahead of the second-place Pyrah. The time was the fastest in the world during that indoor season.

After the race, Frank Litsky of *The New York Times* interviewed the winner. "I heard the crowd and I started flying," Julius told Litsky. "I was smoking. I didn't feel confident about the race. I had hurt my knee and didn't work for five days."

Cook marveled at Julius's performance, range, and promise. "He can run the 800 in 1:45.6 and 10K in 29 minutes plus," the coach told Litsky. "He just needs to get older and stronger. He's not really fit because he hasn't done the exercises and drills we do. Before he got here, he hadn't lifted a weight in three months. He's very motivated. I think he will be great at 1,500 meters and the mile."

◆ ◆ ◆

Thus began Julius Achon's magical 1996 season. Since 1984, the University of Arkansas had maintained a stranglehold on the NCAA indoor national championships. GMU had come close to unseating the Razorbacks several times but had always come up short. At the '96 indoor championships in March, however, Julius provided just the jolt that Cook had been hoping for. He won the individual title in the mile, with a 4:02.83 performance, finishing nearly a full second ahead of the second-place finisher, Jonah Kiptarus of Nebraska.

Those points propelled George Mason past Arkansas to the overall team title, the school's first national championship in any sport. Moreover, in the course of the meet's multiple heats, semifinals, and finals, Julius recorded a feat for which there is no formal record but that might stand as the most impressive—and, perhaps, self-destructive—achievement of his running career: within a single twenty-four-hour period, he logged three sub-four-minute miles.

Back in Fairfax, on the GMU campus, the team title brought Cook the recognition he had long sought. The university president invited the team to his home. All marveled over the sensational new runner from Uganda, with good reason. Within his first eight weeks on campus, Julius had won a major race against professional competition, claimed an individual NCAA event title, and led GMU to the NCAA team championship. "I began to think that Julius might even surpass Bile," Cook says.

The spring and summer of 1996 promised even greater glory. This was an Olympic year, and Julius's performances had already secured him a spot on the Ugandan team. Before the Games convened in Atlanta in July, George Mason, again led by Julius, would vie to add the outdoor NCAA championship to its indoor title. Julius appeared a lock to win more individual national titles. If he continued to perform at this electrifying rate, even an Olympic medal seemed possible.

◆ ◆ ◆

With so much at stake, so much within his grasp, John Cook threw everything he had at his team in general and Julius Achon in particular. This opportunity came around only once in a career, in a lifetime. When Cook needed to be charming, he charmed: tossing around the nicknames, telling stories like the one about the rock piles in Munich, communicating in ways spoken and unspoken that he had a special understanding of his foreign athletes and would always take care of them—as long as they performed, put up the numbers.

But if they slacked, if they fell short, Cook transmogrified into a near caricature of the authoritarian coach, screaming that he'd send their sorry asses back to Africa if they didn't get on the stick. And Cook drove himself just as hard, supervising the drills down to the finest detail, plotting matchups, counting points, holding back runners at certain times and working them relentlessly at others.

Cook forged a special bond with Julius. His nickname for the runner was "Chief," which defined Julius in all senses of the term. It wasn't often that the team's star performer was also its moral leader and role model, the hardest and most disciplined worker, but Julius filled all of those roles. It was easy to forget that the kid was just nineteen and had joined the team only a few months earlier.

Julius took to Cook's drills like no runner he had coached before. Especially in the United States, young people typically turned to distance and middle-distance running because they couldn't excel at sports that were more popular, were more enjoyable, and gave them a better chance of attracting a boyfriend or girlfriend. Julius, by contrast, was a superb natural athlete with exceptional strength, coordination, and muscular explosiveness. He was also mentally strong, intensely competitive, with an innate sense of pace and an instinct for matching his resources to the challenge at hand. He didn't overthink, like many American athletes, and thus rarely beat himself.

But did he love the sport, did he run for its own sake, in the manner of many Westerners? On the level that Julius and other elite East African runners operated, that was an irrelevant question. Were Cook's drills of fundamental benefit to Julius? Wouldn't he have been just as successful, just as much the pure middle-distance runner, without them? Maybe. One thing was for sure—Cook wasn't going to play favorites or cut his meal ticket any slack.

"Dammit, Chief, what the fuck are you thinking? Ten reps, not nine! Your shoulders are rounded like a ninety-year-old granny's! You think you're special? You think you're different? You don't think I'll kick your butt back in the damn river with the crocodiles if you don't shape up?"

Julius would buckle down, do just what Cook said. But underneath there was a riptide of barely suppressed hilarity, as if Julius knew what Cook was up to and was in on the joke. There was a conspiratorial bond between the two men, similar to the one that showed between Julius and Kristina when his mother chased him into the bush after he broke one of her clay jars. At times, while ragging on Julius, Cook had to bite back laughter.

The coach hustled to stay one step ahead of his athlete—to keep him busy, hungry, and just the slightest bit off balance. He knew that Julius trusted him totally, without question. This was terrific, but it was also daunting. Cook made sure he was worthy of that trust. Also, he didn't want that other thing to surface with Julius, the mysterious element in his character that could ride him off the rails.

What was this thing? Cook didn't really want to know. He didn't want to hear about it. He knew it had to do with Uganda. Cook would joke about Africa, but he didn't want to learn about the place. He didn't want Julius to think about it, any more than Cook thought about his boyhood in Munich—the thunder of the bombs, the parachutes opening like orchids against the gray sky.

So far, so good. The Chief appeared 100 percent locked in. No tics, no faraway eyes. The bubble around Julius remained intact and airtight.

◆ ◆ ◆

On April 27, 1996, at the Penn Relays at Franklin Field in Philadelphia, one of the oldest and most prestigious track meets in the nation, Julius won three races (the mile, the 4 x 800 relay, and the distance medley relay) and was named MVP of the meet. Then Julius and his teammates returned to George Mason for weeks of intense training, during which Cook would prepare them for the crucial competitions later in the spring and summer.

Track training was a matter of peaks and sloughs, hard days and easy days. You planned your athletes' training so that they hit the big races with their blood-oxygen levels at the highest possible reading, with glycogen flowing through muscles dense with fast-twitch fibers, and with their nervous systems firing. Many coaches around the world illicitly employed erythropoietin (popularly known as EPO), anabolic steroids, and other performance-enhancing drugs to help their runners attain this peak. Cook had observed plenty of juicing during his time in Europe but says he never doped his own athletes. Instead, he employed every possible legal technique to, in effect, simulate a doper's advantage.

Although he was no fan of some of the often hypocritical NCAA rules governing issues such as "amateurism," Cook scrupulously adhered to doping regulations, which, he believed, spoke to the core of his vocation. If everything went exactly right, he thought, a clean runner could compete with the cheaters. "Beating the juicers entails paying attention to your runners 24/7, not just while training," he says. "You monitor their eating, sleeping, every aspect of their physical, mental, and emotional functioning. You put it all together for the big races and tear it down afterward."

In early May, after the Penn Relays, Julius entered one of those tear-down phases, undergoing a draining regimen of drills, weight-lifting, and sprint sessions. The work left him with heavy, tired legs, and Cook decided to hold him out of a conference championship meet that GMU was hosting that weekend.

The meet was on Saturday. On Thursday, Julius logged an especially taxing workout: 20 x 200 meters, with each rep run at 26.3 seconds and just 45 seconds' rest between each rep. Afterward, he dragged himself back to the apartment he shared with a few other foreigners on the team. It was the same sort of arrangement as in New Orleans: mattress on the floor, training shoes by the door, warm-ups in the closet, a pot of rice on the stove, all of it forming that hut that could be collapsed and moved anywhere at a moment's notice. He grabbed a bag of ice from the freezer for his legs, flopped down on the couch, and was just dozing off when the phone buzzed: Coach Cook.

"Chief, how do you feel about running the 800 on Saturday?"

And with that the stage was set for the signature moment in Julius Achon's athletic career: a scintillating, ultimately self-immolating performance in the race he almost sat out—a race that, by the conventions of his sport, he had no business running.

Feeling flat, expecting nothing, Julius toed the line for the 800 meters at the Saturday meet. It felt like his legs were encased in plaster casts. After 500 meters he was running in eighth place, dead last. Moving to the outside lane, he launched a kick that he assumed would amount to little. Instead, it was as if a giant hand picked him up and flung him forward. "The strange thing was it felt so easy," Julius recalls. "I didn't feel like I was moving all that fast."

With 100 meters to go, he found himself in front, moving effortlessly, with the other runners fading behind him. Julius rode the wave the rest of the way home. When he crossed the line and looked up at the stadium's digital clock, he thought it had malfunctioned. It read 1:44.5, which, if accurate, would be an NCAA record.

Of all the great college middle-distance runners in U.S. history— Glenn Cunningham, Jim Ryun, Marty Liquori, and others—none had run the distance that quickly. It couldn't be true. But then again, it *had* to be true, because his teammates were rushing forward to embrace him and, across the infield, Coach Cook was grinning.

In a race that he was not even supposed to run, Julius had broken the NCAA record for the 800 meters.

◆ ◆ ◆

If the future looked bright for Julius before that record-setting performance, it now appeared limitless. There was every reason for Cook to think that he had the generation's next great middle-distance runner on his hands and every motivation for Julius to keep following his coach's leadership. There was no intimation that Julius's debut season was too good to be true; no evidence suggesting that Cook had raced Julius too often, gone to the well too many times. Or perhaps, with his long career culminating in such triumphant fashion, when he was so busy preparing for the critical summer season, Cook simply overlooked the warning signs.

Next up on the schedule were the NCAA outdoor championships in June at the University of Oregon in Eugene. For the first time, Arkansas or LSU or Stanford or one of the other glossy, name-brand programs wasn't favored to win the team title. Those teams were loaded with lissome suburban-bred female distance runners and clean-limbed male runners who'd come of age playing youth-league soccer. The sprinters tended to be pop-muscled, dreadlocked guys on loan from the football team and women who eased into the starting blocks wearing spandex tights.

The favorite in 1996 was George Mason, a commuter school in the Virginia suburbs, its team composed not of native-born U.S. blue-chippers who'd won state titles in high school but of village-bred East Africans and American kids who went unrecruited by the glamour schools and were now molded and nurtured by a self-taught former soccer player, the son of a Luftwaffe officer and the stepson of a Georgia red-dirt top-sarge who'd survived two tours in 'Nam.

On the NCAA form charts, most of the GMU runners ranked fourth through eighth in their events, each performance good for a few points toward the team title. At the top of the card, meanwhile, projected to rake in twenty total points with expected wins in both the 800 and 1,500 meters, stood the Chief.

His accomplishments over the previous five months had been astonishing: the win at the Mobil meet in New York City; the three sub-four-minute miles in a twenty-four-hour period at the NCAA indoor nationals; the MVP, three-race performance at the Penn Relays; the 800-meter NCAA record run on stale legs. Along with these races, Julius had logged countless hours of high-intensity training.

Looking back, Cook recognized that he might have struck a Faustian bargain with Julius. But at the time, the coach had a lot on his mind. For years, Cook had been waiting for a team of this quality and depth. And a college coach's job was to promote the welfare of the team, not any single performer.

Besides, Julius was only nineteen years old. Sure, Cook was demanding a lot from him, but he would make it up to the kid. "Just get me through the NCAA in June, Chief. You're going to make the Ugandan Olympic team without raising a sweat. After the NCAAs, I'll take you to Europe to train. When you come into Atlanta for the Olympics, it will be your moment, Chief."

◆ ◆ ◆

The George Mason team flew out to Oregon for the NCAA championships. The meet was at historic Hayward Field, where the legendary coach Bill Bowerman had developed Steve Prefontaine, the late great charismatic middle-distance star of the 1970s, and where Phil Knight had competed as an undergraduate before founding, with Bowerman, the company that would become Nike. Hayward Field was hallowed ground for the U.S. running community, but the mystique meant little to Julius. But while he didn't feel intimidated, he also didn't quite feel himself. He felt tired, on the edge of a cold, and was having trouble sleeping. It wasn't nearly as humid in the Willamette Valley as in Virginia, but the air felt heavy in his lungs.

The 800 came first, the heats one day, the finals the next. Julius finished second in his semifinal race, but ran 1:45.95 in the finals, more than a second slower than his NCAA record performance a month earlier. He finished third, earning six valuable team points, but not the ten that Cook and others had anticipated.

That disappointing pattern repeated in the 1,500. Julius felt exhausted by this point and oddly dehydrated. As a boy in Awake, he could run all day in the equatorial sun on a few scoops of ditch water, but now, in the green, mild Pacific Northwest, he felt parched, dried up. His stride lacked its customary pop, and this time, unlike his NCAA record run, no magic hand flung him forward. Again, Julius finished third in the finals, putting up another six points for his team. At meet's end, the George Mason men finished second overall, trailing LSU by fifteen points.

You could hardly say that Julius cost GMU the title—the team couldn't possibly have gotten so close without him—but he felt that he'd let his coach and teammates down. For almost any other runner, two third-place finishes in a national championship meet would form a crowning achievement. For Julius, the performance felt like failure.

There was little time for disappointment, however, because the Olympic summer was dawning. Not only would Julius be representing his nation at the Games, running the 1,500 meters, but he had been chosen to carry the Ugandan flag into the Olympic stadium during opening ceremonies. Julius would have exulted if he didn't feel like he was moving underwater.

✦ ✦ ✦

In late June, Cook traveled to Europe to prepare several of his runners for the Atlanta Games. With the support of the Ugandan federation, Julius moved his bubble to the Swiss Alps.

Along with training at altitude, he would enter some tune-up races on the European circuit. Track and field was still a major spectator sport on the continent and in the United Kingdom. Diamond League meets formed the top tier, with lucrative races staged at major stadiums in the capital cities. Nearly every week through the summer, regional cities hosted meets that offered smaller pots of prize money. These meets were popular among younger and aspiring pros, especially runners from East Africa. Between weekend races, the athletes shared cheap apartments close to an airport or train terminal. More established runners and their coaches were put up at hotels by their sponsoring shoe companies. Elite performers with world-class credentials established their bases at off-season ski resorts.

The camp that Cook led in Switzerland was somewhere in the middle. Besides Julius, Cook was also supervising Abdi Bile, who would be representing Somalia in the Olympics for the second time. Along with the opportunity to work with experienced Olympic-level runners, Julius began learning about the business of his sport. His breakthrough rookie season at George Mason had made him a marketable property.

An agent from Germany approached Julius, hoping to entice him to leave school and turn professional. The agent could guarantee Julius a base annual income of around fifty thousand dollars, but of course he was capable of earning far more, because the agent could hook Julius up with a French doctor who could "supply whatever he needed."

Julius wasn't tempted by the offer of PEDs, but the prospect of making that much money per year caught his attention. He had become the breadwinner for his large family back in Uganda. The thousand dollars he'd given Kristina in December 1994 was still supporting the family nearly two years later. His sisters and brothers didn't have to jump out the window when the teacher came around to collect school fees. Imagine how much support he could provide with such a princely regular income! Moreover, there were other financial considerations. What if Julius turned down the agent's offer, returned to George Mason and the NCAA's indentured-servant system, and suffered a serious injury that ruined his professional athletic prospects? What other future was open to him? Julius was holding his own in his college classes, but it wasn't as if he were studying to become a corporate attorney or orthopedic surgeon.

If he signed with the agent, however, Julius would forfeit his NCAA eligibility and his scholarship to George Mason. He turned to Cook for advice. The coach knew that he and the university had already received a handsome return on their investment in Julius. The big payoff—the previous winter's NCAA indoor team title—had already been deposited, and now only interest would accrue. On the other hand, Cook sincerely believed that Julius wouldn't reach his peak until 1997, after his body had further matured and he'd benefited from a full year of Cook's guidance.

"Hell, Chief, a year from now, at the world championships, you're going to smoke all those juicers in the 1,500 and be standing up on the medal podium. You're going to have the top-shelf agents fighting to sign you instead of this palooka. Stick with me, Chief. Have I lied to you so far?"

Julius followed Cook's advice and rebuffed the agent. At this point, he wasn't about to strike off in a new direction. In Switzerland, he labored through his workouts and logged a few strength-building 5,000-meter races on the second-tier European circuit.

Occasionally, catching a snippet of a BBC newscast on the TV in a hotel lobby, he would learn of developments in Uganda. The news wasn't good. Joseph Kony had moved his terrorist franchise south, into Langiland.

◆ ◆ ◆

By 1996, emboldened by his success in evading Museveni's forces, well equipped and armed by his Sudanese hosts and sponsors, and having plundered and terrorized his native Acholiland until there weren't many more children or cattle left to steal, Kony began deepening his thrusts into the south, raiding villages around Lira district. To protect the population and deprive the LRA of willing or unwilling support, the Ugandan government had established a network of IDP (internally displaced person) camps across the north. Many terrified villagers abandoned their huts, livestock, and garden patches to seek safety in the camps. Many others were driven by government forces into the camps, where they could be more easily controlled.

But what was going on in Awake? Was Julius's family safe? There was no way to know, no reliable means of communication. He worried that something awful was afoot. Julius couldn't get Kony out of his brain. Could this be the same man he'd watched that day years ago in the Soroti camp? There seemed no way to square the red-eyed stoner who preached from atop the anthills, promising his ragged Alice Lakwena remnants that they'd soon be rich, with the powerful commander now terrorizing the north. There were stories so terrible they could barely be spoken of. Little boys forced to drink their mothers' blood. Men buried alive.

And now, there were the IDP camps, where the suffering apparently was even more intense than in the villages. Julius could not picture these places; he couldn't fix an image in his mind. For Julius, the landscape of his home had always been fixed and immutable. The huts might be torn down and reconfigured, the herds of cattle might wax and wane according to the weather, the season, and the prevalence of the Karamojong, but the lineaments of the villages never changed. Since time immemorial, before the creation of some of the anthills, the same boundaries prevailed.

But now the landscape was changing. If the Langi were fleeing to the camps, who would tend the goats and chickens, harvest the mangoes, turn over the soil in the sweet-potato patches? During his six years out in the world, Julius had been able to forget Awake because, paradoxically, he saw it so indelibly in his mind, a picture that might change with the slant of light during various seasons but essentially remained unchanged. For six years, Julius had only sporadically thought of home. Now, Awake wouldn't leave him alone.

◆ ◆ ◆

Julius kept up with his work. The drills, the track intervals, the long tempo runs on mountain trails. He laughed and joked with his training partners, but now, on the edge of his consciousness, Uganda and Kony lurked. The images were so subtle, so pervasive, that he was barely aware of their presence.

To sharpen his speed, he entered an 800-meter race in Belgium. Midway through the second lap, 150 meters to go, just as Julius launched his finishing drive, a shout of pain rose from his right hamstring. For the first time during a race, he pulled up, stepped off the track, did not finish. He looked down glumly at his thickly veined thigh, which had never failed him before. This was the first significant injury of his career.

Would it have happened if Julius had been more focused, if the bubble around him had remained intact? Perhaps. Or maybe it was inevitable, given the incessant hard training and racing he'd logged over the long year. But Julius knew that stress and worry had been factors, and Cook sensed a similar dynamic. The injury sidelined Julius for two critical weeks, the key training sessions before breaking camp and heading back to the United States for the Atlanta Games.

◆ ◆ ◆

It should have been Julius's crowning, John Akii-Bua–like moment: the nineteen-year-old boy from the bush carrying the Ugandan flag into the Olympic stadium while, around the world, a billion people watched on TV. Julius marched proudly, but there was a wiggle in his brain. Millions of eyes fastened on him, and yet he felt alone. The people that mattered most—his family—would be nowhere near a TV screen. The troubling images kept wheeling through his mind: a teeming, amorphous IDP camp; Joseph Kony wagging his finger and preaching in his blasphemous singsong.

First heat, 1,500 meters. There were no Americans in contention for a medal, so the stadium was only about half full, and half of that crowd seemed to be heading to the concession stands or reading their programs. When the PA voice called Julius's name, there was little reaction.

Per protocol, Julius stepped forward. He waved and smiled, his image huge on the stadium's video screen. Half empty, the stadium seemed even larger than it had with every seat filled at the opening ceremony. He flashed on that moment a seeming lifetime ago, when he won the national junior race in Kampala. He had just crossed the finish line. He glowed with pride, but had no teammate, friend, or family member with whom to share his good fortune. He couldn't even look busy by changing his shoes or putting on warm-ups. All he could do was stand there, alone, hands empty, waiting in awkward silence.

The gun cracked and Julius took off, hoping that some magic might descend, the way it had back on May 6, when, despite his tired legs—maybe *because* of his tired legs—he had relaxed enough to let the power rise and popped that NCAA-record 800. But no magic today, no pixie dust. His hamstring was tight, his stride constricted, and when the time came to goose it on the gun lap, his body couldn't respond. He ran 3:43.08, a respectable time, but far short of what he needed to qualify for the semifinal round. It was one race and done for Julius Achon in Atlanta.

He sat in the stands for the 1,500-meter final, watching the two reigning masters of the distance, Noureddine Morceli of Morocco and Hicham El Guerrouj of Algeria, hammer at each other, El Guerrouj tripping and falling on the third lap and Morceli going on to claim the gold medal in 3:35.78, a clocking still within Julius's range. He was young yet and his hamstring would heal; Cook had promised him that he wouldn't peak for another year. Great things awaited, glory and good money.

Julius was starting to feel like himself again, just starting to patch up his bubble, when a boom sounded, a rending blast. It was neither a fireworks display nor an accidental gas explosion. In Atlanta's Centennial Olympic Park, an anti-abortion terrorist had left a backpack full of explosives on a bench. The bomb detonated, killing one woman and injuring 111 people. Even as it signified something horrific in the present moment, the sound returned Julius to the camp in Soroti and the strafing *sombiye*. Julius left his first Olympics under a deepening shadow.

◆ ◆ ◆

The triumphant year of 1996 was heading for the homestretch. Julius was back at George Mason, inside the bubble, living in an apartment near campus with other foreign runners. After a few weeks of rest, his training cranked up again. Unlike football or basketball, Division I running doesn't have an off-season. You run indoor track in the winter, outdoor track in the spring and summer, and cross-country in the fall. Outside of the team, did anyone on campus really care? It often didn't seem that way. GMU was building its men's basketball program, selling out a new ten-thousand-seat arena. But another cross-country season was coming up, and Cook drove his athletes to put up the numbers. Drills, sprints, lifting, stretching, tempo runs . . .

His leg felt strong again. Physically, Julius was almost back to where he had been in May, before the NCAA championships, his hamstring injury, and the anticlimax of the Olympics. And mentally he was recovering: The change in Uganda, and the silence from Awake, took up receding territory in his consciousness. Back to Plan A: Follow Coach Cook into the bush. Base mileage, tempos, sprints. English class, psychology lecture, biology lab.

He was the Chief, the happy-go-lucky guy with a smile and good word for everybody. But each afternoon, before workouts, Julius would go to the student union and anxiously page through *The*

Washington Post and *The New York Times* for some scrap of news about Uganda. In the evening, after his workout, he would turn on the network news, hoping for an image from anywhere in sub-Saharan Africa.

Usually there was nothing. No news was good news, right? If the LRA infection was spreading there would be news. If the camps were filling up there would be news. No news, no news, and then one afternoon in early October, Julius opened the paper, and there was Uganda splashed across the front page.

At St. Mary's preparatory school in Aboke town, 139 girls between the ages of eleven and sixteen had been abducted by the Lord's Resistance Army. Aboke was not in the north, in a distant quarantine region near the Sudanese border, but south of Awake, deep in Langiland. St. Mary's was a school much like the one at Aliwang, run by the Comboni order of missionaries from Italy.

As Julius read the newspaper account, he could clearly picture the events in his mind. The school had been guarded by government soldiers, but they had been called away and the rebels came during the night. The sisters locked the doors and bolted the windows. They thought they had protected the girls, but when dawn came more than a hundred of them were gone. A few survivors wandered around, dazed and hysterical. And then Sister Rachele Fassera, a tough, unyielding nun like the ones who used to keep the children in line at Aliwang, had trailed the rebels through the bush. She caught up with the band and confronted the leader, who, like the children at Aliwang, relented under the nun's unbending will.

Sister Rachele succeeded in bringing back a hundred girls, while the LRA kept more than thirty. Julius knew that the incident had made international news only because of the heroism of a white person, but that didn't bother him. He imagined the scene in detail: the chaos, the terror, the movements in the night. Would Aliwang be next? Had Aliwang already fallen? What about Awake?

The story stayed alive for the next few days. Grief-blasted mothers wailed; government officials issued vague, evasive statements; pundits weighed in; and Western celebrities such as Hillary Clinton registered outrage. Outside of the African Studies department, no one at George Mason seemed to pay much attention to the story. Sensing that something wasn't quite right with his runner, however, Cook called Julius into his office.

"Chief, forget about all this African witch-doctor tribal stuff, all this rebel civil war junk. That's behind you now. You're in America, hoss. You've got a chance to take it all the way—shoe company contracts, appearance fees, Olympic medals, the whole nine yards. But you've got to stick to your knitting. You can't let yourself get distracted."

Julius managed a smile. "God has a plan for my life, coach," he said.

Cook shook his head. Where was God in the Dachau concentration camp, or in Munich when the incendiary bombs lit up the city? The coach didn't have a religious bone in his body. Yet at the same time he respected Julius's faith and integrity. In fact, he almost envied the kid for his sense of destiny. He was a good man. John Cook knew that might mean a lot of trouble for Julius Achon.

◆ ◆ ◆

Despite his preoccupation with Uganda and his lingering weariness from the 1996 season, Julius continued a standout athletic career at George Mason. In the fall of '96, he won the individual conference cross-country championship, and in March of '97, he successfully defended his indoor NCAA title in the mile—though the GMU men failed to repeat as team champions, as Arkansas resumed its dynasty. But his times hadn't improved since the previous year, and Julius didn't run with quite the same dominance or flair.

The drop-off was partly due to over-racing in 1996, but also due to his heaviness of heart, his guilt toward his family, and his anxiety about their welfare. His decline accelerated during the spring and summer. Injuries forced him to drop out of both the 800 and 1,500 at the outdoor NCAA championships. And at the 1997 world championships that summer in Athens, in the 1,500-meter competition that Cook predicted he would win, Julius failed to advance past the first heat. "Running for a college takes a lot out of you," he says.

"Racing every weekend kills the body." And now there were no agents taking him out to lunch to offer a professional contract. Julius had no choice but to return to George Mason for another year yoked to the collegiate running wheel.

"Julius had so much talent," Cook says. "He and I were amigos. But I had sixty other athletes to look after. He talked about villages being attacked. I didn't listen as well as I should have. He was on a mission to do something for his people. He wanted to go back to Uganda, but if he did that he would never return. I didn't want him to go back. He was just on the edge of realizing his gift. If he committed 100 percent, didn't get distracted, then he could take it all the way. Then, he could really do something for his people. The other thing was, running was all he had. School was hard for Julius. He would get discouraged."

◆ ◆ ◆

And now, early in 1998, Cook suddenly found his own village under attack. The coach took a dim view of NCAA rules that he deemed hypocritical or harmful to his athletes, and was sensitive to their financial struggles. "I knew that Julius needed some new clothes," Cook says. "It was important to him to look his best when he went to church on Sunday."

Everybody at George Mason was benefiting from Julius, including Cook, so why shouldn't the kid be able to buy a cheap sport coat? And if sleet was drilling down and those poor bastards who'd grown up in equatorial Africa and had 3 percent body fat were walking across campus to class, shivering their bony asses off, there was no way on earth Cook wasn't going to stop and give them a ride in the school van and hand them towels to dry off with and tell them sure, fuck it, keep the damn towels.

And yet, on these latter grounds, Cook says that a GMU administrator summoned him into his office. "That's an NCAA violation, and we could get our national title vacated," Cook remembers the official saying.

Cook forced himself to remain calm. "I had been brought in for a come-to-Jesus meeting," he says. "I understood politics. I recognized right away this wasn't a game I was going to win."

The administrator, Cook says, brought up other matters. A professor was questioning the extra tutoring that runners had received—where had the money come from to pay the tutors? And how come Achon dresses so sharp? How does he pay for the nice clothes he wears on Sunday? And then a more troubling question: How about this money that Achon was paid for running a race in Japan over the summer?

Cook had helped arrange for Julius to run the 1,500-meter race at a track meet in Japan. Had Julius been a professional athlete, like every other runner in the race, the meet promoter would have paid all of his expenses, plus five grand for an appearance fee. But because Julius was a good soldier who wanted to keep his NCAA amateur status—because he'd agreed to win more races to make the university and the athletic director look good—dirt-poor Julius, who couldn't afford a pair of shoes until he was almost twenty, had turned down the up-front payments.

But after the competition, when the meet director, without Cook's knowledge, offered Julius two thousand dollars to cover some of his travel expenses, Julius accepted the money; the practice was standard in elite-level track meets around the world. Indeed, before track became openly professional in the 1980s, Olympic-level American runners derived much of their income from these kinds of under-the-table payments.

Somehow this incident got reported, probably by a rival college coach who got wind of it. In NCAA Division I athletics, coaches ruthlessly exploit every possible advantage. Cook acknowledges that, given the opportunity, he might have done the same thing. But now he had to protect his star athlete.

At that point, Cook had already put in for retirement. He speculates that he was called in because George Mason was growing, and the school was establishing a high-profile men's basketball program. "Men's hoops is a huge moneymaker, and the school wasn't going to let some issues in a quote-unquote minor sport risk any sanctions."

Cook says that the administrator said that Julius could stay in school, but his scholarship would be revoked for the coming semester. He would have to pay tuition, fees, and expenses out of his own pocket.

John Cook was fifty-seven years old and had his NCAA title. He had made good money organizing the Mobil meets and qualified for pensions from his various teaching gigs. GMU had gotten what they wanted out of Cook—the championship banners to put up on the athletic center wall, a ton of credibility—and now, apparently, they no longer needed a first-rate track program. Let some university official tell Julius Achon that he had to pay his own tuition, Cook decided. He was out of there.

Cook retired, barely saying goodbye to the runners he had gathered from around the world. "When I leave something," he says, "I'm pretty good at cutting the cord."

Julius was stunned. He repeatedly telephoned his mentor, the captain he had followed into the bush, but Cook neither took nor returned the calls. "That's how I am," Cook says. "When I'm done, I'm done. Julius would be okay. A new coach was coming in, and I didn't want to mess with their relationship."

◆ ◆ ◆

Julius would be okay. Julius was always smiling, always up. When other guys got pissed off or discouraged, Julius would always be there with the right word, joke, or gesture. People took their troubles to the Chief. Julius never got tired, he could live on air and water. . . . Cook needed to believe all that.

"John Cook refused to pick up the phone," Julius says. "He just told me, 'Stay at George Mason and get your degree.'"

The captain was gone. Cook would not pick up the phone, and the university had turned on Julius. Every day he worried more about the situation back home. Kony and the LRA were on a rampage, and the IDP camps were overflowing. His anxiety about his family felt like a fever. What could he do to help them? He considered returning to Uganda but decided that the best thing was to send more money. All Julius knew was running. He didn't have a green card, so the sport was his only option. Had he saved that German agent's phone number? No, well, certainly, other agents would call. God would provide.

On a practical level, Julius had to decide if he was going to turn professional immediately or stay on at George Mason. Earning a degree had seemed difficult enough before Cook left. Now, without the coach's support, the goal seemed unattainable. Before the Atlanta Games, when presented with an opportunity to leave school and turn pro, Julius had chosen to stay, because Cook was there to guide him. It made little sense to make the same choice again, now that the coach was gone. Finally, Julius was already being penalized for, in effect, turning professional. Why not make his status official and try to benefit from it?

In January of 1999, Julius withdrew from George Mason University. He was all alone in the United States, with only an expired student visa for cover. He still had the money from Japan, along with small pools of cash from other sources. Where should he go? What should he do? Which new captain should he follow? He had survived his time with Kony and run forty miles from Awake; he could find his way now. His contacts within the sport advised him to start in Albuquerque, New Mexico.

He had visited the city two years before. During winter break in '96, when the other George Mason runners went home for the holidays, Cook had sent Julius to train at altitude in Albuquerque. It had been similar to his time in Kampala as a schoolboy; Julius had been on his own for Christmas. No gathering of clans down by the river; no fires at night to ward off the demons. Deeply missing his family, Julius burned off his sadness and homesickness with searing ten-mile tempo runs on the 9,000-foot-elevation trails along the snowcapped Sandia Mountains.

It had seemed like the most difficult few weeks of his time in the United States, but now he looked back on those days with nostalgia. Kony remained bottled up in Acholiland, and Julius was in the midst of his magical year of running. When winter break was over, he had returned to a secure American home at George Mason. Now, two years later, the LRA was tormenting the Langi, Julius's running had hit a sore patch, and he was on his own.

◆ ◆ ◆

With its high altitude, abundant sunshine, access to mountain trails and other training venues, cheap rent compared to similar western cities such as Boulder and Flagstaff, and good airline connections, Albuquerque had long been a favored base of operations for professional runners. The city first attracted foreign athletes in the 1960s, when the University of New Mexico started recruiting European runners. Since then it had increasingly drawn Kenyans, Ethiopians, Russians, Brazilians, Mexicans, Moroccans, and many others. Their numbers included established Olympic-level performers as well as aspiring athletes hoping to attract an agent who would negotiate a shoe endorsement contract and plug the runner into big-money races around the United States and other parts of the world. A kind of gold-rush mentality prevailed, and by 1999, Albuquerque was recognized as the Deadwood of the sport.

It was the place where the oddballs and pilgrims landed to try to strike it rich on the American road running circuit, a wild-west crossroads rife with performance-enhancing drugs and sexually transmitted diseases. And sooner or later, almost every elite runner in town visited the home of Eddy and Shawn Hellebuyck. A 1996 Olympic marathoner for his native Belgium, Eddy made a living through prize money won at second-tier road races around the world. A native of the Chicago area, Shawn was Eddy's wife and agent. The couple also made money by renting out rooms in their house to foreign runners.

For a few hundred dollars a month, a non-African runner could get his own bedroom and hang out with Eddy and his circle, many of whom used EPO, anabolic steroids, and other performance-enhancing drugs. Eddy Hellebuyck would eventually get caught for EPO violations in 2004. The alleged drug supplier in Albuquerque was Leonid Shvetsov, Eddy's Russian housemate and training partner. Shvetsov, also an Olympic marathoner, was said to store his

EPO next to the orange juice in the house's communal refrigerator. Eddy kept his stash in a small refrigerator in the master bedroom, where he stocked his private supply of beer.

And the African runners? They slept in the Hellebuycks' basement, in bunk beds stacked like in a submarine or a mining camp. They were assumed to require fewer comforts than the white athletes, and Eddy and Shawn adopted a paternalistic attitude toward the Africans. For a percentage of their winnings, Shawn arranged their travel to races and deposited their earnings in a bank account in New Mexico. The Kenyans and other East African runners eagerly accepted these services, even if it took them a long time to draw their money through Shawn. Sometimes Eddy would "ask" them to wash his car or rake his yard.

According to a longtime resident of Albuquerque who helped coach several Kenyan runners at the time, "The Hellebuycks' attitude seemed to be, 'Hell, they're just Africans. We're doing them a big favor. Where would they be without us?' "

Julius bunked down in steerage, experiencing this quiet but corrosive racist dynamic for the first time. He wasn't in college anymore, was no longer the rising star. He was just another aspiring professional runner competing with scores of other aspiring pros for the few bucks out there on the circuit. The economics of professional track and road racing were cruel: The very top athletes earned seven-figure incomes, while the vast majority, runners with times only a split second slower, earned little or nothing. Shoe companies offered endorsement contracts to attractive, personable American runners; black African runners of equal or higher caliber were judged of negligible marketing value.

Julius trained hard through January and February, but he was already orbiting in a vicious circle. Without a good agent and coach, he would never break through to the next level of performance. But until he demonstrated some superior performances, he couldn't attract a good agent or coach. In his present circumstances, the best he could hope for was to maintain fitness and not regress further. He had to run hard to stand still, in other words. Julius felt like he was back in the training camps of Uganda, as if he'd never gotten anywhere in the last few years. Soon there would be little choice but to sign with Shawn Hellebuyck and become another East African cog in the combine.

Meanwhile the family silence from Uganda continued, along with the stream of disturbing news reports: Kony on the prowl; one of the kidnapped Aboke girls, escaped from the LRA, reporting torture and sexual slavery.

At night, Julius lay awake in his bunk, while his fellow Africans—Kenyans, Ethiopians, Somalians, Moroccans, Eritreans—slept all around him. Every guy in the room was as different from one another as a native Frenchman was from a native Texan, but in the eyes of most Americans, they were the same. There was nobody for Julius to talk to, either upstairs or downstairs, about his shameful past or his worrisome present. He still had his talent and his sense of destiny. He still had that two-grand stake from Japan, and—the last vestige of his GMU scholarship—an open return airline ticket to Entebbe. Julius decided it was time to use it.

◆ ◆ ◆

In the late winter of 1999, he traveled back to Uganda for the first time in more than four years. It would just be a visit, he assured himself as the airliner arrowed over the dark Atlantic. He was not returning in defeat like his brother Jasper. Following Julius's path, Jasper had developed into an outstanding sprinter and had won a scholarship to the University of Arizona. Lacking his older brother's discipline and grit, however, Jasper left Arizona after just one semester and returned to Uganda—a fate common to many young Africans overwhelmed by the outside world. Julius assumed he had already married, built his hut on the family land in Awake, and was sleeping in the elephant grass at night to escape the LRA.

Julius wasn't going to be like Jasper. Nor was he going to be like the successful expats making return visits to Uganda, who strutted, caroused, and bragged about their wealth and accomplishments, which most often were quite modest. Julius was on a different sort of mission, although of what nature even he could not say. He had run in the Olympics, set an NCAA record, and, even after his recent slump, was still the top-rated middle-distance runner in Uganda. His name still meant something there.

Francis met him at the Entebbe airport, and they rode in a taxi van the thirty miles to central Kampala, a trip that would take twenty minutes on an American freeway. Here it was a jouncing, exhausting two-hour ordeal. The air was thick with smoke, exhaust, body odor, and the brackish effluvia of Lake Victoria. And Julius had forgotten the unrelenting din of Uganda: shrill voices, amplified music, the whine of traffic and blat of the horns.

Finally they arrived at Francis's house. His cousin appeared fit and seemed like his old, cheerful self. He caught Julius up on the bad news first: The war had picked up pace in the north. Then the good news: So far, Julius's family remained safely in Awake. No one had been killed or wounded, and none of the children had been kidnapped. Then more bad news: "It is too dangerous to travel north of the Nile, Julius. You must stay here in Kampala."

"Do you mean that it's impossible to travel north, Francis? Or that the journey might be difficult?"

Francis smiled. "Same old Julius," he said. "The buses still head north, but you hear bad stories. Rest up for a few days, and then we'll send you on your way."

"Thank you, Francis, but I will go tomorrow."

◆ ◆ ◆

The next morning, Julius continued his journey home. He rode in a taxi to the downtown bus station. He told one of the station boys that he would give him five shillings to help him carry his Mizuno gear bag to a bus headed for Lira. When the boy heard the destination—the north—his mouth tightened. He led the way to two large buses in the corner of the depot. Armed soldiers stood next to the buses, eyeing the passing crowds. Julius paid the ragged, barefoot boy a few shillings. When the boy gave a long look at the shiny Mizuno bag, Julius added another shilling.

Once the buses were full of passengers, the convoy—a military

vehicle out in front of the two buses, another traveling behind—
ground out of the city and started traveling north. Riding in the
second bus, Julius automatically shifted to war mode, every nerve
straining, as if he'd just escaped the rebel camp the day before. His
muscles were rigid, and he observed every detail. His ears pricked
at each sound resonating from inside and outside the bus.

Uganda was supposedly at war, but the scene along the road appeared unchanged: the usual parade of schoolchildren, the usual
slalom around ruts and washouts, and, when the bus stopped to dis-
charge or pick up passengers, the usual press of village women
hawking skewers of roasted goat-meat chunks. The war, apparently,
had not traveled south of the Nile.

As they continued north, the landscape bleached and flattened,
the villages grew fewer and more threadbare, and none of the children wore shoes. The conversation dwindled inside the bus, and as
the convoy approached Karuma near the bank of the Nile, the talk
died altogether. The convoy lurched to a halt at the town, and a
soldier stepped on board. Raking his eyes up and down the rows of
passengers, he ordered everybody off the bus.

Remaining outwardly calm but on interior high alert, Julius as-
sessed the soldiers' positions and plotted escape lanes among them.
He located the unit commander and kept him at the edge of his
vision at all times.

Two lines! Two lines! the soldiers ordered. Formerly a sleepy
crossroads selling sodas and trinkets to the trickle of foreign tourists
who, before the war, made their way to Murchison Falls, Karuma
now bristled with military. The two long lines inched glacially toward a checkpoint where soldiers inspected documents and screened
the passengers. With his passport and student ID card from George
Mason, Julius felt amply documented. Perhaps the soldiers would
recognize him as the celebrity Olympic runner. But at this moment,
Julius hardly felt like a celebrity.

In fact, the means by which he had temporarily escaped
Uganda—running around in circles faster than the next guy—
suddenly seemed like a pathetic sham. This desperate journey and

the verdict of the frightened, illiterate young soldier about to inspect Julius's passport: This was reality. He had been living in a fantasyland the last few years, protected by a provisional membership in one of the lucky countries. Through a series of events that he'd been powerless to influence, Julius had let that membership expire. Now he was alone and vulnerable. The faint scar from carrying Captain John's rifle still creased his right shoulder.

After a long, tense study of the documents—what seemed like a hundred suspicious glances back and forth between the passport and Julius—the soldier returned the documents and waved him back onto the bus. Other soldiers stood around, glowering, but none signaled for a bribe or payoff, the standard operating procedure for any official transaction in Uganda. This must be war, Julius thought.

The buses resumed the journey. Julius remained on high alert. Despite the tension and fear at the checkpoint, this had been the easy part of the trip. On the far side of the Nile, the wild north awaited.

◆ ◆ ◆

The buses left the town and headed for the bridge. The chimps and monkeys watched from the bluff above the river. Absorbed in the scene, looking back at the primates, it took Julius a moment to realize that something had changed. Where were the army vehicles? What had happened to the escort?

Across the river—beyond the foaming cataract of the great Nile—more heavily armed vehicles surely waited to shepherd the buses through the rebel-infested north. But no military vehicles appeared. It took a moment for the penny to drop for Julius, as he had gotten soft in America. Why should he be surprised at this development? Government soldiers would fight to the death to keep the south secure, but they didn't really care what happened in the north. Julius remembered once again that he was back in Africa.

During the stop at the checkpoint, the two northbound buses had been separated. The first bus had drawn a mile ahead of the vehicle in which Julius was a passenger. The driver hurried to catch up, but you could only go so fast on the rutted, crenellated road. Julius gripped the back of the seat in front of him.

There were no people on the road. No schoolchildren, no women with swaying hips, no men pushing bicycles. The anxiety among the passengers ratcheted up a notch. Rumbling down a short hill, the bus rounded a corner through a thick patch of bush by a brackish pond. They came upon the first bus, upended, lying on its roof.

It took a moment for Julius to process the surreal sight. At first he thought it was an accident, which were common along this poor road traveled at high speeds by old, unsafe vehicles. He then realized that the first bus had been ambushed. The ambush was the favored tactic of all guerrilla armies in Africa. When you operated amid punishing heat and impenetrable jungle, why go to the trouble of hunting for the enemy? Just wait beside the road or trail and let the victims come to you.

For a moment—an instant—the bus driver hesitated. Wild-eyed, he scanned the roadside bush for rebel soldiers. The passengers gave a collective intake of breath, bracing for rocket-propelled grenade rounds. The driver slammed the accelerator, blowing by the stricken bus. Julius gaped helplessly: Seventy-five people lay inside, amid the wreckage of their mangoes, chickens, and modest hopes and dreams.

Later that day, in Lira, officials confirmed that all the passengers on the ambushed bus had perished. Why had Julius's bus been spared? The guess was that the rebels mistook it for a government military vehicle and ran away, but no one knew for certain. Like all aspects of war, the matter really came down to luck or, if you preferred, the will of God.

◆ ◆ ◆

Lira seemed a town transformed. The IDP camp was growing, and a siege mentality ruled the crowded streets. The calls of the merchants at the marketplace seemed urgent to the point of desperation. The stalls were full, and food remained in ample supply, although the prices were twice as high as what Julius remembered.

Still, by the standards of the outside world, staple items cost virtually nothing. He bought fifty-kilo sacks of beans, rice, and cornmeal, fifty dollars' worth of food that would feed Awake for three months. Transporting the goods formed a stiffer challenge.

Government troops maintained a perimeter around Lira, and, after the trauma of the ambush, Julius was tempted to linger in town. If the road from the south had proved so deadly, how could he survive a forty-mile thrust deeper into the kill zone? Asking around, however, Julius learned that most of the raiding and fighting had moved to the south and east. You couldn't travel anywhere at night—if you ventured a mile out of Lira after dusk, your death was certain—but if you traveled toward Otuke in daylight, when the government troops patrolled the road, you might be okay.

Julius hired a pickup truck—despite the fraught circumstances, there was a certain exhilaration to operating with such command; in the United States, he moved at the pleasure of others—and helped the driver load the food. Julius had carried his national flag into the Olympic stadium, he'd been quoted in *The New York Times*, and now he was throwing a sack of beans into the bed of a pickup truck, headed deep into rebel country.

They departed Lira in the morning, driving past the limestone outcropping. The driver rushed because at all costs, they must not be traveling after dark. The traffic seemed of normal volume. Even whipping by on a truck, however, Julius recognized the strain and fear on people's faces.

Aliwang Mission came into view, the school grounds and churchyard swollen with refugees. Julius had always thought of Aliwang as an oasis, an island of order and stability. Now it seemed like just another node of chaos.

As they approached the turnoff for Awake, Julius's stomach knotted with commingled anticipation and dread. The last mile seemed to take forever, but finally they made it. There was the hut where he'd been raised, and there was his mother, standing in shocked stillness at the truck's approach.

Only later, after they had reunited, after the clanswomen ululated and his father smiled and his sisters and brothers hopped with joy at the gifts Julius had brought from the United States—an assortment of George Mason T-shirts—did Kristina explain her response.

"A truck only comes when it carries a dead person," she said. "I thought they were bringing your body. I thought you were gone for good."

• • •

Julius stayed five days in Awake, his first visit since that happy, triumphant Christmas of 1994, just before he'd left for the United States. Now, instead of a thousand dollars, he delivered rice, beans, and cornmeal, but his parents welcomed the staple items as if they were gold.

Around the fire, Julius did not speak of his triumphs out in the world. With trouble and danger pressing from all directions, it seemed gratuitous to recall the Olympic stadium in Atlanta. Instead, he described American cars and shopping malls and the glut of goods in the village-sized supermarkets. In America, Julius explained, people kept animals not for food or hunting but as surrogate members of the family; whole aisles of the supermarkets were laden with pet products. Just as he spoke of lions and crocodiles to American audiences, he told of house cats and yard dogs for Ugandan listeners.

He caught up on the family news. Jimmy, his next-oldest brother, was in business college in Lira, and Jasper had joined the government army. Kristina, Charles, and the younger children were getting by the best they could here in the village. Although thankful for his family's safety, Julius was disturbed by the condition of Awake.

The rebels and government soldiers had taken all of the cattle and most of the goats and chickens. Every few weeks, Kristina would wring the neck of one of the scrawny surviving chickens (which she had bought at the market with the dregs of the money that Julius had left four years earlier) and boil it into a thin soup that provided protein for the immediate family and several relatives. The exceptionally poor nutrition rendered the children more than usually susceptible to malaria and respiratory infections. The garden produce had been similarly decimated; both the LRA and the government soldiers grabbed what they wanted. Each night for months the family had left the hut to sleep out in the bush to avoid the rebel raids.

But thus far, with the exception of Julius years earlier, none of the children had been kidnapped. Although hungry and frightened, they were surviving. Most important, the family had been able to hang on in the village. They had not been forced into the IDP camp at Aliwang, a place of grinding misery, where food was even more scarce than in the countryside and death was more likely to come through disease or starvation than by direct LRA violence.

"So we are safe now, and maybe Kony has gone away for good," Kristina said.

Julius took a less optimistic view. While it was true that the family was better off in the village than in the camp, it was folly to think that their good fortune would last. Sooner or later they would be forced out of Awake, by either the rebels or the army. Where would they go? That was largely up to Julius to decide.

Even while living halfway around the world, he served as the de facto head of household. He assumed that role when he brought back the money from Kampala in December 1994. That money had provided a lifeline, and the payments had to continue. Indeed, instead of escaping the obligations of a firstborn son by going to America, Julius's ties to his family had only deepened. In a further paradox, to continue protecting his parents and siblings here in Otuke, he again needed to leave them. Julius had to make money; nobody else in the family could do it. He couldn't make any money in the bush, nor were his prospects much brighter in Lira or Kampala. He must return to America and pursue a professional running career. But before leaving, he had to figure out a place of refuge; a fallback position for his family, an alternative to the camps.

◆ ◆ ◆

During his visit, Julius never missed a day of running. Training—or at least maintaining some semblance of base fitness—was more crucial than ever, as both a means of livelihood and a routine to build his day around.

Each morning he ran the same route as when he was twelve years old and just back from his time in the bush. Then he ran barefoot and bare-chested, in a pair of raggedy, ballooning gym shorts; now he ran in high-tech training shoes and wore Lycra tights to ward off the morning chill. This exotic getup aroused no end of amusement and fascination; the village children chased after him in flocks, laughing uncontrollably. Just as they had when he'd started to run, the village women chastised Kristina: "What is wrong with Julius?"

After five days he traveled back to Lira, where he located a one-acre plot of land near the edge of town. The property had good drainage and space to drill a well. There was a clutch of huts on one side of the plot and an auto repair shop on the other, with a decent dirt road connecting to the artery into town. He made some inquiries and eventually found himself across a desk from an Indian businessman.

Migrants from the Indian subcontinent arrived in Uganda at the beginning of the twentieth century, when the British were building the railroad that Winston Churchill likened to a thread of civilization drawn across chaos. The British administrators couldn't find skilled local workers, so they imported laborers from India, another colony, to clear the bush and lay the tracks. The work was brutal and many workers died from malaria, fever, and lion attack. Unfortunately, the slender thread of the railroad quickly dissolved back into jungle, as quixotic a hope as the dam at Murchison Falls.

But thousands of Indian laborers had remained in Uganda. They worked diligently, built small businesses, and came to form the backbone of Uganda's mercantile class. The Indians had survived the British, the lions, and the depredations of Idi Amin, who temporarily forced them out of the nation at gunpoint. Some Ugandans resented the Indians for their success, but Julius never felt that way. In fact, now, bartering with this broker in Lira, Julius was heartened by the businessman's brisk, efficient manner and practical acumen. If the Indians had prevailed over persecution and hardship, so could the Langi. Indeed, the nation as a whole could survive.

Two thousand dollars, the disputed money that caused him to leave George Mason, paid for the acre. "You will not be sorry," the broker told Julius, shaking his hand. "Land will never fail you."

◆ ◆ ◆

Julius made his way on to Kampala, satisfied that, under the circumstances, he had done his best for his family and that thanks to his efforts they stood a chance of weathering the conflict without undue further suffering. Now he was eager to return to America and begin his professional running career properly. The sooner he could start, the sooner he could wire funds back to Uganda. But in the capital, to his shock and dismay, Julius discovered that there was no going back to the United States.

After withdrawing from George Mason, he no longer qualified for a student visa. He could apply for a tourist visa, but that carried certain restrictions, such as proving that he could travel to the States with sufficient funds to return to Uganda. After buying the property in Lira, Julius was broke. He was also on his own; there was no longer a John Cook pulling bureaucratic strings for him on the American end.

Julius rushed back to the U.S. embassy, hoping to connect with the secretary and ambassador who'd been so attentive when he first traveled to the States in December '94, but both had moved on to other postings. The new secretary greeted him with a blank smile and instructed him to wait until his number was called.

◆ ◆ ◆

As Julius stood on the street outside the embassy, pondering his next move, the city pulsed around him, everybody walking and talking, absorbed in their own private dramas, oblivious to the nightmare unfolding in the north and to Julius Achon, the former national sportsman of the year, who had somehow managed to squander a golden opportunity for a life in America. Mr. Banage and John Cook had warned him not to return to Awake, but he had ignored his mentors' advice.

Given his responsibility as a firstborn son, however, what choice did he have? He wished that he could have been one of those people who, once they escaped, never looked back. But such tunnel vision was beyond his capacity.

And now he couldn't waste any time feeling sorry for himself. He moved into an apartment near Francis's house and resumed training. He hooked up with the national training camp in western Uganda and started preparing for the 1999 world championships in Seville. At that meet, however, due to spotty training, lack of coaching, and general anxiety, he again failed to make it to the finals in the 1,500. Disappointing performances at major competitions were now forming a pattern.

"It was too much responsibility and uncertainty," Julius says. "I was thinking always about the welfare of my family in the village. I didn't have any money and I was miserable, worrying all the time."

He spent the next year shuttling between the training camp and Kampala, competing in every professional track meet that would pay his expenses, with the longer-range goal of the 2000 Olympic Games in Sydney. Whenever he won money, he funneled some of it to Lira to begin construction on a house and security wall on the property he'd purchased the year before.

Early in 2000 he won the 1,500 at a track meet in Osaka, Japan, which yielded two thousand dollars in prize money. It was his first good race in months. Maybe he was back on track; maybe Julius could ride this momentum into the Olympics, get noticed by a European or American agent, and attain the career that he still dreamed about, the level he knew he deserved.

His victory—and the amount of money he'd won—made the newspapers in Kampala. Julius flew home to Entebbe feeling better than he had in months. The check was in his gym bag. Francis dropped him off at his apartment, and he cleaned up and crawled into bed. He was just dropping off to sleep when seven gunmen broke into his apartment. They threw Julius to the floor, badly wrenching his back, and got away with everything of value in the apartment, including the gym bag containing the prize money. Such crimes were common in Kampala, but Julius was devastated.

All he could do was press on. He made it through the selection process for the Sydney Games. The Ugandan federation appointed him team captain, but he had the same results as in Atlanta. Julius finished fifth in his qualifying heat. The twelve fastest runners advanced to the semifinals and Julius was number thirteen—a number fitting his long run of bad luck. Moreover, in Sydney, unlike in Atlanta, there was no flag-bearing glory to compensate for the disappointment or to augur glories to come.

◆ ◆ ◆

Dejected, he returned to Kampala. Not even thieves bothered to greet him now. For the first time, Julius contemplated quitting the sport. Perhaps he could resume his college studies, earn a degree, and become a teacher and coach like Mr. Banage. Feeling his hopes fading, his world constricting, Julius went out walking one day, not moving toward a workout or any other errand, but just walking, in the way that the average Ugandan walked, moving for its own sake. Julius went walking and was rewarded with a vision.

She was moving toward him on one of the dusty back lanes of Kampala. From a main thoroughfare, a visitor to the city would never imagine that an unmarked side alley could lead to a distinct neighborhood with stores, schools, hostels, mosques, churches, and thousands of dwellings and that an unmarked alley in that hidden district could find its way to yet another full-fledged community beyond, the districts spilling down the hills into the baked ravines in seemingly endless profusion, one opening to the next in the manner of a Russian nesting doll.

Julius lived in one of these neighborhoods near the center of the city. Like most Kampala districts, it was a place where the destitute and desperate lived alongside families that were relatively prosperous, where open-air hovels stood beside stucco homes owned by civil servants and police officers.

He was drifting uphill and she was on her way down, so the relationship began with Julius literally looking up at his future bride.

◆ ◆ ◆

She had a smooth teardrop face and bright brown eyes, and she cut along the rutted street with a lithe, sure-footed stride. It was late afternoon and the mosques were calling the faithful to prayer, and the churches summoning their believers to vespers. As the young woman approached, Julius beamed her a bright smile, throwing all his energy her way. She must have caught the bolt, because she looked at him, giving a frank appraising glance that nearly knocked him over. Then she continued down the hill, disappearing into the crowd.

Julius was no longer depressed. He went to meet his brother Jimmy, who was going to school in Kampala. Julius described the young woman in such detail that his brother laughed. "I know that girl," Jimmy said. Her name was Grace and she lived in the neighborhood—a churchgoing girl from a good family. Through Jimmy, Julius made arrangements to meet her. In traditional courtship manner, he presented himself at her family home and met her mother and father. After living so long amid the fast, loose ways of the West, Julius found the ritual appealing. Everything about this girl was appealing.

Her father was a prosperous accountant, and Grace—the eldest of nine children, just like Julius—attended college, studying to become a social worker. "I noticed Julius that day as I was walking to church," she remembers. "He came to see me, but at first I was not impressed. I didn't know anything about his career as an Olympic runner, and I already had a boyfriend."

Also, like many Kampalans, Grace knew nothing of the war in the north. She had no inkling that schoolgirls were being torn from their dormitory beds or that people were starving in IDP camps. Julius found her innocence comforting. Knowing that Grace was the one, he doggedly continued his suit. A plan was afoot, and his time in Kampala was growing short.

◆ ◆ ◆

Julius had passed the previous eighteen months in limbo, with his running career in suspended animation. There was not one standard-dimension running track in the entire nation. Even modestly equipped gyms were scarce, and massage therapy or chiropractic services that runners in the developed world took for granted were basically nonexistent. More important, there were no first-rate coaches in Uganda. Julius employed many of John Cook's drills and techniques, but that wasn't the same as working under the eyes of a competent, trusted coach on a daily basis.

Living in Uganda also limited his income opportunities. Julius lacked access to agents and training centers like the one in Albuquerque, which, for all its wildness, offered a community of professional runners. On his own, Julius couldn't acquire a visa that would allow him to live and train in the United States or Europe, and his times weren't quite good enough to elicit the interest of a foreign coach or agent who would work on his behalf.

Meanwhile, precious time was slipping away. A middle-distance runner's window of opportunity doesn't stay open for long. Fast-twitch muscle fiber and general explosiveness both peak in an athlete's twenties. VO2 max—a measurement of the maximum amount of oxygen available to the body—declined by small yearly increments, but an inch was all that separated standing on the medal podium from loading cornmeal onto a pickup truck in Lira town. Julius was zero for two at the Olympics, and by the time the Athens Games came around he would be twenty-eight, borderline elderly for a professional athlete.

In the winter of 2001, while training for the world indoor championships in Lisbon in February, Julius hatched a plan to get out of Uganda, covertly negotiating with a representative from Portugal about seeking asylum in that country. Ever since his triumph at the 1994 world juniors, he'd been well thought of in Lisbon. Seeking expiation for its colonial past, moreover, Portugal maintained a liberal asylum policy toward Africans. Julius would have preferred the United States, which was more familiar and offered a richer running environment, but beggars couldn't be choosers. He also felt vaguely guilty about vying for an asylum spot; compared to the hundreds of thousands of northern Ugandans suffering in IDP camps, Julius lived like a sultan. But his family was on the firing line, and Julius was its sole outside support. He couldn't worry about the delicacy of his feelings.

On the eve of his departure for Lisbon, he went to see Grace. He hadn't told her of his asylum plan, which he'd promised the Portuguese authorities to keep secret.

"I'll text you every day," Julius vowed. "And every night I'll think about you, no matter how long we have to be apart."

Grace was mystified, but pleased.

◆ ◆ ◆

His first job in Lisbon was to run the 1,500 at the world championship meet, strive to finish in the top five, and win some prize money. Julius ran hard, he always ran hard, but at surge time, 500 meters out, where the contenders separate from the field, and again over the final 100 meters, where the leaders unleash their kick, Julius couldn't find the higher gear, the gear that was available only to runners who had logged the requisite speed work and strength work, followed a healthy and carefully calibrated diet, slept eight to ten untroubled hours each night, traveled regularly to the mountains for weeks of altitude training, received twice-weekly massage therapy, and exploited every other opportunity available to a world-class middle-distance runner.

Lacking these opportunities, Julius finished a flat, dispiriting ninth. No money again. After the race, per his plan, he filed for political asylum and moved into quarters at the Benfica Sporting Club in Lisbon. Although it was one of the oldest and most prestigious sports clubs in the nation, Julius slept on a cot in a storage room in the dank, unheated basement.

The largest sports club in Portugal, Benfica featured a solid track and field program, but, by far, its main sport was soccer. Track was

Julius Achon, competing in a heat of the 1,500 meters at the 2000 Olympics in Sydney. The runner in the green singlet is Hicham El Guerrouj of Morocco, the world-record holder at the distance, who won a silver medal at the 2000 Olympic Games. POOL JO SYDNEY 2000 / GAMMA-RAPHO VIA GETTY IMAGES

Charles, Julius's father, works his land in Awake village.
LOVE MERCY FOUNDATION

Children of Awake. JOHN BRANT

The road to Lira, hard as iron during the dry season, is a gumbo of mud during the rains. ACHON UGANDA CHILDREN'S FUND

A Cents for Seeds meeting under the mango tree in Awake village.
COURTESY OF THE FEE FAMILY

The Nile River at Karuma Bridge. The Nile divides Uganda in every conceivable manner. JOHN BRANT

Seeking shelter from the equatorial sun in the hut where Julius grew up.
ACHON UGANDA CHILDREN'S FUND

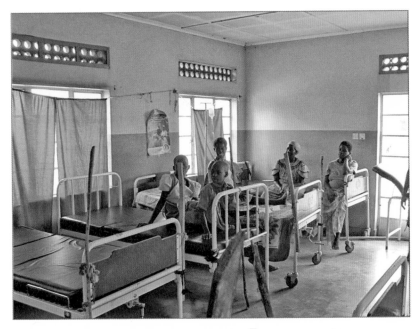

A ward at the government hospital in Otuke. JOHN BRANT

Kristina's grave in
Awake village.
JOHN BRANT

Julius and his grandmothers in Awake village. JOHN BRANT

Jim Fee and Julius Achon: Their stories rhymed. COURTESY OF THE FEE FAMILY

Jim and Julius on the Nike corporate campus.
COURTESY OF THE FEE FAMILY

Jim Fee and Julius in western Uganda, visiting the Engeye Clinic. For years Jim resisted going to Africa, but he quickly learned to love it.

COURTESY OF THE FEE FAMILY

Julius Achon's rules for his high school runners.

JULIUS ACHON

DEAR ATHLETES:
I WOULD LIKE TO THANK
EVERY ONE FOR THE HARDWORK
1. BE LIKE A SOLDIER WHEN
COMPETING [FIGHT]
2. SLEEP 6 - 8 HRs DAILY.
3. TRAIN HARD AND BE POSITIVE
4. EAT GOOD FOOD & DRINK FLUID
5. ACT LIKE A CHAMPION.
6. STAY INJURY FREE.
7. AVOID RUNNING ON ROADs.
(HARD SURFACE)
8.
8. DON'T OVER DO A LOT OF
MILEAGE.
9. TALK TO YOUR COACHES ALWAY.
10. NO LAME EXCUSES.
COACH JULIUS ACHON.
NB: PRAY AT ALL TIMES.
4/29/07

Julius visits his former primary school.
LOVE MERCY FOUNDATION

Angela and Jim Fee with the Lira orphans. ACHON UGANDA CHILDREN'S FUND

*The bore-hole well
in Awake village.*
ACHON UGANDA CHILDREN'S FUND

The waiting room at the Kristina Health Center. ACHON UGANDA CHILDREN'S FUND

Assembled dignitaries at the dedication of the Jim Fee memorial wing at the Kristina Health Center, February 2014. ACHON UGANDA CHILDREN'S FUND

The blue-roofed buildings of the Kristina Health Center bloom like a dream among the thatch-roofed huts of Awake. ACHON UGANDA CHILDREN'S FUND

Julius's brother Jimmy and his wife, Florence, lead a meeting under the mango tree. JOHN BRANT

Julius and his family at the orphanage compound in Lira.
JOHN BRANT

Grace Achon, Jayden Achon, and family, outside their new house in Kampala. JOHN BRANT

Kristina Health Center in Awake. ACHON UGANDA CHILDREN'S FUND

Children rest in the shade at the Kristina Health Center.
ACHON UGANDA CHILDREN'S FUND

Julius and his family outside their house in Kampala. JULIUS ACHON

Dedication of the Jim Fee memorial wing, February 2014. JOHN BRANT

Mike Fee and a friend at the Kristina Health Center. JOHN BRANT

Julius runs with the children at the first Nike-sponsored cross-country meet in Otuke province.

a comparative afterthought, and Julius soon recognized that, as an African sleeping in the basement, he was an afterthought to an afterthought. Because he was a Ugandan citizen, he couldn't compete for a slot on Portugal's national team and thus could deliver the club no Olympic luster. Other than altruism, there wasn't much payoff to hosting Julius.

When the custodian opened up the club in the morning, Julius made sure to keep out from underfoot. Wherever he'd boarded before—Makerere, Southern, George Mason—he had more than earned his keep, offering excellent returns on the investment lodged in him. Now, in Lisbon, he felt like dead weight. "I was running 3:39 for the 1,500," Julius says, "and the other guys were running 3:38."

Moreover, he had shown up in March, and there were no paying track meets scheduled for months. Julius didn't know the language and, outside of a few people in the club, knew no one in the city of nearly three million. Lisbon had a sizable community of African immigrants, but they almost all came from former Portuguese colonies such as Angola, Cape Verde, Guinea-Bissau, and Mozambique. They typically struggled in the city, working as domestics, dishwashers, and roofers. Crowded into poor, graffiti-covered neighborhoods, African immigrants suffered attacks from right-wing skinheads. When a Ugandan walked the streets of these neighborhoods, he drew cold looks from all sides.

Julius hammered solitary intervals on the Benfica track. He logged endurance runs through the city's Monsanto Forest Park. On weekends, he took the streetcar or hitched rides to 10K and 5K road races around the area. They were local events designed for citizen-athletes, but to boost their profile organizers offered modest cash prizes for professional runners. Typically, a hundred euros went to the winner, fifty to the second-place finisher, twenty-five for third place, and a handshake and T-shirt for everybody else. Julius approached these venues out of necessity. Road-race winnings formed his only available income stream.

Road racing presented a new challenge for Julius. A track-oriented runner struck a Faustian bargain with the roads; the money was better, but too much time on the roads would ruin you for the track. The pavement took its toll on your joints and gradually murdered your speed. A professional long-distance runner could concentrate on the marathon and earn a decent living, but a professional middle-distance runner, whose performance and financial cycles centered on the Olympics, could go to the roads only once his best days on the track were past.

Julius was only twenty-five, far from finished on the track, but once again, he saw no other choice. Almost every weekend he won a 10K and took home a few euros, half of which he'd wire to Jimmy in Kampala to distribute to the village. Julius was popular at the road races. He would make happy sign-language conversation with the locals, most of whom assumed he was Kenyan. He grinned for countless cellphone photos. He then traveled back to the Benfica basement.

◆ ◆ ◆

When he wasn't training, racing, or trying to make himself useful around the clubhouse, he walked the streets alone. He'd buy a kilo of rice at the street market and cook spartan meals on his hot plate, one a day to economize. His cheekbones and shoulder blades jutted, and he worried constantly about his family. Only a trickle of news from Uganda reached Portugal, mostly through the BBC. The climate was sunny in Lisbon, but the days passed in a gray wheel: run, eat, walk, worry, run some more. There wasn't much time or opportunity for drills or weight training, so his muscular explosiveness, the key to speed, dwindled.

Almost like an outlaw scouting the next convenience store he was going to rob, Julius would pore over a map, plotting the route to the race he would run that weekend. Early on Saturday or Sunday morning, he would catch the day's first subway to a suburb or small town, step to the starting line, shoot to the lead, whip across the finish, collect his check at the awards ceremony, and then go home. Some of the more prominent races weren't so easy to win, and if an elite-level Portuguese athlete was running, he would get paid more than Julius.

For the first time in his life, Julius Achon was lonely. Even during the worst of his previous struggles—in the bush with Kony, in his first semester at Makerere College, sleeping in the elephant grass to escape the Karamojong—however severe the hardship, he never felt alone. Even in Albuquerque, he had felt part of something. If nothing else, Julius always had his dreams for company, the certainty that he was getting faster and moving in step with his destiny.

But now, in Lisbon, he felt cut off from any sustaining connection. Even his running had regressed; at this point he was no better than a journeyman pro. His only solace was knowing that the trickle of euros he sent to Uganda was keeping his family alive and out of the IDP camps; that, and dreaming about Grace.

◆ ◆ ◆

As the months passed she grew only more distinct in his mind. He thought about her frequently—her smile, her laugh, the way she moved, the sense of calm she conveyed. True to his vow, he texted Grace daily, and the chain of their messages got him through the hours. Summer, fall, another winter: Julius watched the light change through the filmed windows of his basement room. At this stage of the Olympic cycle, he should be thinking hard about Athens, with each moment meted to that purpose. Instead he thought about his family, he thought about Grace, and he was haunted by Joseph Kony.

The misery and violence kept ratcheting up in northern Uganda. Aided and sheltered by the Sudanese government, the LRA operated with near-total impunity. The kidnappings and murders and torture kept spreading, and the IDP camps kept swelling. At all costs his family had to avoid rebel mayhem, but the camps were in many ways more of a threat. How much longer could they hold out in Awake?

About a year after arriving in Lisbon, Julius made a brief trip back to Uganda. First stop was in Kampala to woo Grace. The fact that he had traveled from Europe to see her impressed the young woman and her parents. Convinced of Julius's intent, they granted

permission for the relationship to deepen. He then made the difficult journey to Lira. His family could no longer remain in the village. It was time to settle them on the property in town.

The compound now consisted of a small stucco house; a clutch of
circular, bush-style huts; and an eight-foot masonry wall around the
perimeter for security. Lira was a city under siege. Its population
had swelled grotesquely and the IDP camp festered just a few hundred yards from the border of the property. No person in the region
had gone unscathed by the rebels. In characteristic understated
Langi fashion, citizens would downplay their suffering, at first say
that the rebels hadn't hurt them. Dig a little deeper, however, and
you learned otherwise. The twelve-year-old boy who—driven from
his village, his parents killed—subsisted on a diet of leaves and
twigs. The teacher haunted by the fact that he could not protect his
pupils from being kidnapped and who had watched his son be shot
and killed.

"My wife and I have ten children, and we lost one daughter to a
fever when she was small," the teacher said. "It is normal to lose a
child in that manner. To lose a son in the manner of the LRA is not
normal."

Given the danger and hysteria, Julius wanted to stay in Lira to
help his family get established, but after a few days his parents
urged him to leave, and not for his own safety. Charles told him that
for the sake of God he must return to Portugal—to the world—and
keep sending the precious euros.

◆ ◆ ◆

So Julius returned to his underground shadow life in Lisbon and
clawed more desperately than ever at his running. He applied six
times for a visa at the U.S. embassy and was six times denied. He
ran his weekly road race, swept up around the club, ate his one
spare meal a day, and walked the streets alone.

All this while maintaining a front that nothing was wrong. He
could not appear in need. At all costs Julius must not show weakness. He could not reveal the truth or tell his story, either to white

people or to the city's African diaspora community, whose citizens had their own stories of persecution and woe.

In 2003, at the heart of his Portugal exile, when it seemed that the situation couldn't get any worse, Jimmy called from Lira, finally delivering the news that Julius had been dreading for years. The LRA had taken one of the family.

"My God," Julius said. "Not one of the girls?"

"No," Jimmy said. "They took Father."

◆ ◆ ◆

The arc of Charles's ordeal in 2003 in many ways mirrored the ordeal of Julius fifteen years earlier. An LRA patrol grabbed Charles when he had returned to Awake to check on the family property. On the first day he was forced to march forty miles. "I saw many battles," he says. "I saw the rebels kill people, beating their brains out with rifle butts, using the *panga* because they didn't want to waste bullets. The spirit of killing was with them. They killed for nothing. You walked all day under the sun with no water or food, you sat down to rest for a moment, and they killed you. I was very strong. I had to walk long distances with a heavy load on my head, but I never sat down."

The rebels would move through the bush in vast numbers, three hundred soldiers and captives in a line, the latter tied together with rope like slaves. "You just walked," Charles says. "They allowed no talking. Your pockets had to be empty. If they found anything in your pockets—a picture of your family, a piece of cassava root—they killed you."

This went on for three months. Charles expected to die at any moment. "One day when we walked, the rebels abducted a boy, maybe fourteen years old. He cried, he wept, so the rebels killed him, with rifle butts to the head." Charles pauses, thinking. "We walked on. They killed very many people. We walked very far with no food, and we were very hungry."

Charles's escape was also similar to his son's. "A government helicopter bombed us, so we scattered," he says. "We were near a big river, and I swam across where the water was deep. It was twilight, nearly evening, so I was hidden. I got to the other side of the river, and I was so tired I thought I might die then and there. I rested for a moment and prayed."

A villager came upon him. Each man was terrified of the other. The villager asked Charles what had happened to him. Charles explained that he'd been taken by the rebels, the helicopter had bombed them, and he had escaped.

The villager thought for a moment. Charles was sure the man was going to lift his head and ululate, give the Uganda 911, alert the rebels of his presence to avoid getting killed himself. Charles would not have blamed the man. He might have done the same had the situation been reversed. The man stood, and Charles waited. It was, he figured, God's will. He was too exhausted to fight the man or to run any farther. Instead of ululating, however, the villager reached out his hand. "Come with me," he said.

The villager put Charles in his cart and covered him to avoid detection. He carried Charles to his village, where he spent the night and rested until he was strong enough to follow a sort of underground railroad to get home.

"My wife and children could not believe that I had survived," Charles says. "They wept to see me. I couldn't talk or walk. I had to be taken to Lira for treatment. After one week in the hospital I was able to walk home. I can't now think of the past."

◆ ◆ ◆

During the time of his father's abduction, Julius toiled on in Lisbon. He didn't have the emotional energy to worry about Charles, so he assumed that he was dead. By the same token, news of his father's return elicited more relief than joy.

By this point, Julius had lost all illusions about the profession of running, including the Olympics. Willy-nilly, he had made the shift from the track to the roads, sacrificing the speed that carried him to elite-level performances in the 800 and 1,500. He knew he was finished as a medal contender, although he still might compete at the

Athens Games in 2004, this time for Portugal rather than Uganda. He had begun the process of becoming a Portuguese citizen. Better that than return to Uganda. If he went home, stopped sending money from abroad, it would mean misery and possibly death for his family. Looking beyond the war, there was no good life for a former sportsman in Uganda—or anywhere in Africa.

Julius remembered what he'd observed during his stint in Albuquerque. The Kenyans and Ethiopians who were finished as professional runners, the ones who had failed to make enough money to go home and buy a farm or hotel or some other business, stayed in the United States, sometimes legally but more often without documentation, working at the airport, ferrying passengers around in electric carts. Or they worked as cashiers in the exit kiosks of parking garages or as home health workers for the elderly. In Uganda, however, even these survival-mode, minimum-wage jobs did not exist.

Julius was determined to write a different kind of story. He'd been rejected six times for a visa by the American embassy because he didn't have family in the United States or enough money to support himself. On his best days at road races he was earning three hundred or four hundred euros and wiring at least half of that to Lira, where Jimmy said that the population inside the family compound had swelled exponentially with clansmen driven hungry and terrified from the countryside. The number of refugees in the camps outside the walls was growing even faster, with only sporadic food shipments arriving from the UN to keep people alive.

Julius was developing a reputation in Portugal. Unlike the migrants from Mozambique or Cape Verde, he didn't remind the Portuguese of their shameful colonial past. He was reasonably certain that he could make a living here. And occasionally he would pop a good workout that made him think the magic could return: 6 x 1K at 2:33 per rep, for instance; or a road 8K in 22:51. He might even consider the high-risk/high-reward proposition of a marathon.

In 2003, all of these forces converged: mountains of worry and trouble, with a thin vein of hope running among them. He was about to sign the application for Portuguese citizenship when his cellphone buzzed. It was another international call—what sort of blow would fall this time? But instead of the voice of doom, Julius heard the raunchy, raspy voice that he still equated with America.

"Pack your fucking bags, Chief," John Cook said. "You and I are going to Oregon."

◆ ◆ ◆

After leaving George Mason University—getting out before he was forced out, before trouble descended, before the shadow he'd been racing since Munich caught up with him—John Cook found himself without a definite portfolio but in considerable demand. His long, successful tenure at GMU had made him a legend in the sport. Starting with nothing, he had built one of the best and most consistent programs in the nation. His reputation for developing middle-distance runners was unparalleled. A number of Cook's disciples, former assistant coaches such as Jama Aden and Scott Raczko, had established their own successful programs based on Cook's ideas. His revolutionary work on drills, stride mechanics, and applied sports science was gaining credence.

Cook and his wife moved to Florida, to the sunshine that the native German craved, but he traveled frequently to coaching clinics and consulted at running camps. Still, he didn't feel quite finished with his career. He felt that he had more to learn, more to offer, perhaps in the realm of professional running—not as a consultant but as an actual coach, again molding athletes.

Out of all the work he'd done in the past, meanwhile—all the runners he had cajoled, educated, charmed, and reamed, from pimply high schoolers to Somali thoroughbreds—there was only one piece of business that felt unfinished, one ghost that still haunted him: Julius Achon. Cook's hunger for more action and his need for expiation came together in an unexpected way.

Alberto Salazar, three-time winner of the New York City Marathon in the 1980s, an icon of that era's running boom, had been chartered by Nike to develop a stable of professional American runners that could eventually challenge the East Africans who had dominated track and road racing for decades. Based at Nike corporate headquarters near Portland, the team would be called the Nike Oregon Project.

"Alberto wanted my technical knowledge," Cook says. "He wanted me to be in charge of conditioning and sports science for the project. Alberto had a direct line to the king, Phil Knight, and said money wasn't much of a barrier. I could hire who I wanted. I went out and got Dan Pfaff and Vern Gambetta, pioneers in the field of functional training, guys I learned a lot from. I decided I needed a pacer for the group, a guy who understood my system and could model it for the other runners. I immediately thought of Julius."

Salazar agreed to the hire. He would help Julius acquire a visa and pay for travel from Portugal, put him up in a house in Portland with the other runners, and pay him an annual stipend of twenty thousand dollars. It wasn't a high salary, and the support role represented a distinct comedown from his former world-class stature, but Julius was desperate in Lisbon, his family even more desperate in Lira town. For the second time, Julius gratefully accepted John Cook's offer to come to America.

But first, Julius said, he needed to return home to check on the welfare of his family. Cook advised against it. However, he knew that, regarding Uganda, there was no stopping Julius Achon.

◆ ◆ ◆

He traveled back in that familiar, commingled key of hope and dread. He finally had good news to report—the new job in America, the prospect of more money coming in—but the situation in northern Uganda had grown dire.

The countryside in Langiland had emptied, and two hundred thousand people now crammed into Lira town. Late in 2003, the Museveni government unwittingly provoked Kony by launching Operation Iron Fist. A major offensive thrust across the border into Sudan intended to root out the LRA once and for all, Operation Iron

Fist instead induced the rebels to filter back south, to regions in Uganda that government troops had just vacated. The scourge of the Langi began in earnest.

In less than a month, the number of displaced persons in the region swelled from sixty-five thousand to two hundred thousand. Each day, an average of fifty-eight children under the age of five were dying. From June 2002 to May 2003, more than eighty-four hundred children were abducted by the LRA. By August 2005, 1.5 million people—95 percent of the population of the north—were living in IDP camps.

According to a Human Rights Watch report, in two northern districts in 2002, the LRA burned upward of 1,946 houses and 1,600 storage granaries; looted 1,327 houses, 16 villages, and 307 shops; stole 911 goats and 1,335 chickens; stole or burned 130 bicycles; and attacked 18 schools and 5 health clinics.

"The situation in Uganda is worse than in Iraq," United Nations official Jan Egeland said, referring to the war in the Middle East that commanded global attention. "I can't find any other part of the world that is having an emergency on the scale of Uganda that is getting such little international attention."

In Lira, within the walled compound, Julius's family would often go days without food. Twenty huts were now shoehorned into the one-acre property, with one well and no plumbing or electricity. Kampala, however, when Julius arrived there in October 2003, appeared the same as always. He made a quick stop to see Grace. He told her the news about America and promised that she could join him there once he got established. He kissed her goodbye and then struck north toward Lira.

The bus station, the checkpoint, the monkeys, the Nile, and the wasteland beyond the river. No traffic, no people, nothing at all. On Julius's last visit, during the day, there had been a modicum of activity, but now all was still. The countryside lay smoking and ransacked. The only thing moving was the bus, with its escort of wired government soldiers ready to blast away at the crack of a branch or the flit of a bird above the water ditches where bloated carcasses of cattle floated. Around every corner, from every swatch of elephant grass, Julius tensed for the ambush, the AK-47 or RPG round that he'd been expecting since the day he was taken in 1988. But no ambush descended, at least not today, and after what seemed an endless journey, the convoy approached Lira town.

◆ ◆ ◆

Then he saw a mass of what looked like hundreds of children emerging from a side road to the left. They must be soldiers, Julius thought, and this must be an ambush.

But they carried no weapons, not even *pangas* or clubs, the traditional weapons that had come back in vogue as the spirit of killing had come to rule the north, when the killers outnumbered the rifles available. The children were ragged and dirty and emaciated to such a degree that Julius had to turn his head away. And yet the mob kept advancing, reaching the main road and turning as one toward Lira town, moving not with the surge and leap of school-bound children but with a grim, implacable pulsing.

"Night commuters," the passenger next to Julius said. "They need to get to Lira town before sundown."

To avoid kidnap by the LRA, the man explained, thousands of children throughout northern Uganda left their camps and families each evening, trekking for miles into towns and urban areas, where they took shelter wherever they could—under a doorway or in a public square. In the morning they trekked back to the camps. Julius was appalled, but the passengers in the bus, as well as the soldiers in the convoy vehicles, stared at the children with flat, impassive eyes.

That was only the beginning. Lira, the provincial city he'd once mistaken for a thriving metropolis, that he'd first approached by running along a chain of silver heat-shimmer lakes, had metasta-sized into a nightmare. The city was basically one massive IDP camp, centered at the stadium where he'd raced as a barefoot boy.

The camp was a malodorous swarm of thatched huts and flimsy tin lean-tos, laced by rivers of mud and human waste. People squatted in aimless clots, and the night-commuting children seeped to every corner of the town like a black tide. The government soldiers behaved more like guards at a prison camp than defenders against outward attack. The United Nations teams were able to dispense just enough food to keep most camp residents from starving. With little clean water and no sanitation, dysentery and typhus ran rampant. A fog of fear hung as thick as the smoke from the cook fires. The fear tipped into panic as night closed down.

Julius made his way to the family compound, the shape of Lira so blurred and broken that he took several wrong turns in the town he knew so well. To his relief, the wall around the property was intact. Inside, however, conditions were only a notch or two better than those of the camp. Twenty circular thatched-roof huts belonging to clansmen and extended family were crammed into a space that, out in the bush, would accommodate only two or three. Kristina, Charles, and the older children were hollow-cheeked and reeling. The smaller children regarded Julius with dull eyes and bellies swollen from hunger. Grit and filth blew everywhere. Julius felt ashamed of his health, strength, and unpatched clothing. He dispensed the small gifts he'd brought and berated himself for not bringing more.

Still, Julius recognized that this rudimentary haven had saved— or at least extended—the lives of his family and clan members. With the money that Julius provided each month, Kristina and the other women were able to go out to the market and buy a chicken or a goat and in the corner of the compound plant a patch of cassava and yams. And thanks to Julius's money, Charles and the other men were able to pay off the soldiers so that they wouldn't rob or otherwise harass the family.

Julius told his parents about the new opportunity in the United States, but in these circumstances, its promise sounded almost obscene. Kristina had made a place for him in the house, but Julius said no, give the space to the children. For a few shillings, he would find a hotel room in town.

◆ ◆ ◆

He went out of the compound and was immediately engulfed by swarms of children, the night commuters, begging for anything and everything this obviously privileged man had to give. Julius put on a hard face and waded through them. He couldn't stop, couldn't say yes to one child without saying yes to all. What little he possessed, he needed to save for his own family. "It made me nearly blind with anger, to have to tell them no," Julius says.

Julius found a small hotel where he rented a room for the equivalent of two dollars a night. He couldn't bring himself to stay in the family compound, but the hotel presented its own difficulties. Each morning during his visit, walking from his lodgings to the compound, he was besieged by petitioners, children and adults, people who knew him and strangers who had taken note of his relatively prosperous appearance. The former voiced schemes that required Julius's "investment," and he was obliged to listen politely. The latter simply held out their hands.

The Langi assumed that Julius had made his fortune out in the world and that therefore, by tribal custom, he would share it. They should see my basement room at the sporting club, Julius thought. They should see me diving for the finish line to make one hundred euros at a road race. But by the standards of northern Uganda, he realized, his modest home and profession did make him a wealthy man. He could sleep soundly at night, his room secure from attack, and whenever he wanted he could brew a cup of tea on his hot plate. Julius felt guilty about having so much. He felt even guiltier for not having more so that he could truly be of use to his people.

As the days passed, however, and the incessant demands continued, Julius felt himself harden toward his countrymen. This perverted world was starting to seem normal to him. He endured the days by imagining the America that awaited him. The dream world seemed most vivid and comforting when he ran. Even among these ruins, Julius had to train. In truth, it was more important now than ever. Running wasn't merely his own life raft; it kept scores of others afloat as well. Also, he couldn't disappoint John Cook or his new boss, Alberto Salazar. Finally, Julius couldn't disappoint himself. How many more chances would he have at the dream?

But each day when he stopped running, the dream world faded. He would look down to find yet another child staring up at him, hand outstretched. The dead were accumulating, both in town and out in the countryside. There was no longer even the pretense of a motive animating the violence. The rebels killed for the sake of killing. Even Father Guido, the priest who had baptized Julius in Aliwang, had been ambushed.

One day that winter the priest drove out to a village to pick up a sick child and bring him back to the mission hospital. Father Guido was returning from the village, the child in the backseat, when bullets raked his vehicle. Father Guido crashed the rig into a ditch. An AK-47 round had ripped through his hand. He looked in the backseat and saw a red pulpy mass where the child had been sitting. Father Guido reeled out of the vehicle and fled into the bush. He crouched and watched as the rebels torched the vehicle with the child's body inside.

"You have seen how a chicken is slaughtered, no?" an LRA bush doctor told an interviewer. "Here the death of a person is no different from a chicken. At least a chicken is killed when a visitor comes, and is eaten. Here nobody cares about the death of a person."

Still, people left the camp, venturing beyond the fortified city in search of food. Their hunger trumped their terror, and a certain fatalism prevailed. Sometimes, the rebels wouldn't attack for weeks. Other times, they seemed more numerous than mosquitoes during the rains. Out in the countryside, when confronted by a rebel, people immediately turned and ran, hoping to be killed quickly by a bullet rather than be dismembered by *panga*.

◆ ◆ ◆

In Lira, Julius preferred to run in the early morning, before people were around to petition him. In the predawn darkness, moreover, he felt less self-conscious about wearing training shoes that sold for one hundred euros in the Lisbon shopping malls.

One morning near the end of his visit he set out on a ten-mile tempo run. He ranged around the sleeping town, his chuffing breath and chocking footfall ghostly in the packed, fetid silence.

He finished his hour-long run at the bus depot in the center of Lira.

As the first light rose, in that long moment before the camp and city burst into life, Julius saw a mass of children lying beneath a bus. He counted eleven bodies, sprawled at awkward angles. Who knew how long they'd been lying there or where they had died? Perhaps they'd been dragged in from the countryside and left by the rebels as a warning.

Julius kept his distance from the bodies. What if they'd been tortured, had their lips or ears cut off? Or as was the case with Julius's boyhood friend, what if their skulls had been crushed like eggshells by a rock or a rifle butt? Or maybe these children had merely starved to death or died from malaria or typhus or from AIDS or measles, the disease that had appeared to kill Julius when he was seven years old. Death was everywhere in Lira town; the dead were so many that you learned not to see them.

But then, just as the young Julius had sneezed in his burial sheet, one of the children stirred. Julius realized that the kids weren't corpses; they were night commuters drawn to the meager shelter offered by the bus, whose cooling engine ticked out faint pulses of warmth during the night.

The stirring child wakened and saw Julius, who tried to look away, but it was too late. The child—a boy who might have been anywhere between six and twelve—rose and approached him, holding out his hand in a manner less beseeching than demanding. Julius's shorts and training shoes gave him away: He must have money.

"I have no money," he told the boy, showing him the empty key-pocket of his shorts. "I'm a runner. I am going to train." He realized how meaningless that sounded to the boy. He might as well be speaking Chinese.

The boy kept on staring at him. Julius told himself to say no, just as he had scores of times each day as he made his rounds in Lira. He told himself to turn and run—his outfit gave him that license—but he couldn't move. Nor could he look away.

Julius understood the primal instinct to survive that drove a boy to lie in the dirt all night beneath a bus; he had also suffered under Kony. Or perhaps the anger engendered by having to choose between his family and his community—saving a few people while keeping so many others at bay—cleared Julius's sight. Or maybe he had simply lived too long straddling Africa and the West. He had lost the tunnel vision that came with unalloyed citizenship, the luxury of being at home in the world.

Julius saw this boy and the other children, and could not pretend otherwise.

♦ ♦ ♦

Acting on an impulse at once rash and the product of a lifetime, Julius gathered the children and brought them to the family compound. He fed them bowls of beans and rice and made a space for them to lie down in the shade. After they had rested, Julius told them that it was time for them to return to their camps. But the children showed no signs of leaving. Finally one of the boys told Julius that they had no camp to return to. The rebels had killed their parents. The eleven children were orphans.

Julius pondered the situation. Since he was leaving in a few days, there was no time for him to find another place for the children, and his conscience wouldn't allow him to turn them out. As Julius struggled to reach a decision, the orphans, unbidden, went out to help the compound children tend the fire in the trash pit. They were bush children who knew how to work.

Kristina accepted their presence as a matter of course and calmly directed their labors. That evening, Julius handed a bowl of soup to each of the orphans. They slept under the lean-to roof outside the house, and the next day passed in a manner similar to the previous one. Julius realized that the decision had been taken out of his hands. He told his father that the children should stay. To support them, Julius would increase the monthly remittance he sent from the United States. Charles accepted the arrangement equably. It would be no problem, he assured his son, as long as you keep sending money.

And so the orphanage was born. To the average American it

seems a crushing burden, but in Uganda it wasn't as big a deal. In a land with so little, paradoxically, people didn't mind sharing what little they had. Boarding eleven children entailed ladling out that many more bowls of rice and beans once a day. And in Uganda, the next chore was always at hand; the children would earn their keep.

◆ ◆ ◆

The time came for departure, for Julius to take a second stab at America. He hated leaving his family in these desperate straits. True, the wall around the compound was holding, but how much longer could it stand? And now, albeit for sound reasons, Julius had added to the number of people straining the compound's capacity.

But his family didn't feel deserted. They understood that the money Julius sent from the outside world was all that kept them alive. On the morning of departure, he stood in the heart of the cramped, smoky compound, the children running around with a modicum of abandon unavailable to kids beyond the walls. Kristina and Charles stood with him to say goodbye.

Charles shook his hand, his eyes rheumy and unfocused by years of liquor and his own searing months with the LRA. Kristina, by contrast, looked into her son's divided heart with clear eyes. She said that she thanked God every day for all that he, Julius, had provided the family. "Look at the condition we're in," she said without irony. Kristina was genuinely grateful for this blasted acre.

"You were right all along," she told her son. "All those times I doubted you, all the times I insisted you get married and settle down with us—if you had followed my advice, where would we be? Where would you be? You made the right decision to go out in the world. And it's right for all of us that you go back to the world now."

By Langi tribal custom, she did not embrace Julius before he left. He shook hands with his mother and with her blessing resumed his journey.

◆ ◆ ◆

On a dark afternoon in December 2003, John Cook drove to Portland International Airport to meet Julius's flight. Cook wanted Julius to join him in Oregon for a number of reasons. While he prided himself on his lack of sentimentality, his willingness—often, his eagerness—to cut ties with his past, Cook had never quite let go of the Chief. Over the last several years, the two men maintained a sporadic email correspondence and occasionally talked on the phone. Cook didn't feel guilty about leaving Julius behind at George Mason, but he did feel a debt. He had never quite squared the Chief's account.

Well, here was a second chance for both of them. He would get Julius out of Portugal and set him up in the United States with a modest but steady income. In return, Cook would have company in this alien country of Oregon. He would have an "amigo," and the team would have a pacer who could also model the drills that were Cook's signature. And maybe, just maybe, Cook could take up where he'd left off with Julius, quietly feed him drills and workouts and gradually rebuild his strength and speed to an Olympian level.

As soon as Julius stepped out of customs at the airport, however, Cook saw that any dream of restoring him to a world-class level was fantasy. The Chief looked like hell. He was thin, drawn, exhausted.

On the drive into town, Cook almost felt like apologizing for the dismal weather. The Oregon rain was bad enough, but the winter darkness was worse. It got dark around four in the afternoon and by five the night had clamped down, a dense rain-forest darkness that almost felt solid; a quality of night that took Cook back to the Black Forest winters of his Munich boyhood.

Julius, for his part, was sanguine about the weather. At least Portland wasn't Lira, he thought. Their car wasn't going to get ambushed on the way to the freeway.

Cook drove Julius to the Oregon Project headquarters, a Nike-owned house in northwest Portland. The place was already famous, Cook explained. It was called the Altitude House because the air inside was filtered and treated to simulate living at ten thousand feet of elevation, which, in theory, would boost the runners' red blood cell levels, giving them a legal performance enhancer. The Altitude House embodied Alberto Salazar's fascination with high-tech training tools and, together with his celebrity past, had already brought the Project a fair amount of media attention. *Wired* magazine had done a big feature story on the high-tech angle.

Cook took a dim view of all this. For all his reliance on physiology and sports science, he was not a fan of fancy equipment.

"OK, Chief, step into the Batcave."

Until he found a condo of his own, Cook explained, he was living in a bedroom upstairs. Julius, for his part, would be bunking downstairs. It was a finished room with a private bathroom—once again, Julius Achon would be the African sleeping in the basement.

◆ ◆ ◆

The next day, Cook drove Julius out to the Nike corporate headquarters in suburban Portland. They got on Highway 26 westbound, then drove through the West Hills tunnel into the teeth of heavy commuter traffic. It was almost nine, but it seemed like dawn had barely taken hold. They took the Murray Boulevard exit, turned left on Murray, and continued another half mile.

"There it is," Cook said. "The gates to the kingdom."

Where? Julius wondered. All he saw was a long landscaped levee broken by a gate that was almost starkly decorated with a single Nike swoosh. Cook turned right into the gate, into a version of Oz: sparkling white office buildings, wide sweeping lawns, a lake, an immaculate soccer pitch, laboratories, and gyms. The buildings were named after famous Nike-sponsored athletes, and they had parking spaces reserved for them, as if Bo Jackson or Tiger Woods were going to drive up for a meeting at any moment. Cook showed Julius a Tartan running track with a forest of fir trees growing in the infield; you couldn't see one side of the track from the other. If you could imagine a place in the world that was the opposite of an IDP camp in northern Uganda, it occurred to Julius, it would be the Nike corporate campus.

And yet, both places were built on dreams. Just as no logical reason stood behind the depravity of the IDP camps—nothing beyond a warlord's cracked vow to rule according to the Ten Commandments—nothing tangible was made on the Nike campus: The shoes and apparel were manufactured in Asia by contract laborers. The campus

produced ideas, designs, and images. But while Kony's fantasies re-
sulted in incalculable suffering, the ones spun here yielded fortunes.

At a recent shareholders' meeting, Phil Knight, the company's
co-founder and CEO, announced record revenues and profits. The
shareholders learned that the last significant challenge to the Nike
empire—a lawsuit related to protests concerning the working conditions of those Asian contract laborers—had been successfully rebuffed. Mark Parker, a vice president Knight was grooming to
succeed him as CEO—he would be named to the position three
years later, in 2006—unveiled a new marketing and advertising
campaign centered on the emerging basketball star LeBron James,
who at the time was about to enter the NBA as the most highly
touted high school athlete to enter the league in a generation or
more.

A Nike interviewer observed that "We promised LeBron James
more money than he could ever spend." Parker responded, "LeBron
is one of those very special athletes with the rare level of talent and
charisma that gives us the license to take the consumer somewhere
totally new. So in a sense, that makes it a bargain."

Then one of the company's star shoe designers took the stage.
"On the product side, we're excited about Nike Free," he announced.
"A footwear technology designed to mimic the bare foot."

"You'll appreciate that, Chief," Cook said sarcastically. "You guys
in Africa had the right idea after all."

Julius, processing all this information, made no reply. "Now
here's the part where we come in," Cook said. "Okay, at the end of
the shareholders' meeting, Chairman Phil gets back up onstage.
'One more piece of good news I forgot to mention. Right here on
the track on our campus, a young Oregon boy named Galen Rupp
just ran 4:01, the state record for the mile.'"

Cook explained that Galen Rupp was the key to the whole Oregon Project. Salazar had discovered Galen when he was a fourteen-
year-old soccer player. With no specific training as a runner, the
kid could run a half dozen sub-30-second 200-meter repeats like
he was eating popcorn. Salazar told Knight—Alberto sat close to
the king—that Galen could be the next Steve Prefontaine.

Cook then explained that Phil Knight, a middle-class kid from Portland, had gone to the University of Oregon in the early 1960s to run the half mile on the track team coached by the legendary Bill Bowerman. After graduating, Knight started a small business importing track shoes from Japan, which he sold out of the back of his station wagon. The business grew, and Bowerman bought in as a partner. One day, fooling around with his wife's waffle iron, Bowerman came up with the waffle sole for running shoes. The advent of the new sports shoe technology coincided with the birth of the running boom in the United States—Bill Rodgers, Frank Shorter, Jim Fixx, and many others—while at the same time helping to create the boom. Thus Nike was born, establishing its bona fides through Bowerman and the great charismatic, James Dean–like running star of the 1970s, the U of O's Steve Prefontaine.

From those humble, track and field, Oregon origins, Nike grew into a multinational corporation that appropriated the superstars of the TV sports and buffed them into postmodern marketing gods. Knight's heart, however, still lay on the rain-swept Hayward Field track, with the crowd clapping rhythmically for "Pre." But where was the twenty-first-century incarnation of Prefontaine, the charismatic American runner that Nike's master marketers could forge into a peer of Lance, Tiger, or LeBron? Nowhere to be found; the sport once ruled by Americans such as Pre, Shorter, and Joan Benoit was now dominated by wave after wave of Kenyans and Ethiopians who, in the Western world, had the marketing potential of a picnic table.

"All due respect, Chief," Cook said. "Nothing personal."

So now with every other obstacle surmounted and rival vanquished and Phil Knight approaching his legacy years, the chairman was going back to his roots, chartering Salazar (there was even a building on campus named after Alberto) to develop the next great American distance runner. The project was so dear to Knight that he had to tell the shareholders about Galen running a 4:01 mile, and the shareholders had to act interested.

"That's why we're here, Chief," Cook said. "We're here to make this kid Rupp. Forget all those other guys. The only one who matters is Galen. That might seem like small beer compared to all of this"—Cook made a gesture, a wave encompassing the magnificent campus—"but the fact is, in some ways, we're right in the heart of this place."

✦ ✦ ✦

Julius was put to work right away. He had not met Salazar before but knew of his reputation. In the early 1980s, Alberto Salazar won three consecutive editions of the New York City Marathon and set a world record in the distance. In 1982 he won the Boston Marathon, prevailing over Dick Beardsley in a race remembered as the Duel in the Sun. Salazar achieved his success not through great talent but through an obsessive work ethic. Now he brought a similar intensity to his coaching career. A devout Catholic, Salazar was a man of mercurial temperament, secretive and obsessively protective of his turf and athletes one moment, funny, charming, and generous the next.

From the start, Julius's relationship with Salazar was distant and formal. Julius wasn't really a member of the Project, he was an employee. Salazar was his boss, not his mentor. Julius's job was to pace and guide Galen. Whatever Alberto ordered for the boy, Julius would do beside him.

At 10 A.M. on that first day, Julius reported for duty at the campus track. He and Galen warmed up with a few miles on the campus trails. The kid was eighteen but could pass for fourteen, with his flaxen hair, high-pitched voice, and baby face. He seemed at once powerful and fragile. He ran like a horse, but it seemed like a stiff wind could blow him over. Despite his natural athletic talent, the boy appeared to be sickly, suffering from asthma and hay fever and other allergies.

Style-wise, mechanics-wise, Rupp was a good-looking runner, his stride already polished and buffed by Salazar. Was he truly special? Not by African standards, Julius thought, but it was too early to tell. What he had going for him was this extraordinarily close relationship with Salazar and Nike. During the warm-up, Julius kept waiting for the boy to ask a few questions, extend a welcome, but he was too shy to say anything.

They arrived at the track to begin the speed work. Today, 10 x 400 meters. Julius wanted to make a good first impression. Run a quarter, a minute's rest, and then another quarter. Galen, blond hair bobbing, was a white shadow at Julius's shoulder. A few Nike executives ran on the outside lanes. Julius knew they looked right through him to focus on Rupp. Salazar watched stony-faced, holding a stopwatch. One quarter, then another. Finally they finished. Rupp went off to the gym in the Lance Armstrong Fitness Center to do some core-strengthening drills under Cook's supervision. "Okay, good," Salazar said to Julius. "Back here tomorrow, 10 A.M."

The workouts varied: long, draining tempo runs along the Leif Erikson Drive in Portland's Forest Park. A track session might consist of 12 x 1 mile at 4:30 pace, or 16 x 1 mile at 5:20 pace. There were drills and exercises before and after the runs. There wasn't much time or energy for conversation.

By design, Rupp's training partner was basically invisible. That was all right with Julius. He was grateful for the job. He couldn't let them down, there was no margin for error. The checks started to come, and he saved $150 out of each to send to Jimmy in Lira.

So far as his living arrangement, Julius again climbed inside the bubble, but this one felt different than others. The community at the Altitude House hadn't developed organically. It should have been a blast—a bunch of guys in their twenties, living in a cool city with nothing to do but train in the best facilities in the world, bivouacking in an experimental structure that drew the attention of *Wired*, engaged in a Nike-financed attempt to resurrect elite American distance running—but the runners lived and worked under considerable pressure.

That applied to Cook as well as the athletes. He knew that Alberto didn't have first-rate horses in the stable. Other than Galen, nobody under contract had the potential to reach a world-class level. The relatively bleak competitive prospects put Cook in a more irascible mood than usual. Mostly, Julius escaped the pressure. No one was watching him or expecting him to improve, which made his work easier on one level, but more difficult on another. Other than a paycheck, there was no purpose to his pain. Julius was invisible, and if he stayed invisible, he knew he was doing his job. The checks would keep coming, and he could keep funneling the money to his family in Lira town.

Once again, Julius assumed the role of the happy-go-lucky African living in the basement. He gave no indication of his worries or concerns, but he never stopped thinking about Lira, the camp, and now the orphans. And of course he said not a word about his boy-soldier past. He knew that he couldn't show weakness or present as a problem. Salazar had enough problems with his roster runners and didn't need his pacer presenting more. A problem pacer could always be replaced.

Nor could Julius fully confide in John Cook. Cook didn't need another problem, either. After their reunion in December, the meeting at the airport, Cook became somewhat distant. He was under the gun, too. Sure, the Oregon Project was a dream job, but Cook also had to prove himself to Salazar. After almost thirty years of calling his own shots, it wasn't easy to work for somebody else. Cook was in no mood to listen to stories about Uganda, which he'd always warned Julius against anyway.

Grace joined him and shared his room in the Altitude House basement. It was a comfort to have her beside him, although Grace, like Jasper, was overwhelmed by America and rarely ventured out of the basement. Francis came over from London, where he'd been living, and found a job as a home health aide in Woodburn, a town about twenty miles south of Portland.

Overall, Julius was grateful for the arrangement. Even a modest regular paycheck was the dream of most professional runners. After so long living underground in Lisbon, he was used to a shadow life. In Portugal he had stopped competing for himself, and his role now continued the evolution. He had lowered his professional expectations, or perhaps more accurately, he had adjusted them. His hopes for others now superseded his hopes for himself. He now approached running as a business, a trade not much different than shoemaking or plumbing.

◆ ◆ ◆

February 2004 marked the nadir for conditions in northern Uganda, the darkest spell of a seemingly endless terrible time. Operation Iron Fist was still going full blast, Museveni's troops pouring north into Sudan and LRA rebels pouring just as profusely south, filling the vacuum left by the government army. Sixteen years had passed since Julius had been kidnapped. Kony had ravaged the north for an entire generation.

In Oregon, Julius and Francis sucked up every scrap of news they could find about the situation in Uganda. There wasn't much to be found. The BBC was the best source. The national and local media proved useless. Their international coverage was dominated by the Iraq War. If the average American knew anything about Africa, she knew about Nelson Mandela in South Africa or the Tutsi-Hutu horror show in Rwanda. The almost surreal level of carnage in Uganda raised barely a blip on the American radar.

"Once every week or two, Jimmy would telephone from Lira," Francis remembers. "Our conversations were mostly obituaries. 'Remember Oscar, who was so good at soccer?' Jimmy would say. 'He was kidnapped and we'll never see him again. Remember Sally, the cute girl everybody wanted to dance with on disco day? The rebels raped her and cut off her head.'"

Out at the Nike campus, profits kept rocketing. "I can unequivocally report that we are having the best year ever," Phil Knight wrote in a letter to investors. The company kept finding emerging markets—everyplace in the world, it seemed, but central Africa. Portland in general was booming, shedding its provincial past as a town reeling from the decline of the logging industry, retooled as a haven for hipsters and cutting-edge sporting-industry companies, much of the creative energy derived from Nike's growth.

The Oregon Project steamed into an Olympic year. Galen Rupp wasn't quite ready for the Athens Games, but Dan Browne qualified in the marathon. Pacing the group, Julius humped the miles on the Wildwood Trail, his mind in the wind. In February, just before the team decamped to Santa Fe for a spell of sunny winter altitude training, the LRA and Uganda finally broke through into the international headlines.

◆ ◆ ◆

The town of Barlonyo lay about thirty miles north of Awake, in the heart of Langi country. It was roughly the same size as Lira, and like Lira it had metastasized into an IDP camp holding around thirty thousand people. But Barlonyo, significantly closer than Lira to the Sudanese border and LRA-controlled regions, was even more vulnerable. Government troops guarded the camp, but they had been ordered away by their commanders to serve with Operation Iron Fist in Sudan. Ironically, their LRA quarry lurked under their noses, preparing to attack Barlonyo. In place of the government troops, a squad of ill-trained, ill-equipped local militiamen now guarded the camp.

On that Saturday morning in the dry season, the guards left their posts to stock up on supplies at the local market. They hadn't been paid in months, and morale was low. In their absence, at a ululating signal from the LRA commander, the rebels—AK-toting children, some of them kin to the people inside the fence—descended on the IDP camp. A two-hour orgy of burning, shooting, hacking, and raping ensued. Rebels torched huts and watched them burn while children and mothers screamed inside. More than three hundred villagers perished in the attack.

Similar to the St. Mary's school kidnapping almost ten years earlier, when Julius was an undergraduate at George Mason, the Barlonyo massacre was so egregious that the international media could no longer ignore it. In Portland, Julius read the news reports in near panic. What was there to prevent the same sort of attack taking place in Lira? But there was nothing Julius could do about it. Indeed, the worst thing he could do was let worry detract from his running.

A few days later, while Julius was training with the Oregon Project in Santa Fe, an email message arrived from Jimmy in Lira: Kristina had been shot.

◆ ◆ ◆

Later, Julius would piece the story together from Jimmy's account and the accounts of other family members. He imagined and replayed events so often that he might as well have been there.

In February, when news of the Barlonyo massacre reached Lira, the city descended into panic. Food, already scarce, was no longer available at all. The market stalls were ransacked and empty, the UN food stations overrun. The skeleton-crew detachment of government soldiers, the men who hadn't been ordered north with Operation Iron Fist, were no use at all, stealing food themselves and deserting south toward Kampala. In the Achon compound, the family was still safe, but they were hungry. The children's bellies were starting to swell, and the light in their eyes had gone out.

Kristina, desperate, decided to make a break, to travel to the garden plots of Awake and gather what the rebels hadn't stolen. Why her and not Charles or one of the older boys? Because outside of town, men and boys were instantly, automatically killed or kidnapped by the LRA or summarily executed by government troops who assumed that they were aiding the rebels. For their part, younger women would be abducted to serve as bush brides. Older women such as Kristina were of minimal value to the rebels—they didn't make the best porters or sex slaves—and aroused less suspicion from the government troops.

Finally, a sort of fatalism was at work. True, most people venturing outside of town were killed, but some weren't; some completed their mission and brought sustenance back to their children in the camp. No one could accurately predict the odds, so you rationalized them as 50-50. Moreover, did it make a great deal of difference if they lived or died? Consciously or otherwise, some exhausted Langi gave up, choosing death as a more favorable alternative to the daily hell of the camp. In effect, by leaving Lira, some people committed suicide by rebel.

What other choice did Kristina have? Her family was starving, and she needed to provide for them. So, with a few other women from the compound, she set out from Lira at first light, on foot, repeating in reverse the journey that Julius had taken as a fourteen-year-old boy. Morning was the least hazardous time of day. The night raids of the LRA would be finished by dawn. If luck held, the rebels would be back in their camps, and the government troops would control the road until nightfall.

Perhaps the women could flag down a passing truck. If not, they would walk the forty miles, reaching Awake by sunset. They would gather the crops from the garden and other hiding places, spend the night in the relative safety of the IDP camp at Aliwang Mission, and arrange some sort of transport back to Lira the next day or in the days following. Not the greatest plan, but a plan. What was the alternative?

◆ ◆ ◆

The mission started favorably enough, and Julius could imagine the adrenaline-charged hope with which his mother logged those early miles. He envisioned her moving with a lithe, youthful stride despite her forty-odd years. He thought about her startling at each sudden sound and altered slant of light, and then slightly relaxing as the miles accrued without incident. He imagined his mother whispering prayers for safe passage, and her building hope that her prayers were being answered.

But twenty or so miles into the journey, halfway to Awake, at a crossing over a water ditch, a rebel soldier stepped onto the road. Julius envisioned a dreadlocked boy, no older than sixteen, armed with a *panga* and AK-47.

An instant, unspoken connection might have formed. Both Kristina and the rebel soldier knew the script. Rather than face abduction, slavery, and rape or endure a slow, dismembering death by *panga*, Kristina bolted. She ran with the same girlish stride with which, many years earlier, in commingled anger and playfulness, she had chased her son through the bush when he'd broken one of her water pots.

Running was the only play available. Perhaps the young rebel, footsore and weary after a night of pillaging, would be too lazy to chase an older woman who, by all appearances, was carrying nothing worth stealing. By the same token, why waste a scarce bullet on Granny? The young rebel, conditioned to equate a human life with that of a goat or monkey, but also thinking of his own convenience and comfort, might well have let Kristina run.

But perhaps the boy's captain was watching, or maybe a fresh shipment had arrived from Sudan and bullets were in ample supply, or maybe the boy was egged on by his comrades, or perhaps any one of a myriad of mortal factors came into play. The boy lifted his rifle and, with the same careless gesture with which Captain John punished the villager for refusing to surrender his chicken, shot the fleeing woman in the back.

The boy fired quickly. The bullet ripped through Kristina's shoulder, but vital organs were spared. The wound bled profusely, however, and in the tropical heat infection set in immediately. Had Kristina been an American soldier wounded in Fallujah, her wound would have been cleaned and dressed in the field, and within minutes she would have been treated by surgeons in a military hospital. Had Kristina been a runner for the Nike Oregon Project in Portland, and had she turned an ankle on a Forest Park trail, Salazar would have made sure she was inside an MRI machine within an hour. Had she been the innocent victim of a drive-by gang shooting in East Los Angeles, an ambulance would have rushed her to the nearest emergency room.

Kristina, however, lacked membership in that chunk of the world. Her traveling companions did succeed in flagging down an ox-driven cart headed north. They lifted the bleeding woman on board and, without further attack, made it to Otuke town.

◆ ◆ ◆

In Santa Fe, after returning from a workout at the altitude training camp, Julius opened his email and read the message from Jimmy, who gave a summary of events and made a plea for money. It might be possible to obtain medical care, Jimmy wrote, but it would mean paying off the police, the army, hospital officials, nurses, and doctors: all people overrun by work in the best of circumstances. Given the present violence and chaos, the costs would be multiplied. Fifteen hundred dollars was required right away.

Fifteen hundred dollars? Why not a million? Julius reeled away from the computer monitor. All too clearly could he envision the scene in Otuke. The hysteria, the frantic prayers, the futile ministrations of the witch doctor. Julius's present whereabouts in the southern Rocky Mountains seemed correspondingly unreal. Could he ask Salazar for the money, request an advance on his monthly pay? Julius didn't see how this was possible. The coach was just getting to know him. Julius was a fading African runner who was here only by the grace of John Cook; Julius's role was to do his work and not be noticed. An African shouldn't pose a problem; ideally, he shouldn't be noticed at all. Ask a white person for money, and he would instinctively assume you were scamming.

The other obvious person to ask would be Cook. But that would be a mistake. The afternoon after receiving Jimmy's email, Julius joined Mike McGrath, one of the Project athletes, for a workout. Instead of setting the pace, however, Julius, distracted, near frantic, could barely keep up with the American. Cook went berserk. He had put himself on the line for Julius, and now he was dogging it? Cook had always warned Julius against Uganda and its entanglements. Explaining the situation to him would only invite further wrath.

Above all, Julius couldn't jeopardize his new job and the lifeline it provided the family, and now the eleven orphans, back in Uganda. As the Oregon Project finished training in Santa Fe and headed back to Portland, Julius remained paralyzed with worry. For another day or two, he faked it through the workouts and then rushed back to the phone and computer, awaiting the latest updates from Lira town. Julius racked his brain, trying to think of something. He was sitting there thinking when the email came in from Jimmy, informing him that Kristina was gone.

Now they needed five hundred dollars to bury her properly. With Grace holding him, Julius rolled up in a ball and wailed.

If he couldn't bring himself to ask for money when his mother was hanging on to life, he wasn't about to ask for any now. Pending the end of the endless, purposeless conflict, the family buried Kristina in a friend's yard in Otuke town, about five miles from Awake. On the other side of the world, in Oregon, Julius was consumed by grief and guilt. Why hadn't he been there to protect his mother? Or, in America, in Portland, at Nike, where everybody seemed to be effortlessly and gracefully rich, why didn't Julius have the money to save her?

◆ ◆ ◆

Unmoored, reeling, he decided to drown his sorrow. Through much of his life he'd been surrounded by men who dealt with reality—or tried to escape it—by getting loaded: his father, Captain John, and many of the runners in Albuquerque. Now, for the first time, Julius did the same.

A Nike employee offered to take Julius around to the bars in Portland. They started at a place downtown. The friend knew that Julius was hurting, but he didn't know exactly why. Julius hunched on his stool in the forgiving darkness, regarding the rows of bottles arrayed behind the bar. Wherever you turned, America bludgeoned you with another choice.

"Which one is best for forgetting?" he asked.

His friend ordered tequila, and for an hour or so, as the shot glasses stacked up in front of him, Julius was able to forget. But before long he was heaving in the men's room, sicker than he'd ever been from drinking ditch water in Awake. The next morning he suffered a hangover distinguished less by physical pain—although that was exquisite—than by savage remorse. The losses and failures of his life pressed down so hard he thought he'd suffocate.

"If tequila had worked for me, I think I might have stayed with it," Julius says. "But so much hurt came from the bottle that I had to find another way."

◆ ◆ ◆

At first he thought he would quit running. It seemed that the sport lay at the root of all his misery, and that of his family. If he hadn't been so selfishly determined to escape Awake by becoming a big star like John Akii-Bua, Julius would've been home to shield his mother. But Grace and Cook convinced him to continue. For all his travails and decline, Julius remained among the top-ranked 1,500-meter runners in Uganda and stood a chance of qualifying for the Athens Games in 2004, which would be his third Olympic appearance.

However, meeting the standard times for either the 800 or 1,500 would be daunting. And even if he did qualify, there was little hope of improving on his performances in '96 or 2000. He was still young, only twenty-eight, but he felt much older. The years of road racing in Portugal and half a decade of poor nutrition and inconsistent training had taken their toll. His once-shining gift—the potential to be the finest middle-distance runner of his generation—was now tarnished beyond repair. His times were only a second slower than in years past, but as Julius knew too well, a second, a moment, an instant, meant a world of difference. His destiny denied. One more thing to feel guilty about.

In his more hopeful moments, however, Julius reflected that there might be more to the story. Perhaps the path he'd chosen was only leading to the true path that God intended for him. Like the cityscape of Kampala, where seemingly blind alleys led to hidden neighborhoods, his trail may yet open. He had to keep doggedly following it. If Julius felt empty of hope, he also felt empty of bitterness.

◆ ◆ ◆

One day at a time, one workout at a time, he plugged along in his pacer's role for the Oregon Project. He continued working with Galen Rupp, pulling the boy through his first sub-four-minute mile at an indoor meet in Seattle early in 2005. Dissatisfied with the talent level of his other athletes, Salazar recruited Kara and Adam Goucher, a married couple, two gifted but often-injured runners from the University of Colorado. Under the combined guidance of Salazar, Cook, and the rest of the sports medicine team, the Gouchers started to rebuild their careers, aiming to qualify for Olympic and world championship teams.

Now Julius had three elite athletes to work with—Kara, Galen, and Adam. The Nike campus's sumptuous high-tech facilities gave the enterprise an air of mystery and complexity, but the essence of distance running remained brutally simple. The days were divided, hard ones and easy ones, days of sapping effort and days of relative ease and recovery. But for a pacer, the caddy to the performers, every day was a hard day. Galen would run 12 x 1 mile at 4:30 pace one day and rest the next. On Galen's rest day, however, Kara would go 16 x 1 mile at 5:15 pace. There was only one training partner for both runners: Julius Achon. When he just had Galen to pace, Julius could cop the occasional recovery day. Now, for Julius, there was rarely an easy day.

He understood that he was a cog in a machine. The other runners, he says, displayed little curiosity about his life or background. The long tempo runs passed mostly in silence. Back at the Altitude House, Julius would descend to the basement to be with Grace while the guys played videogames upstairs. After discerning that Julius was unlikely to return to his former world-class level, Cook, in the manner of a physician dissociating from a patient beyond saving, kept his distance. Days went by without the two men talking.

But none of that really mattered, because in mind and spirit, Julius wasn't really there. His body might be blasting 5:20 miles along the Leif Erikson Drive or knocking out intervals around the Bo Jackson turf field on the Nike campus, but his head and heart were in Lira with his family and the orphaned children. They were what seemed real to him. If Julius could find any grace note in the situation, it lay in the fact that providence had dropped these eleven kids into his life at the same time that it had removed Kristina.

Julius was grateful to Alberto Salazar and the Oregon Project runners, and didn't expect more from them than he was getting. His job was to keep running. By economizing in draconian fashion, he and Grace were able to send about half of his fifteen-hundred-dollar monthly retainer check to Lira, where the immediate violence and danger had eased. Museveni had flooded enough troops into the northern districts to drive the LRA across the border into Sudan. The raids had subsided, but the countryside remained depopulated. People hung on in the festering camps out of fear and because they'd lost faith in themselves and in the world.

◆ ◆ ◆

Late at night in the Altitude House, early March, more light each evening but gray winter light, the trails a morass of mud, his workout clothes still stiff with rain and sweat from the last workout. With Cook asleep and the other guys sleeping in their futuristic oxygen-controlled rooms, Julius would take the lightly used training shoes and shirts and other gear he'd collected over the last week or so and pack them in boxes to send to the children at the family compound in Lira town. Some of the shoes had barely been worn. The insoles had pancaked to the extent that an elite athlete could no longer safely train in the shoes, but for a kid in the Ugandan bush they were like gold. Julius had to bend and smudge and nick the shoes, make them appear worthless; otherwise the Ugandan postal or customs workers would steal them. He did the same to the T-shirts emblazoned with the talismanic Nike swoosh.

Julius liked this job. It was a relief to work with his hands. He thought about his mother, drawing some comfort from the blessing she'd given the last time he saw her. More than any other moment during his life in Oregon, this small chore felt real. The money Julius sent traveled by invisible and impersonal electronic pulses; these shoes he could touch and smell. He knew how happy the children would be to receive them. It made Julius think about his own first pair of running shoes and recall the surging hope accompanying his junior world title in Portugal. Now running was a business, the province of scowling coaches and anxious teammates, politics and maneuvers. Was the sport any less corrupt here than it was in Africa? He thought about Galen, Kara, and Adam. Despite their contracts and secure futures, were they any happier than Julius?

Could running make you happy? Samuel, one of the orphans, was already showing promise as a runner. Should Julius encourage him to pursue the sport if it would ultimately, inevitably disappoint him? Was Julius disappointed? He realized that he would never become an Olympic champion like John Akii-Bua, but running had still brought him very far from the hut in Awake.

As Julius worked, carefully but absurdly marring each shoe and shirt so that it had a better chance of arriving at its destination, he felt a surge of hope—a shard of light that faded as fast as it had appeared. If he just kept running, he sensed, the light would rise again.

Like most dream teams, the Oregon Project management eventually proved unwieldy, too loaded with talent to be sustainable. Cook didn't like the entire Nike vibe, the formality of the Oregon Project, the fact that everyone involved with it tended to take it so seriously. Cook took running very seriously, but his boyhood in Munich had established where he stood in the bigger scheme of things. Also, after a career spent as an underdog, working for an unglamorous university, Cook wasn't comfortable working for a top-dog outfit such as Nike. Matters came to a head, Cook says, when Salazar told him to fire Pfaff and Gambetta, the physiologists he had hired.

"I told Alberto, 'Those guys are my amigos. You fire them.'"

Now that a split was imminent, Cook almost felt relieved. "This day was coming from the moment I stepped onto the campus," he says. "I could never quite drink the Nike Kool-Aid."

In 2005, eighteen months after his job started, Cook left the Oregon Project and moved back to Sarasota. He hung out his own coaching shingle, eventually developing outstanding U.S. runners such as Shalane Flanagan, Shannon Rowbury, and Leo Manzano. Julius felt no resentment. Delivering him to America constituted a prodigal gift, and Cook had given it twice. When John Cook had left George Mason, Julius had been free to do likewise. Now he had people depending on him on both sides of the world. He had a man's responsibilities, and now he was just another man, no longer a coddled athlete, a special case. He started the irksome, humbling processes of updating his visa and applying for a green card. He bought a seven-year-old Honda Accord for a thousand bucks.

Most important, he needed to keep his job with the Oregon Project. Salazar agreed to retain him. The team's runners were steadily improving, and Julius had never presented as a problem.

• • •

Beneath the surface, however, the unvarying succession of hard training days, worry about his family and the orphans, and the lingering grief over the death of his mother wore on Julius.

Then, in 2006, even that haven was no longer available. Although he would still employ the building as a training center and as quarters for visiting athletes, Salazar decided to close down the residential program of the Altitude House. Nike now provided portable machines that the runners could use in their bedrooms; the house-wide air-treatment technology had grown obsolete. Julius observed the development with anxiety. He knew that, in essence, he was just another training tool. How long until he, too, became obsolete?

Grace and Julius moved into a modest apartment in suburban Beaverton. Paying rent took another chunk out of Julius's monthly stipend. Since he couldn't cut back on the money he sent to Uganda, Julius and Grace economized even more sharply. They never went out, and they made their one main meal a day even more spartan— often, a meal consisted of peanut butter and tea. To supplement their income, Julius started coaching high school runners on the side and working hours as a clerk at the Nike employees' store.

• • •

Located near the edge of campus, dwarfed by structures such as the Tiger Woods Conference Center and the Lance Armstrong Fitness Center, the employees' store seemed to form an asterisk on the magnificent two-hundred-acre corporate headquarters—and yet, in a way, the store epitomized the Nike enterprise: selling the idea of sport.

In contrast to the company's ubiquitous "factory stores" that dotted outlet malls across the nation, the employees' store offered prototype shoes, apparel, and gear to Nike employees at a fraction of the retail price.

For a resident of the Portland area, a pass to the store was a prized possession, one that company employees dispensed to relatives and close friends as a holiday gift. Tourists in the know bartered for passes on the Internet and made the store one of their first stops when visiting the area. Most of the workers at the store, meanwhile, were recent college grads hoping to parlay an entry-level minimum-wage job into a full-time white-collar position.

Among these eager young people, Julius stood out dramatically. Had Julius cared about status or appearances, he might have felt misgivings about the job. In most regards, he was no different now than millions of other minimum-wage service-industry toilers. He no longer had a franchise as a great athlete. He was just another immigrant scrambling for a handhold in the so-called land of opportunity. Unlike the kids he worked beside, moreover, Julius knew that his entry-level gig was unlikely to lead to something better.

Instead of sulking, however, Julius gave the job his all, always hustling, always smiling, expecting no special treatment because he was an athlete. He anticipated a customer's needs and was a good judge of a product's usefulness, drawing on his deep knowledge of runners and running to make sound suggestions.

Neither his customers nor his co-workers knew that his unfailing good humor only formed a mask, behind which an exhausted man desperately pedaled a treadmill.

A typical day began with Julius pacing the Project runners in the morning. From noon until four, he put in his hours at the store, serving customers and stocking shelves. In the late afternoon, he worked with his high school runners. Around 7 P.M., he made it back to the dank, moldy apartment and his one meal a day with Grace.

◆ ◆ ◆

Of all his jobs, roles, and responsibilities, Julius's part-time coaching gig seemed the least taxing and the most enjoyable. He met with the high school athletes once or twice a week, supplementing the main training they underwent with their school teams. He was more like a tutor or personal trainer than a conventional coach. His clients were the cream of the local prep running community. Julius would run with the kids on the track or on trails through Forest Park, imparting drills and lessons he had learned from John Cook and other coaches and athletes he'd engaged with over his long career.

Julius would chide the athletes with mock gruffness when they complained about a drill or workout he had suggested. "At least you don't have to run barefoot through the bush with the rebels chasing you," he would say, echoing Cook's story of throwing rocks in the Munich refugee camps. Julius wouldn't go into detail—no mention of the orphans or the current state of affairs in Lira or the abduction of his father or the death of his mother, but enough to pique the kids' interest.

"We really liked Julius and were fascinated by his background in Uganda," says Adrienne Demaree, one of the athletes. "We were also in awe of his Olympic background and his NCAA record and involvement in the Oregon Project. He was such a great runner and still so humble and down-to-earth."

Adrienne would go home and talk about Julius to her mother, Ann. Her daughter's enthusiasm, in turn, intrigued Ann Demaree. Instinctively, immediately, Ann knew that Adrienne's coach should meet her boss, a man named Jim Fee.

◆ ◆ ◆

It was January 2007, the darkest and coldest time of the year. For serious middle- and long-distance runners, winter was the time to build up their endurance base, to hammer long, relatively deliberate miles on muddy trails like the ones crisscrossing the Portland hills. Citizen athletes, especially marathoners, often enjoyed these long runs, during which you could engage in deep conversations with your training partners. But Julius, who logged the long runs with the clenched pros of the Oregon Project, rarely took pleasure in them.

This afternoon's run, fourteen miles through Forest Park to Germantown Road, had been especially draining. Exhausted, famished, he and Grace drove toward their dinner engagement that evening. "What are we doing again?" Grace asked, her voice tight with resentment.

He reviewed the background for tonight's dinner invitation. "One of my high school runners, Adrienne—her mother's boss—"

"Boss where?" Grace interrupted.

"A company called Welch Allyn, they make medical technology, all of that stuff in hospital rooms."

Grace remained silent. She hated staying home, being stuck in the dark, depressing apartment, but she hated going out even more. In Kampala she was sunny, open, relaxed, and confident; in the United States she had become a virtual recluse. She felt insecure about her English, her clothes, her general appearance. America for Grace: getting by on subsistence wages in a moldy apartment, eating one meal a day, with no friends, no work permit, no car, and no social life. This was the promised land that Julius had sold her on?

Grace hadn't wanted to go out that night, and neither had Julius. The main draw, frankly, was the shot at a good meal. Adrienne's mom said that Angela, tonight's hostess, was a wonderful cook.

"So this girl Adrienne lives at the house?" Grace was still fighting him.

"Adrienne and her mom will be there for dinner, but they don't live there," Julius explained again. "It's the mom's boss's house. He's a runner, he runs marathons. Adrienne's mom thought he'd like to meet me."

Julius understood that he would sing for his supper, entertaining his host with stories about Galen and Alberto and Kara. Then, inevitably, the man would start talking about his own running. Julius had listened to these citizen runners at the road races in Portugal, out at the Nike campus, and especially now at the employees' store. Julius projected a vibe that made people want to talk to him. Usually he was happy to listen, but tonight he was tired. Tonight he was in no mood to hear stories about a guy running thirty-seven minutes at the Carlsbad 10K in 1983.

He drove out on the Sunset Highway, turned right on Murray

away from the Nike campus, passed Sunset High School where he sometimes met his prep runners, and turned right on Thompson. They were still in Portland, but it felt like the suburbs, not the franchise neon drywall suburbs where Julius and Grace lived but deep, leafy-green suburbs. Grace grew increasingly tight and silent. Finally, Julius pulled into a graceful housing development that reminded him of the wealthy neighborhoods in Kampala. He parked in front of a big ranch-style house in the middle of a cul de sac. It reminded Julius of walking into the U.S. embassy to apply for a visa and his first morning in Portland, when John Cook introduced him to the Nike campus.

"I can't do it," Grace said. "I'll just wait here in the car." Julius was patient with her, and a minute later they were ringing the doorbell.

Later, Julius would remember the aroma of Angela Fee's paella wafting over him as he entered the house. He immediately relaxed. Grace softened, too. Angela and Jim, who hosted big dinners every Sunday, were experts at putting their guests at ease. Ruddy and lean, in his early sixties, Jim Fee reminded Julius of the senior Nike executives he saw running lunchtime laps out on campus.

The fish stew tasted as good as it smelled. Julius couldn't stop spooning it in, mopping it up with sourdough bread. Angela kept subtly and tactfully refilling his bowl, while Jim listened raptly to Julius's stories about his earlier running career: the junior world title, the NCAA record, the Olympic appearances. Then it was time to start talking about the Oregon Project, and after that, Julius projected, Jim would start recalling his own races. That would lead to some specific questions about injuries or shoes, and Julius would be happy to help him because of the food, the warmth, the hospitality. Instead of following the familiar arc, however, Fee asked about Africa.

Julius started on his *National Geographic* rap—giraffes, primates, crocodiles, the lion's pawprint. Fee listened with what appeared to be normal interest. Julius was about to move on to Alberto and Galen when Fee surprised him. "Ann mentioned that you spent time as a boy soldier," he said. He didn't pose it as a question. Julius could take the statement any direction he wanted.

This was true, Julius replied cautiously. For three months when he was twelve years old. He briefly described his abduction and escape. It was the first time he'd talked about this to a white person. He had always imagined it would be a painful ordeal, but the words poured out. In fact, it was an effort to hold them back.

Fee seemed to notice this. "Do you ever go back?" he asked in the same respectful tone. "Do you have family?"

Fighting an impulse to tell this stranger everything, Julius replied yes, he had family, and he had the orphans as well. It was also the first time he'd broached this subject with a white person. He summarized the story of finding the children under a bus and bringing them to his parents' house in Lira. He was about to go into greater detail when Adrienne and her mother got up to leave. Julius regretted the interruption. Now that he'd begun his narrative, he felt driven to continue. It was as if the story were something separate from Julius, possessed an agency of its own. Julius glimpsed that same shard of light that had flashed that night when he packed shoe boxes at the Altitude House.

Fee also appeared to sense this current, hurrying back to the table after saying good night to his guests. At that moment, however, Grace signaled that it was time for her and Julius to leave, too. At the door, Fee turned to Julius. "I'd like to hear more about all this," he said. "Can I take you to lunch?"

"Please, be my guest," Julius said. "Come out to the Nike campus. We can eat at the cafeteria in the Mia Hamm Building."

They agreed to meet the next Wednesday. The ensuing days passed in their usual blur of work, but Julius found himself thinking often about his dinner with the Fees. His story continued to stir inside of him, straining to come out.

◆ ◆ ◆

He met Fee for lunch after an especially hard workout with the Oregon Project in which Julius had paced Galen through an interval session on the wide grass soccer field in the middle of campus. Salazar chose this venue because it was harder to run on grass than the synthetic surface of the track; he relentlessly sought any conceivable edge that would add to the stress of a workout and eventually yield an improved performance for Galen or Kara. For Julius, however, the stress and pain had to serve as their own rewards.

Today's work: fifteen 1K repeats run at 2:55 per rep, 90 seconds' rest between reps. By the twelfth rep, Julius felt like razor blades had supplanted the muscle fiber in his legs; somehow he kept moving. After the final rep, there was a half hour of plyometric drills, exercises that Cook had introduced into the program.

Finally the morning's work was finished, and Julius, running fifteen minutes late, hustled across campus to meet Fee at the Mia Hamm Building. The lunch hour was at its height, the business-casual-clad designers and marketers flowing in and out of the cafeteria; a caterer and band setting up tables in the plaza for an event later that afternoon; a group of Chinese businessmen, managers of the contract factories that manufactured the company's products, huddled together in their dark suits; and a group of wide-eyed little kids on a field trip.

Julius apologized for being late, but Fee waved it off. He liked hanging out on campus, he said. As they entered the cafeteria, Fee explained to Julius that he'd always been a Nike guy. He loved the company's shoes, and once, back in the 1980s, he'd even modeled for a Nike ad in a running magazine. His son David had briefly worked for Nike here on campus after he'd graduated from college. Fee even had his own Alberto Salazar story, although he promised he would spare Julius the telling for now.

They went through the cafeteria line. Fee insisted on paying and Julius, deferring to Fee's age, didn't protest. "So," Fee said when they had settled at a table. "You've started an orphanage?"

Julius immediately resumed the narrative he'd begun at Fee's home earlier in the week. Again, the words seemed to leap out with a force and trajectory of their own. "In a way," Julius said. "The children have a place to lay their heads. They have clothes. They attend school." He repeated the story of how he'd found the children, going into greater detail.

Impressed, Fee shook his head. "I can imagine what Angela would say if I brought home one street kid from the Portland bus station."

As best as he could, Julius described the scope and nature of the IDP camps. Fee said he had no idea that such places existed in the world. "To support the children, I send them a portion of my salary each month," Julius continued. "A dollar goes a long way in Uganda."

Fee thought for a moment. "Forgive me if I'm overstepping, but about how much do you make?"

Julius told him about the twenty-thousand-dollar stipend, which he said hadn't been increased during the three years he'd spent with the Project. After lunch, the two men walked across campus in thoughtful silence. Straight out of high school, LeBron James had signed a seven-year, ninety-million-dollar endorsement deal with Nike. Julius made the barest fraction of that sum, received no benefits, and sent almost half of what he made to Africa to support his uprooted family and the eleven orphaned children.

"Have you thought of starting a foundation?" Fee asked.

Julius carefully replied that the idea had crossed his mind.

"Have you applied for 501(c)(3) status?" Fee said. "That way, companies can match their employees' contributions."

"I think now you are speaking to me in Russian," Julius said. Fee threw his head back and laughed.

Nearing the entrance to the employees' store, where Julius was due to start a shift, they came to an ATM. Fee went to the keyboard and punched in his PIN. Five crisp hundred-dollar bills clicked into the cash tray. He handed the money to Julius. Julius thought about the hundred-dollar bill lying on John Cook's table when Julius had just started at George Mason. Taking Cook's money would have been a serious mistake; without quite understanding why, Julius sensed that refusing Fee's money would be an equally serious error.

"You know, that's about what it costs for a plane ticket to Uganda,"

Julius told the man. "You could go to Africa and see what I'm talk-ing about for yourself."

Fee again laughed, much in the way that Kristina had laughed when Julius told her that he was going to run forty miles to Lira town. Smiling, Julius accepted the money.

◆ ◆ ◆

Over the next few months, Fee and Julius would meet periodically for lunch. With the older man's encouragement and support, Ju-lius's glimmer of an idea gradually put on substance.

In effect, Julius wanted to complete the errand that Kristina had started on the morning she walked out of Lira in search of food for her hungry children. However, Julius refrained from telling Fee about Kristina's death. His story was too big to come out all at once. Mostly, Fee and Julius talked business, the nuts and bolts of starting a nonprofit enterprise. Fee helped with tasks such as designing a letterhead, crafting a mission statement, establishing a rudimen-tary website, and applying for nonprofit status with the IRS. The two men brainstormed a name for the organization: the Achon Uganda Children's Fund.

While thrilled by the progress, Julius confessed to Fee that he felt uncomfortable drawing attention to himself and admitting that he'd served, however unwillingly, with Kony and the LRA. He ex-pressed his reluctance to appear as just another African with his hand out. Fee was sympathetic, but he explained to Julius that he was not asking for charity. Julius had something to offer potential donors, something of value: his story. Paradoxically, if Julius didn't want to come across as the caricature he feared—the needy mi-grant, the African with his hand out—then he would have to step forward. Instead of stifling his story, Julius needed to amplify it, support it with a structure, build an organization around it. Your story is your product, Fee explained to Julius.

At that point, however, Fee knew only part of the story. Each time they met, Julius would tell him a little more. He talked about his time in the bush. He described the elephant grass turning red as the *sombiye* circled. He told of running forty miles from Awake.

The stories came out at odd times—while they were walking across the Nike campus after lunch, during breaks from filling out the mind-numbing mountains of paperwork for the IRS and other agencies. The more Julius talked, the more he wanted to tell, and the more Fee wanted to hear.

Julius was a bit puzzled by Fee. Why was he so receptive? Why was he so eager to help? There seemed little apparent motive. Fee wasn't a do-gooder by nature. He was an observant Catholic and supported worthy causes, but usually with money and usually at a safe remove.

But somehow, Julius got Fee's attention. It started with the running. If Julius hadn't been a runner, hadn't been so deeply engaged with Nike, if he'd been just another migrant, Fee never would have gotten involved. Jim Fee started running as a high school kid, growing up in a working-class Irish-Catholic neighborhood on the South Side of Chicago in the 1950s and '60s. Like Julius, Fee had been a miler, and like Julius he was the eldest of nine children. Fee was born in 1945, at the very start of the baby boom, just after his father, the son of a ditchdigger who'd emigrated from Ireland, came home from the Pacific Theater after the Second World War.

The firstborn of a striving American family, Fee was the vessel of hope, the hardworking kid who had a paper route and caddied at the golf course, who earned straight As in school and made all-city as a miler. He earned an academic scholarship to Marquette University in Milwaukee, where he met Angela while waiting on her table at the dining hall. After graduating and marrying, he began a successful career in medical technology, excelling as a marketer and manager, building teams, shepherding products from design to sales. His career took him and Angela and their three kids from Chicago to Minneapolis to Atlanta to Seattle and finally, for the last twenty years, to Portland.

Immersed in career and family, he drifted away from running. He played golf, he put on some middle-aged pounds. One day in the 1970s, when the running boom was starting, Fee was out on the golf course when a runner glided by, a vision of freedom and purpose, and at that moment Fee decided to give up golf and resume running. He ran with the obsession that characterized the first running boom, piling up hundred-mile training weeks, none of the miles easy. He ran fifteen marathons—including Boston, New York City, and Chicago—with a 2:46 personal best.

In part, he was animated by a vow he'd made back as an under-grad at Marquette. Fee and a buddy had gone to see the Bud Greenspan–directed documentary of the 1960 Olympics, high-lighted by the shots of the Ethiopian marathoner Abebe Bikila gliding barefoot through the torchlit streets of Rome. Inspired, Fee told his friend that over the course of his life he'd personally run in as many Olympic stadiums as he could manage. When Fee resumed running in middle age, he started to make good on that college-boy pledge. He embraced every aspect of the running life, from train-ing to racing to nutrition. He ardently subscribed to the Nike mythos and was a particularly big fan of Alberto Salazar.

Years earlier, Fee had hired Salazar to give a motivational talk to his firm's sales staff. After the talk, as he drove Salazar to the air-port, Fee confessed his anxiety: The next day he would travel to Massachusetts to run his first Boston Marathon, and he was worried that, with all the stress of putting together this meeting, his run-ning performance would suffer.

"Don't worry," Salazar said. "You live and you run on two differ-ent batteries." Fee cherished that line as if it came from Socrates, and repeated it often to his co-workers and family members.

So Fee was thrilled to become associated with Julius, a man so close to the heart of the Oregon Project, and to the heart of Nike. Fee still thought of himself as a runner, even though those thou-sands of hard miles, those scores of savagely contested road races, had done a number on his knees and back. Now he cycled more than ran, pedaling centuries and other bike races, attacking the hills on his expensive road bike the way he once attacked marathon hills wearing his beloved Nikes.

Julius and Fee, so different in almost every regard but running, quickly built a close friendship. Besides the working lunches, Julius and Grace became regulars at the Fee Sunday dinners. Fee and Angela made quarterly donations to the foundation, the money going straight to Julius's brother Jimmy, who was now supervising the orphanage and family compound in Lira; Jimmy would send back detailed receipts and invoices, accounting for every penny spent. Each time Fee wrote a check, Julius would repeat his invitation, which, over time, developed into a challenge: Fee should travel to Uganda and see conditions for himself.

Fee would always demur, saying he'd just get in the way. But Julius never gave up.

◆ ◆ ◆

His story was his product, and now it was time for Julius to offer it to the public. For the first gig, Fee arranged for Julius to talk to a church group in downtown Portland. He seemed more anxious and excited than Julius. Fee had sold medical technology, specializing in automatic defibrillators, the devices that shocked hearts back to life after cardiac events. He had never sold a story before, and he was eager to see if the same principles applied.

The first talk drew only about twenty people, but Fee gave it the full professional treatment, helping Julius prepare a PowerPoint slideshow to go with the presentation. He urged Julius to write out his speech, or at least scribble an outline, but Julius demurred. The Lord will guide my words, he assured Fee.

As Julius took the podium, Fee paced in the back of the room. Had he misjudged Julius, overestimating the power and appeal of his story, and the runner's capacity for telling it? Would other people be as impressed as Fee, recognizing the depth of Julius's integrity and character? What if Julius bombed in front of an audience? What if people couldn't understand his accent or understand the geography or the basic politics of Uganda?

Fee didn't need to worry. Julius started by introducing Uganda, showing the nation on a map, and the rest of his talk flowed from there. Again Fee was struck by how the story seemed to stand by itself, with its own vital force. Julius concluded to a cascade of applause, and the foundation collected almost two hundred dollars in donations. Fee beamed as if it were two million dollars. The next day Julius sent the money directly to Jimmy in Lira to pay for food, clothes, and school fees.

* * *

Thus passed the year 2007, with Julius running in the morning, clerking in the afternoon, coaching in the evening, and working on the Achon Uganda Children's Fund on weekends and in every spare moment. The proceeds, while modest, were enough to provide the orphans with a modicum more food, a slightly wider margin of security and stability. Fee arranged talks at all possible venues— church groups, civic and business organizations, brown-bag lunches at his workplace and other offices, high schools. Julius invariably drew a strong response, the audiences both engrossed by his adventures and impressed by his purpose. He stuck to elements pertaining to his youth and the orphanage: his abduction by the LRA and his eventual escape; the forty-mile run from Awake; discovering the children under the bus.

These set pieces became the staples of his narrative, the core product he was offering. American audiences could relate to the act of directly helping kids orphaned by a madman such as Joseph Kony, could empathize with the suffering that Julius had endured. He sharpened his delivery, but the anecdotes never felt polished or rote. Tears invariably flowed when he described the elephant grass turning red from his friends' blood.

* * *

One day late in the year, Julius told Fee that there was more to his story. There was something else on his mind, something that could affect the future of the foundation. For some time now, Fee had had an idea that Julius might be holding something back. There was something major still to be revealed. Fee steeled himself—would it be something dark and terrible? The real reason this man wasn't better known? Was he about to learn after all these months that, in fact, Julius Achon and his story really were too good to be true?

The buried story was indeed dark, but it hardly reflected poorly on Julius. In detail, he told Fee about Kristina's death: from leaving the compound in Lira on a desperate quest for food to her senseless shooting to her dying from infection and blood loss three days later. It was a death like countless others in northern Uganda, Julius explained, and it could have been prevented with basic medical care.

"I want to build a clinic in Awake," Julius told Fee. "So that other mothers and children don't have to die like that."

Fee considered. Raising a thousand dollars to feed a dozen or so kids was one thing. Building a health clinic in the middle of nowhere was something much different.

Sensing Fee's hesitation, Julius elaborated on his thinking. Despite all good intentions and careful planning, the orphanage in Lira might not last—at least in its present form. The children would grow up and move into lives of their own. Other children might take their place, but the connection to the war would be forgotten. At its heart, an orphanage consisted of people; people changed. The essence of a health clinic was more fixed and tangible—a building filled with nurses dispensing medicines that healed malaria and other maladies of the bush. And unlike the orphanage, the health clinic would rise in Awake, where his mother had lived and raised her family.

That was Julius's vision, the other thing he wanted to confess. Fee was more impressed than ever, more convinced of his friend's integrity. But he also recognized the vast scale of the undertaking that Julius was proposing. Ideally, it would require a full-time commitment by someone with experience in the field. Fee knew nothing about building hospitals. He was just a businessman. In terms of retirement, he looked forward to the usual: travel with Angela, time with the grandkids. Julius suggested a project that would change everything. Perhaps, in this case, Julius was simply asking too much from him.

On the other hand: The more time he spent around Julius, the better he got to know him, the more Fee sensed that he was an extraordinary man riding a powerful wave. Someone was going to help Julius build that health clinic. Could Fee live with himself if that someone wasn't him? Those questions aside, Fee had his own ghost to confront.

When he was a kid back in Chicago, all of his extended family's Irish-American immigrant energy and ambition after World War II landed squarely on his shoulders as firstborn son. Expected to do something great, he always stepped up to the challenge. Thus the top grades, the paper route, the service as an altar boy in a parish that might have been in Dublin, and the scholarship to Marquette. Driving it all was his central ambition: to become a physician. From Ellis Island to medical school in three generations. The American dream personified.

But something happened. Fee ground out the grades in the pre-med courses at Marquette but got rejected by every medical school to which he had applied. At that time there were only a handful of medical schools in the United States. A glut of baby boomers was competing for the slots, and the backdoor routes to the profession that are available to students today didn't exist.

Fee was devastated by the rejection, and his family members felt even worse. Fee rebounded, of course, achieving it all—family, career, affluence, even success in his avocation of distance running. But he still felt that vague, ancient gnaw and ache. He had failed to become a doctor as a young man; now, as an aging one, here was Julius Achon—an agent of fate, a man from the moon—inviting him to build a hospital.

Not long after that conversation, on a Saturday afternoon in spring, Fee borrowed a pickup truck from a neighbor and helped Grace and Julius move from their apartment in Beaverton to another apartment complex close by. The unit they were leaving was dark, moldy, and damp, with paint blistering on cheap drywall and a spotted, lurid-colored carpet. Even during their poorest post-college years, Angela and Jim had never lived in such a depressing place. Julius sensed his friend's dismay.

"It wasn't so bad," he said as the two men lifted a mattress onto the truck. "I could brew a cup of tea whenever I liked. At night, the Karamojong didn't come."

Julius and Fee walked back inside to pick up another load. "Okay, Julius," Fee said. "Let's build that health clinic."

◆ ◆ ◆

In 2006, one year before Julius Achon and Jim Fee started their partnership, Joseph Kony granted his first, and thus far only, video interview. A young British freelance journalist named Sam Farmar had been doggedly pursuing Kony for years. Several times Kony had agreed to be interviewed but always reneged at the last moment, failing to show up for assignations that were months in the planning.

By this time, Kony had evolved into a sort of Scarlet Pimpernel figure in central Africa. The LRA had been ravaging northern Uganda for almost two decades; the children of his first crop of abducted bush brides and boy soldiers were now being kidnapped to serve in the rebel ranks. Despite all of Museveni's efforts within Uganda and major offensives such as Operation Iron Fist that carried across national borders, Kony and his forces remained at large, pulling off large-scale atrocities such as Barlonyo and thousands of smaller-scale ambushes and attacks. Afterward, leaving behind burned villages and traumatized survivors with their lips and ears sliced off and their children stolen, they would disappear back into the bush.

The Ugandan government and intermediaries from neighboring African countries floated peace deals with Kony. There would be initial progress on truces and negotiated surrenders, but Kony would always pull out from the talks, often at the final and most infuriating moment. The warlord proved equally elusive to journalists. Reporters and NGO researchers were able to interview hundreds of boy soldiers and bush brides who had escaped the LRA, as well as mutilated survivors of the rebels' violence, but they were never able to sit down with Kony himself. The violence raged on, and Kony's legend grew.

When he finally thought it advantageous to appear in the media—or perhaps he craved the attention—Kony chose to bypass CNN, the BBC, and other establishment media organizations, instead meeting Farmar, a freelancer who he likely thought would be easier to manipulate. Farmar trekked through the bush to a clearing in Congo, and after days of anxious waiting and further delays, Joseph Kony finally walked into the camp.

The devil appeared in everyday fashion. Like the LRA rebels who abducted Julius in 1988, he looked surprisingly ordinary. Slender, almost willowy, wearing a plain red T-shirt, Kony sprawled in a camp chair, amiably pouring tea for the young filmmaker, amused at the man's anxiety, pleased at the effect he was making. Aware of his reputation as a monster, Kony poked fun at his visitors, mocking the forces that, for all their power, had failed to lay a finger on him.

"These things people say about me aren't true," he said in halting but serviceable English. "I do not abduct children, and I do not torture."

He grew animated. "You see, I am a human being like you! I put my shirt on like you! I have arms and legs and walk and talk—I am just a human being!"

After going on in this fashion for another twenty minutes, Kony rose from his camp chair, and he and his retinue of warriors melted back into the bush. The interview served as his farewell to his native country. Shortly afterward, the LRA retreated deep into the forests of Congo and the Central African Republic. As mysteriously and hauntingly as he'd appeared, Joseph Kony departed Uganda.

◆ ◆ ◆

By June 2007, the Nike Oregon Project was six years old. The team was flourishing, albeit in ways that Salazar hadn't foreseen when he started the program. Originally, the emphasis was on developing marathoners who could compete with the Africans in the sport's most lucrative, high-profile event: an American runner who could match the achievements of Salazar. But no such marathoner had emerged—East Africans continued to dominate the event—and Salazar shifted his focus to the middle distances on the track. Specifically, in Galen Rupp's case, Salazar employed Nike's vast scientific and sports medicine resources to improve the efficiency of

Galen's stride and thus goose his closing speed. In the case of Kara Goucher, Salazar devoted the resources at his disposal to getting her healthy and avoiding further injury.

Julius continued to play his supporting role, showing up whenever and wherever Salazar ordered, running the distance and pace that the coach commanded. He might be valuable, but he was also replaceable. Julius says he received neither raise nor bonus, and when he sustained a hernia he paid for medical treatment out of his own pocket. Ironically, Julius says that medications of various kinds were in ample supply around the Oregon Project, although he saw no evidence of illicit performance-enhancing drugs.

Clearly, the key to Rupp's success was his extraordinarily tight relationship with Salazar. It made Julius think of the bonds he'd forged with coaches—and father figures—such as Mr. Banage and John Cook. Everybody needed a captain he could follow into the bush. And now Kara Goucher was benefiting from the same type of guidance. Galen's development demonstrated Salazar's ability to mold a runner beginning in childhood; Kara's renaissance proved Alberto's gift for reviving an athlete whose career appeared finished.

Despite the time he spent around the Oregon Project, all the miles he logged beside the runners, he felt like he never really got to know them. Their relations were friendly, but essentially Julius remained invisible. At the same time, however, he became more of a presence elsewhere around the Nike campus, particularly at the employees' store. Like the high school runners he coached, his young co-workers listened eagerly as Julius described the elephant grass that turned red and his epic forty-mile run from Awake. From there, word filtered out to the designers and mid-level executives on campus, many of whom would eventually play key roles in the AUCF.

◆ ◆ ◆

In March of 2008, Eloise Wellings, Australia's top female 5,000- and 10,000-meter runner, was ready to call it quits on her long, star-crossed career. At age fourteen, around the same age that Julius

Achon had emerged as one of Uganda's top running talents, Wellings burst on the scene in her nation, dominating junior competitions and excelling in senior-level races. Wellings was bright, personable, and attractive. TV crews visited her school to shoot features, and she beamed out from the front page of the nation's major newspapers.

The girl's timing was auspicious. In 2000, the summer Olympic Games came to Sydney. Her countrymen hoped that Wellings might serve as the distance-running equivalent of Cathy Freeman, Australia's native Aborigine sprinting star who won a gold medal in the 400 meters. Wellings's story, however, proved a little too golden to be true.

"If I could run this fast in the shape I'm in," Wellings remembers thinking, "then how fast could I run if were thinner?"

She started dumping her lunches in the trash and finding excuses to miss meals. She nibbled on energy bars and filled her stomach with water. For a time it worked. For a time Wellings continued to run faster. During some workouts, some races, she felt almost weightless, moved along that knife edge beyond which the body started to consume itself. Instead of being alarmed by the hollow-cheeked wraith in the mirror, Wellings was thrilled. Her fascination, however, was tinged by disgust—she still believed herself to be fat; she could never grow lean enough.

"I didn't have what you'd classify as an extreme case of anorexia," Wellings says. "I was never hospitalized. My life was never in danger."

One day a few months before the Olympics, she went out on a routine training run. She planted her foot as she'd done thousands of times before. A screech of pain lifted from her foot, and she went down as if shot. MRI images showed a stress fracture on her metatarsal. They also showed that she was severely malnourished. "I was seventeen, and I had the bone density of a seventy-five-year-old woman," Wellings says.

Neither the fracture nor the underlying condition of anorexia was severe enough to make her stop running. Wellings kept chasing her Olympic dream, setting her sights on Athens in 2004. She resumed training and racing, but her affliction resurfaced. "Every time I started getting in really good shape, which usually coincided with an Olympic year, I would get another stress fracture and be forced to shut down."

By age twenty-five, she had already suffered eight stress fractures in her feet and lower legs. Now, in early 2008, Wellings aimed for the London Games. Yet again, on another routine training run, a stab of pain lifted from her foot: stress fracture number nine. "I'm quitting," she told her husband. She had the backing of a well-off family, and her side business as a personal trainer was on the rise. "I'm not going through this again," she said.

But her husband and her coach counseled patience. Wellings was sponsored by Nike, and her coach was friendly with Alberto Salazar. Salazar invited Wellings to visit Portland and avail herself of the anti-gravity treadmill and other sports medicine facilities available at the Nike corporate campus. Wellings reluctantly boarded a plane for America. Salazar hosted her at the Altitude House, which was now used as a training center and lodging for visiting athletes.

Wellings spent most of the time in the basement, grinding on the anti-gravity treadmill, a device that provided the benefit of running without the pounding on fragile joints. The Oregon Project athletes came and went, friendly and polite but caught up in their own issues. The one exception was the African guy who worked as a pacer for the group.

Wellings and Julius were separated in every possible fashion—race, gender, class, nationality, even running event—but a bond formed. They were both foreigners and outsiders. Both had experienced repeated Olympic disappointments.

During drives out to the Nike campus on the Sunset Highway, or late in the evening as Julius packed shoes and clothes to send to Uganda, he listened to her tale of lucky-world woe, the skein of pain and frustration unspooling from the self-inflicted, culturally induced blows of anorexia. When Wellings was finished, he said, "You think you have it bad? Wait until you hear what I'm dealing with."

Julius told Wellings his story, from jumping out the school window to getting taken by Kony to finding the eleven kids underneath the bus. Wellings was astonished and humbled. "At first I felt ashamed," she says. "I felt like the biggest baby, whining about my sore foot when this man was struggling with matters of life and death, and carrying a whole village on his shoulders. But the more I listened, the more I saw my own troubles in perspective. I suddenly knew that there was a purpose behind my coming to Oregon. I thought I was coming to rehab my foot, but I was really coming to meet Julius."

◆ ◆ ◆

One morning in June 2012, Jim Fee stepped to the lectern in the ballroom of a downtown Seattle hotel to deliver the keynote address at a national conference of alumni-relations directors from leading colleges and universities. The conference organizers had invited Fee to describe how he applied a businessman's skills to building a nationally recognized nonprofit enterprise. Fee was flattered by the invitation. After four years of booking speaking gigs for Julius, he was getting a chance to tell his own story. "Let me go back to the beginning of my relationship with Julius Achon, which started five years ago. . . ."

Fee explained that running formed the magnet that first drew him to Julius's story. He told of the dinner at his house in 2007 and the subsequent lunch meeting at the Nike campus. He described his epiphany as he helped Julius move out of his moldy apartment in Beaverton. Fee related how, as his role in the foundation deepened, he went down a mental checklist of his key business precepts: finding a trustworthy leader with a strong, clear vision; evaluating all objective factors; but, in the end, going with your gut and instincts. "Running? Check. Helping those in need? Check. Building from the ground up? Check. Was Julius a person who could lead, who had a good heart and strong vision? Two checks."

Julius told his story and set the strategic goals; Fee handled logistics, finances, and tactics. His central challenge: distinguishing the Achon Uganda Children's Fund from 3,776 other NGOs operating in central Africa. Fee determined that Julius's background as an Olympic athlete set him apart. The AUCF would focus its fundraising campaign on the Portland-area and national running communities.

Fee plugged Julius into appearances at running clubs and road-race expos. He knew that, in the United States, runners tended to be affluent, compassionate, and accustomed to volunteering. Fee took special aim at the nucleus of runners and running-related employees on the Nike campus, where Julius had toiled for years. He recruited two prominent Nike shoe designers, Chris Cook and Tony Bignell, to serve on the AUCF board. Fee also worked the media, waging a two-year campaign to persuade *Runner's World* to publish a feature on Julius and his work. The story finally appeared early in 2012, and the nationwide exposure opened a relative floodgate of donations.

At that point Fee paused in his presentation. In hindsight, in a carefully prepared narrative, depicted in a series of PowerPoint photos and charts flashing across a screen in a semi-darkened hotel ballroom, the rise of the AUCF sounded rapid, smooth, orderly. The reality, of course, was far different. Julius dedicated every spare moment to foundation business, while Fee, retired from Welch Allyn, labored more than full-time, putting in fifty- and sixty-hour weeks of grunt work, researching funding sources, establishing contacts, answering email queries, and writing personal thank-you notes for every five- and ten-dollar donation, which, for the first few years of operation, formed the bulk of the foundation's income.

Even modest sums, however, were sufficient to make a difference in Uganda. The money supported the makeshift orphan compound in Lira town and was just enough for Julius and Fee to begin planning construction of a rudimentary health clinic in Awake. At the end of 2009, however, two years into the partnership, it seemed that the work had reached a plateau. Fee had tapped every potential donor he could think of, but no major, sustaining funding source had emerged. For every hour he spent on programs, he spent nine searching for money.

"The needle might have stayed stuck," Fee told his audience in Seattle, "if I hadn't taken my first trip to Uganda—if I hadn't gone and taken a look for myself."

◆ ◆ ◆

For two years, Julius quietly but persistently lobbied Fee to travel to Uganda to observe firsthand the impact of his work. Just as persistently, Fee kept putting him off. He told Julius—and himself—that there was no compelling reason for him to go. Why interrupt a productive rhythm? True, the AUCF had yet to make a major splash, and true, Julius still cobbled together a living out of part-time jobs, but overall the foundation had grown. Along with twenty-five additional children, the eleven original orphans, the kids that Julius had found under a bus one morning five years earlier, were all enrolled either in school or in vocational training programs. Still, if the health clinic was going to be constructed in Awake, someone from the foundation would have to spend time in Africa. Fee thought that Julius should go. Julius countered by arranging with Jimmy for the orphans in Lira to send letters to Fee.

> *Greetings of peace and love to you from Uganda. We hope you are fine and pushing on with life despite the odds. We are really grateful for all the material/moral support you always render to us. We therefore ask God to pour his abandoned blessings upon you so that you always prosper in what you are struggling for. There is nothing in return for all that you are doing for us other than prayers; however there is more blessings in giving than receiving. We wish to meet you physically.*
>
> *Yours lovely, Mugisha Samuel*

Pushing on with life . . . his abandoned blessings . . . yours lovely . . . How could you resist such a letter? Summoning his own competitive will, and perhaps realizing that a journey to Africa might catapult him to a new level of involvement, Fee still said no. He threw down his own hole card. Total expenses for one person making the trip would be around four thousand dollars. Not only would the foundation pay that for Julius; Fee would personally donate that sum to the AUCF general fund.

But Julius refused to take the bait. "No," he told Fee. "You must spend that money on your own plane ticket."

Fee knew when he was beat. He also knew that Julius was right: The time had come for him to set eyes on Awake. By this point the AUCF had about seventy-five thousand dollars in the bank, enough to start planning construction of the clinic. Fee submitted to his six hundred dollars' worth of inoculations and medication, and in January 2010, three years after Grace and Julius showed up at his house for dinner, Fee and Julius embarked on a journey to Uganda.

◆ ◆ ◆

Fee traveled frequently, for both business and pleasure—he'd recently taken the family to Europe to watch the Tour de France—but he'd never been to Africa or anywhere else in the developing world. As the jetliner attained cruising altitude out of Portland International, he felt on edge. Julius, for his part, drifted back to the galley, falling into conversation with the flight attendants. Now that he'd started telling his story, started making connections and raising money toward his goal, he couldn't stop. He handed out his AUCF business card. One of the attendants invited Julius to give a talk to her son's high school cross-country team.

Meanwhile, back in his seat, Fee wrote in his journal, a cloth-bound ledger that he always carried when he traveled. He usually filled it with lists, itineraries, addresses, and other quotidian items, but tonight, outbound to Africa, he was in a more meditative mood. He wrote about the general happiness and satisfaction that characterized his life, and his one major regret: that he hadn't spent more time with Angela and the kids. He lifted his pen, looked thoughtfully out the window to the glowing wingtip lights. He always had to work, to provide, to tick off the items on his checklists, to serve as mentor and role model to the young people in his office. On the weekends there was yard work, house maintenance, and the obligation of his long weekend run—he had to get his miles in, the weekly quota. On Sunday, after early mass, it was race day, including those fifteen marathons that blackened his toenails but made him feel alive.

As the flight droned on, as the napkins and earphones and blankets accumulated around his seat, as his mouth grew stale and his head pounded, the excitement of the adventure faded and for the first time since he'd met Julius, Fee entertained doubts. *Is this man for real?* he thought. *What has he gotten me into?*

Upon reflection, however, Fee felt reassured. Although he'd grown more confident in the years that Fee had known him, Julius, at his core, hadn't changed at all. He certainly looked comfortable in an airplane. Fee took pride in traveling light, but he still bore a load of potions and electronics. Julius, by contrast, traveled with virtually no baggage. No books, no digital devices, no video screens. When he wasn't sleeping or spreading the word about the AUCF to other passengers, Julius quietly studied the Bible.

◆ ◆ ◆

From the moment they touched down at Entebbe, the usual roles of the two men were reversed. Fee relied on Julius for everything. Starting in the airport, negotiating payment for Fee's tourist visa, and changing dollars into a mountain of Ugandan shillings. Outside the terminal, amid the overpowering heat and pungent odors, a dozen men clamored to carry their bags and drive them to Kampala. Showing a hard, almost contemptuous edge that Fee had never witnessed stateside, Julius plowed through the petitioners as he had on that day in Lira on his last visit before Kristina had been killed.

After one night at a hotel in Kampala, they traveled on to Lira. Both men were eager to be free of the capital, Fee because of the noise and confusion, Julius due to the city's prevailing atmosphere of vice and duplicity. Kampala: where a thousand well-planned, well-funded Western NGO projects died before they were born; where bureaucrats sat in offices like spiders in their webs or pythons in the tall grass, patiently waiting for money from the *mzungos* (white people) to come floating by.

Then came the day-long ordeal of the journey up to Lira. Years had passed since Julius had made the trip; he regarded the road through *mzungo* eyes. There were no rules; might and size made right. The largest and fastest vehicles formed the top of the food chain, and all lower forms of traffic adjusted to their movements. But somehow it all worked. You found your slot among the buses, four-wheel-drive vehicles, fantastically overloaded pickup trucks, motorcycles, scooters, bicycles, and pedestrians of all stripes, from pencil-legged children to glacially moving elders. Julius gradually relaxed, but Fee continued to flinch each time their rig blasted by a skittering clutch of children or a group of scrambling women.

◆ ◆ ◆

Arriving in Lira, they went straight to the orphanage compound. Julius had warned Fee not to expect too much, but still, in Fee's mind, an "orphanage" conjured images from his Irish-Catholic boyhood on the south side of Chicago—stark gray buildings, cots lined up in a dormitory, pinch-faced nuns ministering to pale children. The Lira compound, by contrast, consisted of two squat windowless and doorless stucco houses on an acre of dirt surrounded by a concrete wall topped by concertina wire. The sprawling IDP camp that formerly spread to the compound border was now dispersed, but its lingering air of suffering was palpable. This is what Fee had devoted his life to over the last three years?

But his mood soon improved. Fifteen orphaned children, scrubbed and wearing clean clothes washed by Florence, Jimmy's wife, lined up to greet their American benefactor. The boys solemnly shook Fee's hand (including Mugisha Samuel of the "Yours lovely" letter), the girls chastely curtsied. Fee appraised their condition. Most seemed hale, but the two youngest, Monica and Brian, were obviously sick. Florence, Jimmy, and Julius suspected that the children were suffering bouts of malaria. Tomorrow morning, Julius explained, they would take them to the clinic at the government hospital for testing.

The next morning Fee woke well before dawn, and when the light rose he was already out running the dusty streets of Lira town. After breakfast, Julius picked him up and they drove back to the orphanage compound. They picked up Monica and Brian, silent and uncomplaining despite their racking chills and fever, along with the other thirteen children—might as well test everybody for malaria, Julius explained—and delivered them to the government clinic.

For the first time, Fee encountered the desperate silence of an African hospital waiting room. Patients overflowed the benches and lay clenched and bleeding on the filthy floor, waiting with dead-eyed stares. No equipment, no computers, no hygiene, no system, no documentation . . . and apparently no doctor, just a few deliriously overworked nurses.

Mothers holding sick babies looked at the Achon contingent with a flare of hope. A white person such as Fee represented money, magic, order, health. Their hope quickly died when the mothers realized that the American had brought his own sick children for treatment. Of the fifteen AUCF children, twelve tested positive for malaria. They were provided doses of medicine costing about four dollars each. During the testing, Julius noticed that one of the boys had a nasty cut on his foot that was about to become infected. Fee paid the equivalent of three dollars to have the wound cleaned and dressed.

Years later, as Fee described this scene to his audience at the Seattle fundraisers' meeting, the audience listened raptly, no doubt calculating, as Fee had at the time, how much that basic procedure would have cost at an emergency room or urgent-care clinic in the United States.

That evening, Julius picked up Fee at the hotel and drove him downtown for dinner—Julius knew of a good, cheap Indian-run cafe. Before dining, however, Fee insisted on going shopping at the street market. They bought six sets of mosquito netting for four dollars each; six was enough, Julius explained, because the children slept two or three to each mat.

Later that evening, in his hotel room, while the fan turned slowly overhead and the Afro-pop disco music blared from the bar downstairs, Fee picked up his ballpoint and opened his ledger. No sentimental musing this time; it was back to the numbers.

Fifteen malaria tests at two dollars a pop came to thirty dollars. Twelve doses of malaria medicine, four bucks each, came to forty-eight dollars. One dressing for a cut foot: three dollars. A half dozen mosquito nets, four dollars each: twenty-four dollars. So the grand total for testing, treating, and preventing malaria for fifteen kids, plus treatment for a foot injury: 105 dollars. Fee broke it down, and came up with fifteen kids receiving comprehensive medical treatment for seven dollars a head.

And then Jim Fee called home. "For the price of a glass of chardonnay in Portland," he told Angela, "you can save a child's life in Uganda."

◆ ◆ ◆

The next day, Fee asked to take a tour of the government hospital in Lira. Julius advised against it. After Kristina's death, he'd developed a deep antipathy toward the nation's bribe-fueled public health system. Also, when the patients and staff saw Fee, a white man, they would assume he had magically arrived to solve all their problems. When the people at the hospital recognized Julius, the Olympic runner now residing in America, they would think the same thing. The two men's presence would just deepen their woe. Finally, and most urgently, Julius wanted to spare Fee the gruesome sights waiting in the wards.

Charles, Julius's father, went along on the visit. They went everywhere in the hospital. They saw terrible things—amputations, gaping wounds, children suffering. But Fee never looked away. He just kept writing things down in his big notebook.

Julius and his father exchanged a look. "This *mzungo* is tough," Charles said.

◆ ◆ ◆

The next day they traveled on to Awake. The forty-mile journey over the terrible road made the trip from Kampala to Lira seem like a waltz down an American interstate. The countryside was blanched and depleted by years of war. There were virtually no cattle on the road, and even the school-bound children moved with a listless, hollow-eyed gait. Julius kept obsessively checking the speedometer, confirming the precise distance he'd run on that day when he was fourteen years old. Now he was thirty-three. He had made his break from the village half a lifetime ago. It seemed like three lifetimes. And yet, at the same time, Julius felt as if he'd never left.

Three miles past Aliwang Mission, they pulled off the main road, jouncing down the dirt path to the village. The swollen-bellied children looked up like zebras as the vehicle passed. Hidden behind the grass and trees, looking out from the clearings by their huts, dozens more villagers tracked their passage.

Finally, they reached the family huts and ground to a stop. Julius's father climbed out of the backseat and was greeted by his new wife. Fee followed, looking all around, at a loss for what to say. Julius knew what he was thinking. Where was the village he had listened to Julius talking about for the last three years? All Fee saw were a sad scatter of circular huts and faint footpaths trailing off into the deep bush. Dirt, heat, glare, the bleat of a goat, and a clump of women and barefoot children staring at Fee as if he were Winston Churchill. This was where he was going to build a health clinic?

They toured the hut area. Julius showed Fee where he had seen the lion's pawprint and the shea nut tree from which the boy had fallen, toward which Julius had run when he began training as a boy. They walked out past the mango tree to the field where he'd been kidnapped. A dry wind rustled through the elephant grass. Julius had never escaped this place, and yet it had long since stopped feeling like home. It occurred to him that he might never find another true home in this world. He was learning to accept this fact.

They returned to the huts, where Charles, who was recovering from a bout of malaria, rested in the shade. To maintain the momentum, Fee put on his executive's hat. The first task, he decided, was to assess the existing healthcare facilities in the area. That meant driving back down the road to Aliwang Mission.

Despite the wreckage and devastation left by the years of war and the presence of the IDP camp—the hospital ward had been pillaged and ransacked, there was no electricity or running water, patients wandered around stunned—Julius was impressed by Ali-wang. The nuns and priests moved with an assurance and authority that Julius didn't recall seeing as a boy. During the war, they had weathered the worst, experienced humanity at its most depraved. Now, having survived the ordeal, they appeared serene in their minds and steadfast in their vocation.

Father Guido led them on a tour of the hospital, which was barely functioning but cleaner and more serviceable than the blasted wards of the government clinics. Then the three men sat in the priest's office. An assistant delivered bottles of Fanta. Fee was also impressed by Father Guido, who reminded him of the rock-ribbed parish priests of his South Side Chicago boyhood. Father Guido, for his part, had never forgotten that Julius and his family had left the Catholic Church to enlist in the evangelical movement. And now, with his health-clinic proposal, Julius, in effect, threat-ened to cut into the Aliwang territory. When Fee told the priest about the AUCF's plans, he suggested pooling resources and estab-lishing the clinic as an addition to Aliwang.

Back in Awake, Fee was enthusiastic about the idea, pointing out the advantages of joining forces with an existing facility. The AUCF's money would go further there, and they could draw on the expertise of the mission's staff.

"No," Julius said. "We must build here."

Fee looked up at the tone in Julius's voice. "Here in Awake," Ju-lius continued, "where my mother can find rest."

Here in Awake, Fee thought, where there was nothing to build on. But of course he understood that that was the point.

◆ ◆ ◆

On the flight back to Portland two weeks later, Fee's ledger was full of lists with crossed-off items. The tasks ahead, while daunting, were also clearly defined. The orphanage, already on solid footing, would continue to grow, funded mainly through a separate founda-tion that Eloise Wellings had established in Australia. Meanwhile, the health clinic in Awake would form the AUCF's central project.

By any practical measure, that project appeared outlandishly difficult. But on another level, building in Awake would be quite simple—there were no permits required or union contracts to negotiate. Fee had arranged to purchase the land from Charles, and Jimmy had agreed to oversee the hiring of an architect and serve as the general contractor. Now Fee opened his ledger and, for the first time since the outbound flight, recorded another impression.

"I am so lucky to be living in America," he wrote. "I will never complain about anything again."

The trip had also confirmed his faith in Julius, whose commitment to his people was remarkably free of sentimentality. At times it almost seemed as if he disliked the villagers he served. This wasn't necessarily a bad thing, Fee realized, again recalling the lash of the nuns at his South Side parochial grammar school.

Fee was particularly impressed by the way Julius had dealt with the incessant stream of schemes and requests coming his way. In the American business world, you usually responded to those types of pitches with a "maybe." You told the person, "Let me get back to you on that." In Uganda, Julius never said maybe. He responded with an immediate yes or no.

Almost always, the answer was no. Julius understood that his time, energy, and resources were limited and had to go to where they would do the most good. And that way, the guy making the pitch wouldn't go away with false hope. In Uganda, Fee was learning, false hope was more damaging than no hope at all.

◆ ◆ ◆

In the second part of his talk in Seattle, Fee described in greater detail the campaign to build the Kristina Health Center. He reminded the audience about how the center got its name—that Kristina, Julius's mother, had been shot and killed by LRA rebels in 2004. Had she received even a modicum of decent first-aid care, she would have survived. Julius wanted to build a clinic in honor of his mother, so that other villagers would be spared her fate; given Uganda's history there would almost certainly be more wars. Julius was also thinking of his niece, who had died in childbirth, and of Florence and Jimmy; Jimmy had had to sell his car to pay the various fees and bribes so that Florence could deliver the couple's first child by cesarean section.

These were the facts, but the truth went deeper. For Julius, the clinic formed a blow against chaos—building the project instilled a sense of order similar to the one he'd experienced during hard training as a runner. The work formed the equivalent of the to-do lists in Jim Fee's ledger.

"Now, it's one thing to support orphans," Fee told the fundraisers. "It's a whole different story to build a medical clinic in a remote village forty miles away from the next town, with terrible roads and no water or electricity. The huts and other buildings don't even have doors or windows to keep away mosquitoes and malaria."

Fortunately, Fee found a model on which to base the project: the Engeye Clinic in southern Uganda. Engeye was the creation of another American, a young physician named Stephanie Van Dyke. Van Dyke had grown up in Portland, the daughter of owners of a popular downtown restaurant. She majored in humanities at Whitman College in eastern Washington State. After graduating, she went on a global walkabout and ended up teaching English at Masaka village in Uganda. Although spared the war that raged north of the Nile, the Masaka villagers suffered the same deadly but preventable maladies as those afflicting Awake and countless other villages across sub-Saharan Africa: malaria, dysentery, AIDS, tuberculosis, and the like. In the face of such misery, teaching the people English seemed as useful as teaching them ancient Greek.

"Everybody has to die," Van Dyke says. "But these people were dying unnecessarily, and it just wasn't right."

Returning to the United States, Van Dyke changed vocational course, acquiring hard-science credits and eventually graduating from medical school. Her grandmother died and left her an inheritance of thirty-five thousand dollars. Van Dyke used the money to found the Engeye clinic in Masaka, a partnership with local healthcare practitioners, whose aim was to provide basic medical care to the village.

Engeye proved a success, and after handing over the clinic to local control, Van Dyke returned to Oregon to start a public health project in the rural south of the state. Fee and Julius visited her to pick her brain. Van Dyke was impressed. "A lot of us go out to save the world but get bogged down in the difficulty and details and get overtaken by negativity," she says. "But not Julius and Jim. They had a specific idea, they were totally committed, they knew who they were and what they wanted, and approached their goal hurdle by hurdle. You could tell right away these guys were going to make it."

◆ ◆ ◆

In the year following Fee's first trip to Uganda, the foundation grew at a quickening pace. They defined a pool of donors among the local and national running communities. The AUCF formed a relationship with Nike that proved especially key. The link wasn't forged through the Oregon Project, senior management, or the corporation's official charity network. Instead, the relationship built from the grass roots, spreading by word of mouth, as a disparate range of Nike employees finally became aware of—finally saw— the man who'd been working among them for six years.

There were two main groups on campus who became converts to the cause: the recent college grads working minimum-wage jobs beside Julius in the employees' store and the star shoe designers who performed the core work on campus, creating the story, idea, and image of Nike.

Tony Bignell, for instance, headed the Innovation Kitchen, a workshop in which some of the foremost shoe and clothing designers in the world were encouraged to go wherever their imagination guided them. "Phil McCartney, head of soccer footwear at Nike, met Julius and heard about what he was doing," Bignell says. "Phil heard that Julius would take our shoes and cover them with mud before shipping them off to orphan kids in Uganda. Phil told me that I absolutely had to meet this guy. So I went out to dinner with Julius and Jim.

"Julius told all about his mom being killed by LRA rebels. I was just blown away. After that dinner, I invited Julius to come and speak at the Innovation Kitchen's regular Monday morning meeting. Again, Julius was just brilliant."

Bignell brought Jack, his ten-year-old son, to the meeting to hear Julius. "Jack said to me, 'If a dollar goes so far in Uganda, why don't we just go to the Dollar Tree and buy Julius what he needs?' Jack also thought that being a rebel soldier sounded pretty cool. 'They give you a rifle and you get to pee in the woods,' he said."

At Fee's request, Bignell agreed to serve on the AUCF board, eventually becoming a director. "Julius and Jim, working together, just sort of emanated the creative, can-do spirit that expressed the Nike ethos at its best," Bignell says. "You have this wonderful but seemingly crazy idea, and you don't know how you can make it happen, but somehow it comes together and works."

At the time, Bignell says, Nike and Bono, the rock star and philanthropist, were collaborating on a program based on red shoelaces. "It was similar to the yellow Livestrong bracelets. You paid a few bucks for a pair of red shoelaces, and the proceeds went to aid programs in Africa. But exactly where did your money go, and precisely who did it help? There was really no way of knowing. But with what Julius was doing in Awake, you knew exactly where each dollar went. You could see pictures of the women and children, and of the clinic as it was being built."

But something more essential, almost existential, drew designers such as Bignell and Cook to Julius and his cause. "It's sort of hard to explain," Bignell says. "After seventeen years with the company, I was very proud of my work for Nike, but at the same time something was missing. I only became aware of that after I met Julius and learned his story."

On the opposite end of the Nike hierarchy, Julius and his story profoundly affected Tim Schneider, who worked as a clerk at the employees' store. A Wisconsin native, Schneider arrived fresh out of college, entranced by the Nike myth, hoping to use an entry-level position as a springboard to a career with the company.

"During breaks we would gather around Julius and listen to his stories about his boy-soldier days and what he was trying to accomplish now in Uganda," Schneider says. "We all were fascinated. What impressed me most about Julius was his lack of bitterness. After all he'd been through, all the people who'd abused and deceived him, Julius still forgave them. There was this amazing strength and dignity to his forgiveness. The more I listened to Julius, the way he conducted himself and what he thought was important, the more uncertain I felt about what I was pursuing at Nike. Putting a price sticker on a T-shirt just didn't seem that valuable."

◆ ◆ ◆

Julius and Fee made their second joint trip to Uganda in November 2010. Just before leaving Portland, Salazar informed Julius that, due to budget restrictions, his pacer position with the Oregon Project had been eliminated. At age thirty-three, Julius's professional running career, in decline for decades, was effectively over. He would have to make do on his wages from the employees' store, his work as a part-time coach, and a modest stipend from AUCF funds. On the positive side of the ledger, he and Grace had married in 2009. His family was healthy, the orphans were thriving, and the KHC buildings were rising in Awake. For a long time he had felt bad about his running, as if he had failed to make full use of the gift God had given him. But as the foundation grew, he concluded that his disappointments with running were all part of God's plan.

The two men landed at Entebbe and went straight to Masaka for a visit to the Engeye clinic. They consulted with John Kalule, the operations manager, a native Ugandan. During the three-day visit, Fee filled up half the pages in his trip ledger. "Medication is key—available and low cost," he jotted down. "Empanel a local board to gain consensus and input . . . involve community in construction."

Julius, however, noticed that the builders had chosen wood rather than bricks for the clinic buildings, wood that would rapidly decompose in the tropical heat and humidity. It was a typical NGO mistake, but significant in Julius's eyes. Above all, he had determined, the Kristina Health Center would be built to last.

"We traveled through towns and villages and visited four hospitals and five clinics," Fee recalled for his Seattle audience. "As a *mzungo*, sixty-four years of age, I had free access to go where I wanted and see what I wanted. Why? Because the people saw me as their great hope. They thought that I was going to save them."

The expectations often weighed on Fee. He began to understand why Julius appeared so stern to the people reaching out to him: He was trying to protect his countrymen. "At each clinic and every hospital I found wonderful, dedicated staff, but everywhere it was the same sad story," Fee said. "Lack of medicines, no supplies, equipment not functioning, scores of patients lying on floors in ward after ward, waiting all day to see a hopelessly overworked nurse. As far as we could determine, in all of Otuke district, there was not one certified medical doctor."

They toured the government hospital in a town in Otuke district about twenty-five miles from Awake. It was a Level IV facility, meaning that surgery could be performed, but there had been no physician on staff for more than eighteen months—hence no surgery. As Fee interviewed the hospital administrator, Julius noticed an unusual commotion in the waiting room. In almost all cases, no matter how severe or painful their condition, patients waited in silence to be treated. But now a young woman's wail echoed off the walls: She was in the last stages of labor. A nurse explained that the delivery would require a cesarean section. The staff would do their best, but the woman and her baby would likely die unless she made it to the hospital in Lira town, forty-two miles distant. And of course, there was no ambulance, or the semblance of one, anywhere in northern Uganda.

Julius and Fee drove the woman to Lira in their four-wheel-drive vehicle. They watched the woman, by turns wailing and whimpering, be admitted to the hospital where living conditions weren't any better than those of the neighboring prisons.

Julius set his jaw. Fee made a note in his ledger: "Get a vehicle to use as an ambulance."

◆ ◆ ◆

Even when they traveled far into the countryside to visit an existing clinic or make arrangements for the facility planned in Awake, Julius and Fee would return to Lira town to spend the night. Julius would drop off Fee at his hotel and go to sleep at a room in the orphanage compound. In the morning he would return to the hotel to have breakfast with Fee and plan the day's itinerary. No white visitor spent the night in the village, although a few tried; over the objections of Julius and the staff at Awake, a volunteer insisted on staying in the huts while painting a mural before the KHC's opening in 2012. She got violently sick from drinking the water; it took her weeks to recover after returning home to the United States.

One morning during the November 2010 visit, as Fee emptied his instant-coffee packet into a cup of hot water and Julius poured from a pot of milky sweet Ugandan tea, the two men discussed the KHC construction. They had decided that, before building the clinic where patients would be treated, they would put up living quarters for the resident medical staff.

Their reasoning: The clinic would lie forty miles of terrible road from the nearest town. Commuting between Lira and Awake might be possible for *mzungo* benefactors in four-wheel-drive vehicles, but it was far beyond the range of the Ugandan nurses, paramedics, and orderlies, with a typical monthly salary of around fifty dollars. Once suitable living quarters were erected, of sufficient quality to attract medical staffers who could easily find work in Kampala or in relatively well-heeled African nations such as Nigeria or South Africa, then the AUCF could put up the building where they'd actually work.

While Julius and Fee talked, a group of eleven American women, a Rotary group from Seattle, sat down for breakfast at a nearby table. Catching shards of conversation from the next table, they invited Julius and Fee to join them. Maureen Brotherton, the group leader, had been doing aid work in Uganda since 2005, the year after the worst violence of the LRA insurgency, when Kony's forces departed for Sudan and the Central African Republic.

"I was feeling a little better about Uganda by then," Brotherton says. "Compared to those terrible days in 2005, there were more people smiling and more crops growing. But there was still an enormous amount of physical and emotional damage. There were thousands of orphaned children, which you never saw here before the war. Their families had shunned them because the mothers were 'bush brides,' girls who'd been abducted by the LRA and used as sex slaves."

Julius and Fee gave Brotherton and her group a condensed, impromptu pitch on the AUCF. They exchanged contact information and pledged to stay in touch. (The group followed through. The Seattle Rotary evolved into a principal sponsor for the AUCF, eventually paying for a used four-wheel-drive vehicle that the KHC employed as an ambulance.)

At the end of the breakfast encounter, Julius pulled Brotherton aside to warn her about the group's Ugandan driver and guide. "Don't trust that man," Julius said. "No one in northern Uganda who has lived an honest life the last few years could be that well fed."

"At first I thought Julius was being paranoid," Brotherton says. "But later I found out he was right. Our driver was charging us twice the proper amount for fuel and pocketing the difference. I had to fire him."

◆ ◆ ◆

In March 2011, construction began on the Kristina Health Center, with Julius and Fee marshaling the funds and making the decisions back in Portland, and Jimmy, Julius's brother, now on the foundation payroll, overseeing the work on the ground in Awake. Before breaking ground, Julius and Fee had consulted with the village elders, who signed off on the project and gave their opinions on the kind of services the clinic should provide. All of the construction work would be performed by local laborers, and an all-Ugandan medical staff would operate the center.

The staff living quarters was the first structure to rise from the bush, a tidy whitewashed stucco building with a blue metal roof and solar panels that might one day provide electrical power, if someone in Otuke district could figure out the hookup. The building stood near the center of the one-acre family compound, a few yards from the hut where Julius had slept as a boy.

Fee was pleased that the cost for the living quarters came to only twenty-seven thousand dollars. He would have been happy to pay forty thousand dollars, the sum he'd originally budgeted for the first phase of the construction. Aware of this fact, the contractor offered a deal to Julius. He would build the quarters for twenty-seven thousand dollars and bill the foundation for forty thousand dollars. The contractor and Julius would split the thirteen-thousand-dollar remainder, a handsome sum in Uganda, and the *mzungo* would never be the wiser.

Julius rejected the deal at once and fired the contractor. He understood that Ugandans were intractably addicted to graft but had resolved that the foundation's health center and orphanage would be different; perhaps the only two honest places in Uganda. At Fee's suggestion, local laborers produced and laid the bricks used for construction. The workers earned the equivalent of four dollars a day, a windfall for the people of Otuke district.

◆ ◆ ◆

"It's a funny thing about Uganda," Jim Fee said one day in the spring of 2013, during a quiet moment in his home office in Portland—"AUCF World Headquarters," he liked to joke.

"You have these highly organized, well-funded NGOs pouring all their resources into a project—say a bore-hole well and pump. The engineers designing the project know all the pitfalls. They know that you can build nearly anything, but keeping it going is another matter entirely. So the NGO people will make sure to train locals to perform maintenance. They will design the system to be as simple and durable as possible. All that, the well goes online, the villagers ululate, photos go up on the NGO's websites . . . and a year later, the pump is broken and the spare parts sit out in the rain getting rusty.

"And then you see a project like ours, with none of us having any experience in this kind of job, going into it with no idea, no real plan." Fee lifted his hand in a helpless gesture. "And yet, somehow, despite all the mistakes and false steps, against all odds, in the end, somehow it works."

◆ ◆ ◆

In May 2011, a few months after construction began in Awake, Julius and Fee made their third trip together to Uganda. Along with inspecting the progress on the KHC—the traditionally fashioned mud-brick walls erected by local men making four dollars a day— and stopping in Engeye to gather more ideas and information, the men would be hosting Jennifer Kahn, a writer working on a profile of Julius for *Runner's World*. Kahn's presence was the result of a two-year lobbying effort by Fee, a steady drumbeat of phone calls and emails to the magazine's editors. The story came out in 2012, and the nationwide exposure proved a boon to the foundation, providing a donation windfall of more than two hundred thousand dollars, earning Julius a more prominent place in the national running community, and enlisting a number of new volunteers who worked actively for the AUCF cause.

One of the readers was Maryline O'Shea, a resident of Annapolis, Maryland, who called Fee and offered to help in any way possible. At first wary—Fee had learned that oddballs and lost souls, as well as people of means and goodwill, were drawn to the cause—he gained confidence in O'Shea after several phone conversations. Although she had no experience as a fundraiser, she organized an annual road race and auction in Annapolis that raised thousands of dollars for the foundation.

"It's hard to put my finger on the appeal that Julius's story had for me," O'Shea says. "It wasn't just Julius—it was he and Jim working together. Jim was in many ways the radiating force. I felt like I'd known him forever. As much as the AUCF was about Julius, it was also about Jim. He made you feel like part of the campaign, part of this wonderful thing, part of the family. As hard as I worked for the foundation, I always felt like I should do more."

◆ ◆ ◆

The two men departed for Uganda on the day of the Sample Sale on the Nike campus. The event was the brainchild of Cook and Bignell, the shoe designers who served on the AUCF board. Held on campus, the one-day sale offered the prototype models from the Innovation Kitchen and other design groups—the cutting-edge, lighter-than-air shoes and apparel epitomizing the Nike way—at deep discounts. Bignell and Cook had arranged for all the profits of the sale to go directly to the AUCF.

Along with the financial benefit, the event carried symbolic weight. It was organized by runners, practitioners of the sport that had delivered Julius out of Uganda and set him on the course that had brought him to Nike. The sale relied on the Nike myth—the story the corporation told with such imagination and force—and yet it was conceived by mid-level officers of the corporation and executed by its foot soldiers. The sale was projected to raise around ten thousand dollars for the foundation; the recompense of a moment for Phil Knight or LeBron James, but enough money to drill three bore-hole wells in Otuke district or, as Jim Fee had learned, prevent and treat malaria for more than a thousand Ugandan children.

Their flight from Portland wouldn't leave until late afternoon, so there was time for Julius and Fee to attend the first few hours of the sale. Early in the morning, with the dew still hanging on the fir trees sprouting in the infield of the Michael Johnson Track where Julius had paced Galen Rupp and Kara Goucher through hundreds of gut-busting interval sessions, the two men arrived at the Nike campus and walked over to the sale.

They were shocked to discover a quarter-mile-long line of customers lined up at the glass door, hot to acquire costly confections of polymer and air, engineered and advertised to simulate the barefooted grace with which Ugandan children floated toward school over the rutted clay roads of the bush. A few hours later, when it was time for Julius and Fee to leave for the airport, the line to get in still stretched deep into the campus.

The turnout augured well for a solid payday, but amid the rigor and dislocation of the thirty-hour flight, the chaos of arrival at Entebbe, and the Mad Max drive to the hotel in Kampala, the sale turned increasingly abstract. Julius and Fee spent much of the trip poring over plans for the staff residence and attendant outbuildings at the KHC. To keep to their tight construction budget they would have to use second-grade roofing materials. Julius hated the thought of skimping, of detracting from the center's capacity to endure while so many similar projects in Uganda had foundered and rotted under the African sun, but the measure couldn't be helped.

Arriving at the Sports View Hotel, looking out over a ravine and Kampala's main soccer stadium, Fee, exhausted, went straight to bed. Julius decided to check his email before retiring. He opened his in-box and saw a message from Tony Bignell at Nike, with "sample sale numbers" in the subject line. Julius opened the message, hoping for a yield in the twelve-thousand-dollar range, about 20 percent more than projected. When Julius read the news, a bolt of adrenaline shot through him: The proceeds amounted to thirty-two thousand dollars.

He tore out to the hall and pounded on Fee's door. Julius delivered the news. The two men danced around the hotel room. The next morning, Julius called Jimmy in Lira, telling him to order the highest-grade roofing materials for the Kristina Health Center.

◆ ◆ ◆

On August 25, 2012, more than three thousand villagers trekked from the deepest reaches of the Otuke district bush to attend the dedication ceremony of the Kristina Health Center, which at that point consisted of two blue-roofed stucco buildings, the staff living quarters, and a ten-room clinic. The latter included a reception lobby, pharmacy room, lab, office, and four treatment rooms. Between the two structures, a bore-hole well built by Lifewater International, another NGO, provided clean water to the Awake community. Women and children no longer had to walk to the river with clay pots or plastic jerrycans balanced on their heads.

The villagers came out to celebrate and give thanks for the health center and well. They came out to welcome the five-person medical staff—a clinic manager, chief medical officer (the equivalent of a physician's assistant in the United States), lab assistant, and two all-purpose nurses—and the twenty-seven guests who had traveled from the United States and Australia for the occasion, led by Eloise Wellings and Jim Fee. Also attending was the Ugandan minister of primary healthcare, Sarah Achieng Opendi.

Throughout the day, a range of conflicting emotions shot through Julius. He felt much as he had at other triumphant moments of his life—representing Uganda at the Olympic Games, for instance, or winning the junior world championship and the scholarship that had brought him to America: On the one hand it seemed like a fantasy, a dream, but at the same time it seemed ordained and perfectly natural. He also felt the same ambivalence he experienced the day he ran forty miles to Lira when he was fourteen years old: welded to his native place and people, yet at the same time standing apart. He loved the villagers he was serving, and yet, after so long out in the world, he couldn't help viewing their backwardness with a certain disdain. Finally, every villager whom Julius encountered that day wanted something from him. As much as wanted to, he couldn't help everybody all the time, and the tension wore on him.

As he welcomed his guests, greeted the villagers, shook hands with the dignitaries, Julius realized that today marked a beginning more than a culmination. There was so much more work to do, so much more to build. For instance, a maternity clinic, which in turn would require electric power, clean water, and indoor plumbing.

Overall, however, Julius felt deeply grateful. In the far corner of the compound, Kristina lay in a freshly dug grave—the foundation had paid to have her body exhumed from the grave in Otuke and reburied in Awake. Eight years after striking out from Lira in search of food for her children, his mother had finally reached her destination.

◆ ◆ ◆

One year later, in October 2013, for the first time in nineteen years, Julius Achon was home in Uganda for the nation's Independence Day. On both a public and a personal level, Julius had much to celebrate. Up in Awake, the Kristina Health Center was treating five hundred patients a month, providing basic medical care, consultation and treatment, counseling, inoculations, education, and triage to the government hospital in Lira. Every patient was required to pay something for treatment, even if it was only a chicken; in return, they were guaranteed prompt, competent, respectful care. Instead of lying on the floor of a government hospital, patients sat on benches in an airy, brightly painted waiting room. The Kristina Health Center was far from perfect, still lacking electricity and running water, but its reputation was such that some employees of the Lira hospital traveled forty miles to Awake for their own medical treatment.

A week later, the second annual Nike-sponsored Achon Uganda cross-country meet would be held in Otuke district, with fifteen hundred children running, thousands of spectators watching, and Chris Cook on hand, leading a delegation of a half dozen volunteers from company headquarters in Oregon, distributing T-shirts to the participants. In a few days, Fee would be flying in on his seventh trip to Uganda to help supervise.

Uganda was still a young nation: October 9 would mark its fifty-first year of independence. Just over a century had passed since young Winston Churchill lay prone atop Murchison Falls, near the Nile's headwaters, entranced by the power of the water and the beauty and bounty of the countryside, proclaiming Uganda to be the pearl of Africa and a key to the British Empire. Churchill foresaw a dam at Murchison Falls flooding turbines that would irrigate cotton fields that would feed textile mills that would produce the fabric to clothe the world. He failed to foresee a century-long chain of global and regional upheaval—nor could he acknowledge the original sin of colonialism and imperialism that engendered the chaos. Rather than a flood of hydroelectric power, a flood of blood had characterized the modern history of Uganda.

"When I say I'm from Uganda," says Francis, Julius's cousin, "some people ask me, 'Don't you eat people there?'"

You might think that Ugandans would observe their independence day with a certain ambivalence, especially in the blasted north. That wasn't the case. Throughout the nation, the exultation of sovereignty trumped the suffering that, indirectly, freedom had wrought. Independence Day was the highlight of the Ugandan calendar, and Julius had loved it as a boy.

Villagers would spend weeks preparing for the holiday. Julius helped his father apply a fresh coat of red-earth mud and cow dung to the hut's walls. His mother and sisters scoured the family saucepan—almost as valuable as the clay water pot and, later, plastic jerrycan—until it gleamed. Women donned their brightest dresses, men skinned fatted calves, and children played and sang all day. After nightfall, people continued to dance in the village center, which was decorated with dry papyrus, elephant grass, and sorghum stalks. If at all possible, you returned to your native village for Independence Day, and on that December day in 1994, when Julius departed Entebbe for George Mason, the thought of missing the holiday aroused his sharp regret.

That was nineteen years earlier. Half of a lifetime. Now he was thirty-six, and since the day he left Uganda he had run in two Olympic Games and established an NCAA record. He had become a husband to Grace and a father to Jayden, their son, who had been born a year earlier, in 2012. That same year, Julius attained U.S. citizenship. The government of Uganda named him humanitarian of the year. At the end of 2012, finally, Grace and Julius decided to return to Uganda and build a house in Kampala.

It seemed an odd time to leave America. The foundation, after so many lean years, was at last accruing sizable donations and increased media exposure. Requests for Julius to speak, for years a sporadic trickle, had increased to a steady flow. If he remained visible, kept delivering talks around the United States, then a major foundation or donor might eventually provide sustaining funding. Enough so that Fee and Julius could achieve the dream of every NGO operative: They could focus on building the KHC and its programs instead of constantly scrounging for money.

As the foundation grew, so did Julius's personal prospects. Tony Bignell offered to take him on as a full-time salaried apprentice at Nike's Innovation Kitchen. Bignell was mulling an ambitious plan: After learning the rudiments of shoe design and production, Julius would establish and supervise a small-scale factory in or near Awake, employing local residents to manufacture environmentally responsible, African-themed running shoes for an international market. Meanwhile, Julius could continue his public speaking and AUCF work, overseeing the health clinic and orphanage, traveling regularly to the United States on Nike's dime. By maintaining his primary residence in Oregon, he could give his son what Julius once dreamed of: the opportunity to grow up in America.

But Grace had never adjusted to life in the United States and wanted to raise Jayden around her family in Kampala. For his part, Julius had misgivings about working full-time for Nike. Why hadn't the company offered him a full-fledged job, or even a raise to his stipend, in the years when he desperately needed it? Also, despite his growing facility as a public speaker, Julius still lacked the Nike personality, that ease and gleam emanating from every company operative, the guys in the Innovation Kitchen especially. The proposed dream job, Julius realized, wasn't quite his dream, and he respectfully turned it down.

By the same token, he felt ambivalent about the foundation's growth spurt. Julius and Fee had gotten this far because they were amateurs and outsiders who had scrapped for every dollar they were given and accounted for every penny they spent. If they hit upon a sugar-daddy benefactor to pay all its bills, would the AUCF maintain its edge? Wouldn't Ugandan officials swoop in to take their cut? Wouldn't the KHC then suffer the same decline as that of every other well-funded, well-intentioned aid project in central Africa?

In March 2013, after a party at the Fee house in Portland, Julius boarded a jet to join Grace and Jayden in Uganda. The nation had attained a tentative, exhausted peace. Joseph Kony was still at large but had been driven deep into the bush of Congo and the Central African Republic. More than six years had passed since the last significant LRA action in Uganda; the devil had departed as suddenly and capriciously as he had arrived twenty-five years earlier. The IDP camps had dispersed. Beans and cassava sprouted in garden patches, and goats bleated as children led them to the springs. At night the elders told stories around the fires.

Beneath the surface, however, the ghosts still walked. The cattle herds had been virtually wiped out, so the villagers were stripped of their livelihoods and cultural reference point. Orphanages run by outside aid groups, once unheard of in Uganda, now bulged with thousands of children born to LRA bush brides, who returned from captivity to be shunned by their families. The roads and paths were filled with traumatized beggars missing arms, lips, and ears. Unemployed and unschooled young men lounged in the shebeens, drinking to forget the atrocities they committed as abducted boy soldiers. A generation raised in the camps, lacking education and a work ethic, waited in vain for handouts from charity NGO groups.

Nonetheless, Julius's story had found its way into the world. Awake now had its bright, blue-roofed buildings. One village was healing; reason enough to celebrate on this Ugandan Independence Day.

◆ ◆ ◆

On the morning of October 6, three days before the holiday proper, Julius was with his family at the home they were building in Kampala. As a boy and younger man he rose early to train, and now he rose at dawn to attend to email correspondence from the United States and Australia. Early morning, before Jayden roused, was the quietest time of day around the household. Julius typically got messages from donors, links to stories from foundation board members, invoices from tradesmen and contractors working on the fourth building at the KHC complex, a dormitory and kitchen for patients who traveled long distances to be treated at the clinic. A sizable chunk of the messages he forwarded to Fee. "If somebody offered me fifty thousand dollars a year to do this job, I would quit on the spot," Fee often joked. "I only do it for free."

Julius's recent trip to the States had proven especially productive. A fundraiser in Seattle arranged by Maureen Brotherton netted five thousand dollars. A 5K road race held at the Nike campus, organized by Chris Cook, brought in three thousand dollars. At the race, Mark Parker, the Nike CEO, had written a personal check to the foundation. Earlier, Fee had succeeded in scheduling a meeting with Parker, who'd been so engrossed by Julius's story that the allotted fifteen minutes stretched into an hour. Julius had taken a side trip to Amherst College in Massachusetts to speak to a student group. His visit to the United States culminated with a benefit concert at a dance club in Portland that delivered another ten thousand dollars to the AUCF.

Meanwhile, over the past few years, Eloise Wellings had built a network of supporters in Australia that matched the scope of the U.S.-based AUCF. Along with assuming primary sponsorship of the orphanage in Lira town, Wellings's Love Mercy Foundation established a highly successful "Cents for Seeds" program that provided farmers in Awake with materials and training. As her running career continued to prosper, Wellings tirelessly spread Julius's story among her nation's public and media.

On Julius's day of departure for Uganda, Fee drove Julius to the Portland airport. The entire drive they spent calling and thanking donors, Fee via Bluetooth and Julius on his smartphone. As they pulled up to the terminal, they were still talking. Finally, Julius had to leave to make his flight. He and Fee exchanged glancing handshakes and hugs, agreeing to continue their conversation in a few weeks, when Fee arrived in Uganda.

During their six-year partnership they never had a serious disagreement; the closest they came had been on Fee's first visit to Uganda, when he floated the idea of establishing KHC at Aliwang instead of in Awake. Otherwise they worked in harmony.

"Our stories rhymed," Julius says, summarizing his extraordinary friendship with Jim Fee.

◆ ◆ ◆

On that quiet morning in Kampala, with the usually spotty Internet connection working and Grace and Jayden sleeping, feeling better about his prospects than he had for years, perhaps since the day he boarded a jet for the United States half a lifetime ago as a frightened, wild-haired boy, Julius opened his email, expecting a message from Fee.

There was a message in his in-box from Portland, but it came from Angela, not Jim. Julius clicked on the black line. The birds outside his window still clucked and trilled, but he no longer heard them. His eyes darted in pinball fashion over the message. He was unable to take in sentences, only isolated phrases.

terrible accident ... critical condition ... hope we can save him. ...

• • •

Early October was the hottest and most turbulent time of year in California's Central Valley. Furnace winds blew out of the west, the continental land mass sucking air off the Pacific and driving it toward the wall of the Sierra. Jim Fee kept both hands on the wheel as he and Angela drove down I-5 toward Davis, a city ten miles west of Sacramento and about an hour's drive east of the San Francisco Bay Area.

It was an exciting time for Angela and Jim Fee. Molly, their daughter, was pregnant, and eager to become a mother. Fee's son Mike and his wife, Karen, had moved to Davis from Oakland with their three children a few months earlier, during the summer of 2013. This was Angela and Jim's first trip to see the new house. Fee spent much of the ten-hour drive talking about the family and the AUCF. In two weeks, he was scheduled to leave on his seventh trip to Uganda.

The trip would have a packed agenda. Fee planned to look in on the orphanage in Lira, assess the construction of the new dormitory wing for patients at the KHC in Awake, check up on the day-to-day operation of the clinic, explore the possibility of adding a maternity wing, shop for an ambulance vehicle funded by a grant from the Seattle Rotary, and help out with the big Nike-organized cross-country meet. Beyond these tasks, Fee looked forward to hanging out with Julius. Since he'd moved back to Uganda the previous year, Fee missed the daily contact with his friend.

Fee also anticipated spending time in Awake. He tolerated Kampala and the comfortable Sports View Hotel. He enjoyed Lira, where the staff at the Hotel Margaritha felt like family, but he loved leaving town and heading north to Awake, to walk the KHC grounds with Jimmy, have a talk with Charles, share a corn-mush lunch with the nurses, sit with the patients waiting for treatment, and joke with the flocks of children as he walked and ran the paths around the village. Above all Fee relished seeing the sturdy blue-roofed buildings of the KHC rising out of the emptiness. Yes, Fee told Angela as they drilled south on that day in early October 2013, he loved the AUCF work, it was going full throttle, yet at the same time, ever the prudent executive, he realized the necessity of planning on transition.

He was sixty-seven and couldn't keep pounding the fifty- and sixty-hour workweeks indefinitely. He wanted to make more trips like this one—visiting the grandkids. Also, he didn't know how many more thirty-hour plane rides he had in him. Enough money was coming in that the foundation could consider hiring a full-time executive director working out of the United States, fundraising, finding the mainframe donors—a setup similar to what Stephanie Van Dyke had established for the Engeye clinic. Also, it was time to get a more active board of directors.

After a pause, Fee suddenly changed tack. "If anything happens to me on this trip," he said, "you know you're covered."

About an hour north of Davis, Fee's phone buzzed with a text message from Mike. "Want to go for a ride when you get to town?"

There was little need to reply; of course Fee wanted to ride. After a taxing ten-hour drive, most men his age would want nothing more than a tall drink and a flat place to stretch out. Fee wasn't typical. Celebrating their father's most recent birthday by joining him for a hard, hilly bike ride, for instance, Mike and David, a competitive Ironman triathlete, had struggled to keep contact with their father, who rode a road bike with a three-thousand-dollar Pinarello Dogma artisan-crafted frame.

Arriving in Davis, Fee unloaded his bike and followed his son on a ten-mile loop through the fields around the former agricultural town, which now was anchored by the University of California–Davis campus. A strong prevailing wind carried from the west, slowing the riders on their outbound course but speeding their return on the final stretch along Russell Boulevard. A paved bike trail ran parallel to the roadway, but Fee and his son, following the ethic of serious cyclists, stuck to the highway.

◆ ◆ ◆

The day after his parents' arrival, Mike flew to Denver on a two-day business trip. Angela and Jim set to work in Davis, helping settle Karen and their grandchildren into their new home. They cleaned, painted and landscaped, and ferried the kids to their various activities and sports practices. The more Fee saw of Davis, the more he approved of it. For Jim's generation, the vision of the good life unfolded in the suburbs, where Angela and he had prospered and raised their family. For many in his children's generation, the dream country consisted of towns like Davis, urban enclaves that felt like small towns.

Fee figured out the bike routes from Mike's house in north Davis to the downtown hardware store, supermarket, and coffee shop. After completing his chores in the yard and house, he took a long solo ride on the route that his son had shown him the day before.

That night, Mike called from his hotel in Denver. His father gave him a report on his afternoon's ride. Fee said the wind had been stronger than on any ride he could remember. Mike took note of the comment; this from a man who'd been seriously cycling since the 1980s, who loved to attack hills, and who'd ridden through hard country from Central Oregon to the French Alps. Mike had shown his father a new smartphone app by which you could measure your workout against others who'd ridden the same route. It showed that Fee had ridden harder and faster than anyone recording that ride on the app. Mike was impressed, but also a little concerned.

"Dad, tomorrow, take it a little easier," he said over the phone. "Just ride around town, or go out for a long walk."

The next day, in Davis, Fee continued on the yard and house chores. One of the grandkids' rooms needed painting, and Angela and Jim tackled the job. Over the course of their forty-plus-year marriage, the couple had painted rooms in new houses across the continent. They bicycled downtown to the hardware store for supplies, and then Jim suggested something slightly but unmistakably out of character.

"My father lived by the precept of deferred gratification," Mike explains. "He invariably denied himself any reward until after a task was accomplished."

On that morning, however, Fee suggested that he and Angela treat themselves to lattes before they started painting, a small but telling aberration that she would remember later.

Angela and Jim had their coffee, then pedaled home and painted the room. In the afternoon Angela went to pick up the kids after school, and Fee set out on his hour's bike ride on the Davis-Winters highway, the route he'd ridden the previous two days. The afternoon wind again gusted out of the west, but Fee had grown up in Chicago. He wouldn't let a little breeze stop him.

He rode for about an hour and was almost back to town. He had rounded a curve and was working down Russell Boulevard, beneath a half-mile-long row of olive trees. A seven-acre hayfield lay on his right, and a field of sunflowers bloomed to his left. Apparently mindful of the wind and his son's warnings, Fee rode on the flat, straight bike path instead of the road. Then, with wind at his back, amid the olive trees and sunflowers, something happened.

"Coming off the curve, Dad must have been hammering," Mike Fee speculates. "He always rode under control, but he always rode hard."

◆ ◆ ◆

A local rancher named Pete Craig was out for his own afternoon bicycle ride when he saw the man crumpled by the side of the path, a damaged bike lying beside him, about two miles west of downtown Davis. Craig pulled out his cellphone and called 911.

A car approached from the west, heading toward town. Steve Kelleher was driving. Kelleher, a middle school science teacher, wasn't supposed to be on the road that early. He was supposed to be out on the coast at Point Reyes National Seashore with his biology class on its fall field trip. But this was the time of the Tea Party–instigated shutdown of the federal government. Funding had dried up, and the field trip, originally scheduled for three days, had been cut to two days. Kelleher had gotten off the freeway ahead of the worst Friday afternoon traffic.

When he saw the roadside commotion, Kelleher, who'd received advanced CPR training during his military service, stopped his car and jumped out. The man lying on the ground couldn't move or breathe; Kelleher couldn't detect a pulse. For twenty minutes, until the ambulance arrived, he administered mouth-to-mouth CPR, delaying the irreversible brain damage that occurs within minutes when the heart stops beating.

Since there was no motor vehicle or pedestrian involved in the accident, nor any other obvious cause, doctors speculated that a cardiac event may have precipitated the crash. "They questioned my mom thoroughly about the days before the accident, looking for clues in his behavior. But there were no clues, no indication of a heart attack or stroke," Mike said. "We all wanted this to be something more than a freak accident."

After their investigation, the police returned the bicycle to the family. The bike was intact, except for the front wheel. "The spokes were gone, every one of them," Mike says. "The wind must have sent a chunk of debris—a tree limb or pinecone—straight into the spokes, stopping the bike on a dime."

Mike speculates that his father pitched straight over the drop-bar and hit the ground square on his head, breaking his neck. "He didn't have time to try to break his fall," Mike says. "There was no wrist fracture, only a slight abrasion where his scalp got torn by the inner surface of his helmet on impact."

As he rounded the curve on that golden October afternoon, Jim Fee might have been thinking about a cold glass of chardonnay, or about the drive to the Sacramento airport to pick up Mike, or about what kind of roof to put on the new wing at the Kristina Health Center, or about emailing Julius to discuss the ambulance purchase.

There was no doubt about the last things he saw: the hayfield, the olive trees, and a wide, straight bike trail leading him home.

◆ ◆ ◆

Two days after his father's accident, David Fee sat with him in the ICU at the UC Davis hospital in Sacramento. His spinal cord severed at the C-2 vertebra, Jim was permanently paralyzed from the neck down. His heart and lungs no longer functioned; he breathed via a mechanical respirator. Hooked up to the tubes and meters and screens, the coils of sleek plastic and glowing digital readouts that were keeping him tenuously alive, his dad ought to be angry, David thought. By rights he would be raging. Active and fit, comparatively young, loved by family and friends, engaged in a major, flourishing project, Jim Fee ought to be desperately clutching at the day or so the docs said he had left to live. But instead he seemed at peace.

"You're okay with this, Dad?" David said, not sure what he meant. Okay with his death, or okay with his life? But Fee seemed to know. His dry lips twitched into a smile.

The three days passed in a psychedelic blur. A steady stream of family members and friends flowed through the room to receive what amounted to Jim's benediction. "Hold my hand," he would mouth to his visitors. After a while they figured out that he had no feeling in his hand, so the visitors would lay their hands on Fee's head.

In the midst of all this, David had another moment alone with his father. He picked up the conversation where he had left it yesterday. "It's the foundation, isn't it, Dad?" he said. "What you've done with Julius—that's tied it all up for you, hasn't it?"

Jim gave a bigger smile than he'd managed the day before. In fact, for a moment, David's father almost glowed.

◆ ◆ ◆

On the other side of the world, in Uganda, Julius passed the days after Fee's accident in a state of limbo. He went through the motions of the holiday, serving as guest of honor at Independence Day ceremonies in Lira and Otuke. Every few hours a call or email would come in from California, providing updates on Fee's condition. There wasn't much to report. It was just a matter of waiting.

Julius had trouble believing this was real. It was certainly inexplicable. Like everyone else, he at first assumed a hit-and-run driver had plowed into Fee. Such accidents happened daily in Kampala and Lira and on the roads through the Ugandan countryside. Motor scooters and bicycles blasted through unregulated intersections and got T-boned by a truck or taxi. These incidents were much rarer in the orderly United States, but they still happened. It took a while for Julius to understand that his friend had been struck down by an act even more random than his mother's fatal shooting.

Julius pounced on each scrap of news from California, scouring the messages for some glimmer of hope. "We're going to have to let Dad go," Mike Fee wrote in an email. Mike and David explained that friends and family were flying in from around the country to say goodbye. There had been some amazing moments, David said during one phone call.

"I can be on the flight out of Entebbe tonight," Julius said.

"It's okay, Julius," David said. After a difficult moment he added, "We'll let you know about the memorial service."

He knew that David was right. All he could do was hang on in Uganda, waiting and praying. A week earlier, Fee had driven him to the Portland airport. They had made plans to meet here in Uganda just a few days from now. The two men had Skyped twice in the interim, sharing news and ideas, laughing and joking.

There was no accounting for this, no way to make sense of it, no other response than to acknowledge the workings of God and observe an eerie symmetry: A decade earlier, Julius had waited helplessly in Oregon while his mother, lacking the barest semblance of medical care, suffered and bled in Uganda. Now he waited helplessly in Uganda while, in California, his friend and mentor, the man with whom his story rhymed, received the finest medical care in the world. For both Kristina and Jim, however, the end would be the same.

◆ ◆ ◆

The end finally came on the morning of Independence Day, October 9. Julius was in Lira, preparing to travel up to the village and the Kristina Medical Center. At the orphanage compound, Julius arose early to prepare for the forty-mile journey—one that Jim always complained about but at the same time relished—when the email came from California, announcing that Fee was gone.

Three days earlier, when Julius first learned of the accident, everything stopped. Now the world started up again. The plangent sounds of Africa issued through the open windows and doorways, cowbells and motorbikes and birdsong, along with a commingled aroma of jasmine and diesel, cook fires and cow dung.

After a few minutes, Julius went out to deliver the news to his family and the orphans. He did so with the ceremony worthy of the occasion. Fee was a *kwaro,* an elder who had lived a rich, full life, but he was something more: Jim Fee was *dano adana,* a human person.

Julius gathered Grace and the baby, Charles and Jimmy, and the eleven children—now young adults—he'd found lying under a bus ten years earlier. Gina, twenty, who was studying to be a midwife, was especially close to Jim.

Dano adana oto tin, Julius said: A human person has died today. Gina started to weep. Julius didn't have to say another word.

EPILOGUE

The cellphone sounded at 3 A.M. at the orphanage compound in Lira town. Julius battled out of a deep sleep to answer the call, which, due to its spectral message and his REM fog, seemed to extend a portent-laden dream.

Up in Awake, one of the cows about to be slaughtered for this afternoon's feast had broken loose from its tether and vanished into the bush. The voice on the phone sounded frightened and worried. He kept apologizing for disturbing Julius's rest. Once he was certain he was no longer dreaming, however, Julius assured the man—the night watchman at the Kristina Health Center—that he'd been right to call.

More than a thousand villagers would attend today's ceremony marking the opening of the Jim Fee memorial wing at the clinic. They were drawn in part by the prospect of singing and dancing and honoring their late American benefactor, but mostly due to the promise of protein. In the months ahead, Julius knew, the Langi villagers would discuss today's meal in exhaustive detail, analyzing the texture of the cuts and the size of the portions, comparing it to earlier feasts provided by the health center.

The cow, at all costs, must be retrieved.

Julius moved out to the yard. Stars burned down in the only time of day when cook fires and diesel exhaust didn't foul the air. It was nearing the end of the dry season. Frogs were starting to croak, meaning the rains would soon come. Out in the bush, it was time to turn over the soil in the cassava patches and gather the elephant grass to re-thatch the roofs of huts. Out in the world, back in the cold drizzle of Oregon, though it was still technically winter, spring's first daffodil shoots would be sprouting.

"Look down by the river bottom," he instructed the worried night watchman. Julius was fully conscious now, his dream vapor dispersed. "Where the sugar cane grows."

Forty minutes later, after a half dozen calls and texts back and forth, that's where the searchers found the cow. Julius returned to bed, but he was too wired to sleep. He thought about how Jim Fee would have loved this scene with the cow. Julius would have told him the story during one of their weekly Skype sessions, and Jim would have laughed. Then, looking to the day ahead, Julius thought about how Fee had introduced him at speaking gigs.

"Ladies and gentlemen, Julius Achon: boy soldier, Olympic athlete, humanitarian! It's rare enough to be one of those things—how many people are all three?"

Several items concerning that intro at first bothered Julius. Number one, by Langi tribal custom, he resisted individual distinction. Second, he'd spent twenty years of his life deeply ashamed of his time with Joseph Kony; if you made it out of the bush alive, you never talked about it. Third, humanitarian? Perhaps. Although, in large part, the foundation work made it possible for Julius to live with himself. Fourth, something about the packaged quality of the introduction annoyed him, as if Julius had consciously plotted the epic course of his life with a career in mind.

Over time, however, he had learned to accept the label, which, as Jim had promised, separated the AUCF from hundreds of other nongovernmental organizations working in central Africa. The blue-roofed buildings of the Kristina Health Center bloomed like a dream amid the thatched-roof huts of Awake. After less than two years in operation, the clinic treated five hundred patients a month and was already recognized as one of the best rural healthcare facilities in northern Uganda.

After a half hour of tossing and turning, Julius gave up on sleep. He had learned to get by on little. On the long flights between Africa and the United States, however, while the mostly *mzungo* passengers, aid workers traveling to and from assignments, writhed in their coach seats, staring stupefied into their video screens, Julius would zonk out for eight or nine hours at a stretch.

He slipped out of bed and went to work loading sacks of rice and beans and cases of soft drinks into the back of the foundation-owned four-wheel-drive Toyota. After a few minutes, his brother Jimmy came out to help him. At dawn the compound awakened, and beyond its walls the city came to life, not gradually in the manner of Western cities, with a slow rising of light and building din of traffic, but all at once. One moment darkness and silence, and the next dazzling light and a welter of noise and movement—the crow of roosters, blat of motorbikes, and creak of pump handles. Julius told the exhausted night watchman that he could go home.

Since the war, Uganda had assumed a schizophrenic identity as an extravagantly friendly and hospitable nation whose citizens lived in perpetual fear and mistrust of one another. Soldiers, police, and private security guards were everywhere—even at the orphanage compound. Going downstairs to breakfast, a guest in a tourist hotel would encounter a watchman sitting at every shadowy landing. Visit a mid-level government functionary at his cramped office in Kampala, and a big man—a bodyguard—would be sharing the small space.

After loading the Toyota, Julius washed and dressed. He wanted to look his best for the government dignitaries. There was a chance that President Museveni himself might attend the dedication. Once reviled in northern Uganda—as much the author of the region's misery as Kony himself—Museveni was now moderately popular north of the Nile. He had delivered a fairly solid peace to Uganda.

With an election scheduled for next year, the president wanted to continue his twenty-five-year rule with a clear mandate. He was eager to align himself with a successful healthcare project led by a nationally famous athlete, one of a handful of Ugandans equally respected by their local tribes and the country as a whole.

Julius dressed accordingly in a sharp dark-gray suit, a pink pinpoint-collar shirt, and Cole Haan loafers. He'd bought the shoes—Cole Haan was Nike's dress-shoe brand—at half price, using an employee discount. Whenever he wore them, he was reminded of a humbling fact. Here in Uganda he may be courted by the president. In America, however, Julius had been just another migrant from an unlucky country, hustling back to the storeroom to fetch a pair of size nines.

An hour later, Julius was driving across town to pick up the Fee family at the Hotel Margaritha. He drove past the grandiloquently named John Akii-Bua Stadium, where he ran his first important races as a boy, and continued past the crowded market with its hundreds of stalls, everybody selling and enough people somehow buying for the whole careening enterprise to make it through another African day. He passed the men's prison, the women's prison, and the government hospital.

Half a mile farther on, Julius threaded the Toyota through Bomba Circus, a major traffic rotary, where a small granite marker lay on the edge of the weedy lawn.

THIS MONUMENT WAS BUILT IN MEMORY OF THOSE
WHO LOST THEIR LIVES AND THOSE UNACCOUNTED FOR
DURING THE 20 YEARS OF LORD'S RESISTANCE ARMY
INSURGENCY IN LANGI SUB-REGION AND
NORTHERN UGANDA AS A WHOLE.

The marker had been commissioned by a charity group from Norway, and Europeans and Americans were the only ones who came to look at it. Confronting the past, remembering and naming the evil, the rational process of healing and reconciliation so central to the Western mind, ran counter to the Langi way. Naming the evil would only invite its return. The Langi believed that, at night, the dead still walked among their blasted villages, where, in one of them, Julius had conceived a different sort of response to the evil.

Shooting out of the traffic circle, he hung a left at the boyhood home of Milton Obote, Uganda's first president after it gained independence in 1962, and proceeded through the security gate of the Hotel Margaritha. Kevin Fee, Jim's brother, younger by two years, emerged from the building first. Kevin looked so much like Jim that, when he'd checked into the hotel, the desk clerk mistook him for his late brother. Seeing him now, moving so much like Jim, Julius's heart dropped. Next came Angela Fee, looking drawn and pale but resolved to meet the rigors of the emotional day.

She was followed by Michael and David, arrived in Uganda for the first time to observe their late father's legacy. The brothers wore cheap, ill-fitting sport coats and ties hurriedly purchased at the Lira market; they had learned just the day before that they'd be speaking at today's ceremony. Julius settled the family into the Toyota, left the hotel, and proceeded out of town along a boulevard shaded by plane trees planted by the British during the days of empire.

After a quarter mile, Julius angled the Toyota right off the paved boulevard and onto a clay road shooting northwest into the bush. On the right, a limestone outcropping jutted two hundred feet above the surrounding scrub flats. One day a few years earlier, on one of his first trips to Uganda, Jim Fee had run out to the mountain from the hotel in Lira, a distance of four miles, on a blazing dry-season morning.

"And he didn't carry a water bottle," Mike Fee said from the backseat. Mike had heard the story often around the dinner table back in the States.

Obama, yes! Fee had called to the ragged kids who followed him, fascinated by this exotic sight, hoping that the nutty old *mzungo* might cough up a few shillings. But Fee carried no money, and when the sun started to hammer he stopped at a market stand and bought a bottle of water on credit. Later that day, after his run, he made a point of returning to the stand and paying his debt.

Julius smiled at the story: the exuberance, the risk, the responsibility, and the confidence that one's goodwill toward the world would always be returned.

The mountain and the story behind them, the travelers fell silent, settling into the journey to Awake. Julius hunched over the steering wheel, intent on reaching the village before the government officials might arrive, but also because you had to drive fast on the clay road, whipping over the ruts that were hard as iron in this dry season. Otherwise the Toyota would be rattled to pieces, along with the bones of everyone riding inside.

This being a Sunday, the road was relatively uncrowded. No barefoot, ebony-skinned children walking to school in their spectacularly colored uniform blouses, drifting like blooms of tropical fish in the waters of a coral reef. But there was still plenty of traffic. Clots of women walked with plastic jerrycans of water balanced on their heads. Men teetered on bicycles, with fantastic loads of sugar cane hanging over the handlebars.

Julius glanced in the mirror. He could imagine how disappointing the landscape appeared to the Americans. Angela and her sons stared out at a flat, scorched, seemingly featureless savannah. Thorn trees, scrub brush, dry red earth, the occasional towering anthill. There was nothing here to attract tourists—no mountains or whitewater rivers, no gorilla parks like in the southern part of the country. In Uganda, however, the invisible world was often more vivid than the palpable one. Julius wanted the Fees to see some of what a Langi saw. All that was lost, and all that still lived, if you looked with the right eyes.

"Once there were giraffes along this road," he said. "You would see the water buffalo. As a small boy I got up one morning, stepped out of our hut, and found the pawprint of a lion in the dust."

There was an uptick of attention in the backseat. "Then the war came," Julius went on. "Within one month, all the animals left this land. They walked from here up to the national park near Gulu. For a week it was Noah's Ark. It was a freeway of giraffes and elephants. Then the animals were gone, and they have not returned."

There was one more ghost that Julius could point out, one more unseen thing that belonged so intrinsically to the place that you could almost touch it. Far in the distance, a small chimerical figure moved toward them on the clay road. It might be a stray goat or cow like the one that had escaped Awake the night before. But no, the apparition was of a barefoot fourteen-year-old boy, moving with an implacable loping stride unlike the wayward gait of school-bound children or the plod of toiling adults.

There was an air of relentless purpose to the boy. He had been running for hours, but his pace was unflagging. There was something at once terrible and hopeful to the way he ran, as if he were delivering the outcome of a great battle, or warning of a looming catastrophe, or fleeing an unspeakable evil, or pursuing a shining dream.

In his mind's eye, steering his four-wheel-drive Toyota, wearing his sharp suit and Cole Haan loafers, at age thirty-seven, with the AC rocking full blast and the rig full of Americans, with the president on his way from Kampala to shake his hand and the cow retrieved and slaughtered for the day's feast and the villagers starting to gather; with the lion now absent from the land and Jim dead and his mother dead and his fellow boy soldiers dead, their blood jumping from the elephant grass as the government jet strafed and strafed again; with so many dead, so much departed, in the ghost-clotted emptiness of the road this morning, Julius Achon can almost see himself, a ragged, barefoot boy running forty miles from Awake.

ACKNOWLEDGMENTS

Separately and together, two extraordinary men, Julius Achon and Jim Fee, made this book possible. With the same patience, perseverance, and vision with which they built the Kristina Health Center, Julius and Jim guided me through the gathering and telling of this story. They opened their homes, minds, and hearts; stood stalwart through the storms and stills of developing this book; and, most important, adopted me into the warm and gracious communities they have created in Uganda, the United States, Australia, and around the world.

The Achon and Fee families provided unfailing support, often under the most trying circumstances. Julius and Grace welcomed me into their world in Uganda. From the huts of Awake to the avenues of Kampala, their hospitality was impeccable. The Fee family based in Portland, Oregon—Angela, Michael, David, Molly—seems less a clan than a generous and benevolent act of nature.

In a similar vein, the people of the Achon Uganda Children's

Fund form more of a family than an NGO. Jimmy Okullo, Dave Devine, Tim Schneider, Chris Cook, Tony Bignell, Kristen Hewitt, Stephanie Van Dyke, Maryline O'Shea, Maureen Brotherton, Frank Weigel, Fred Cason, and many others lent their time and insights. The Ugandan staff at the Kristina Health Center serves with extraordinary competence and grace.

Love Mercy Uganda, the AUCF's partner organization in Australia, proved equally supportive of this project; special thanks to Eloise Wellings and Caitlin Barrett.

My agent, Sloan Harris, believed in Julius's story from the moment I mentioned it. My editor, Mark Tavani, saw a golden thread running through Julius's odyssey, and never let me lose sight of it.

I deeply appreciate John Cook's honesty and insights. I very much enjoyed banging around Lira and Awake with my excellent traveling companions, Kevin Fee and Giovanni Cucchiaro.

My love and gratitude go to Patricia Gregorio and our children, Tom and Mary, who inspire every good sentence that I write.

Finally, thank you to the nameless and departed of Uganda. They still walk the road to Awake.

ABOUT THE AUTHOR

JOHN BRANT is the author of *Duel in the Sun: Alberto Salazar, Dick Beardsley, and America's Greatest Marathon;* a writer at large for *Runner's World;* and a contributor to publications ranging from *Outside* to *The New York Times Magazine.* Brant's stories have appeared numerous times in the annual *Best American Sports Writing* collection. He lives in Portland, Oregon.

achonugandachildren.org

ABOUT THE TYPE

This book was set in Walbaum, a typeface designed in 1810 by German punch cutter J. E. (Justus Erich) Walbaum (1768–1839). Walbaum's type is more French than German in appearance. Like Bodoni, it is a classical typeface, yet its openness and slight irregularities give it a human, romantic quality.

ABOUT THE TYPE